CULTURAL IDENTITY IN THE ROMAN EMPIRE

This provocative and often controversial volume examines concepts of ethnicity, citizenship and nationhood, to determine what constituted cultural identity in the Roman Empire. The contributors draw together the most recent research and use diverse theoretical and methodological perspectives from archaeology, classical studies and ancient history to challenge our basic assumptions of Romanization and how parts of Europe became incorporated into a Roman culture.

Cultural Identity in the Roman Empire breaks new ground, arguing that the idea of a unified and easily defined Roman culture is over-simplistic, and offering alternative theories and models. This well-documented and timely book presents cultural identity throughout the Roman empire as a complex and diverse issue, far removed from the previous notion of a dichotomy between the Roman invaders and the Barbarian conquered.

Ray Laurence is a Lecturer in the Department of Classics at the University of Reading. He is the author of *The Roads of Roman Italy: Mobility and Cultural Change* (Routledge 1999) and *Roman Pompeii: Space and Society* (Routledge 1994).

Joanne Berry is Rome scholar in Italian studies at the British School at Rome. Her research interests are Pompeii, artefact assemblages and the Roman house.

CULTURAL IDENTITY IN THE ROMAN EMPIRE

Edited by
Ray Laurence and Joanne Berry

London and New York

First published 1998 by Routledge

This paperback edition first published 2001
by Routledge
11 New Fetter Lane, London EC4P 4EE

Simultaneously published in the USA and Canada
by Routledge
29 West 35th Street, New York, NY 10001

Routledge is an imprint of the Taylor & Francis Group

Typeset in Garamond by Keystroke, Jacaranda Lodge, Wolverhampton
Printed and bound in Great Britain by Biddles Ltd., Guildford and King's Lynn

British Library Cataloguing in Publication Data
A catalogue record for this book is available from the British Library

Library of Congress Cataloging in Publication Data
A catalog record for this book has been requested

ISBN 0–415–24149–9 (Pbk)
ISBN 0–415–13594–X (Hbk)

CONTENTS

CONTENTS

PLATES

FIGURES

TABLES

CONTRIBUTORS

Joanne Berry is Rome scholar in Italian Studies at the British School at Rome.

David Braund is Professor of Black Sea and Mediterranean History in the Department of Classics and Ancient History at the University of Exeter.

Mark Grahame is a Lecturer in the Department of Archaeology at the University of Southampton.

Valerie Hope is a Lecturer in the Department of Classical Studies at the Open University, Walton Hall, Milton Keynes.

Raphael Isserlin is Assistant Archaeologist at Central Archaeological Services, English Heritage, Fort Cumberland, Eastney, Portsmouth.

Ray Laurence is a Lecturer in the Department of Classics at the University of Reading.

Kathryn Lomas lectures in the Department of Classics at the University of Newcastle.

Eireann Marshall is Temporary Lecturer in the Department of Classics and Ancient History at the University of Exeter.

David Petts is a Research Student in the Department of Archaeology at the University of Reading.

Peter van Dommelen is a Lecturer in the Department of Archaeology at the University of Glasgow.

Alex Woolf is a Lecturer in Celtic and Early Scottish History and Culture at the University of Edinburgh.

ACKNOWLEDGEMENTS

This volume arose from two sessions on the subjects of cultural identity and acculturation at the Theroretical Roman Archaeology Conference held at Reading in April 1995. We would like to thank all who participated in those sessions, in particular Eleanor Scott, who chaired them. Also, we are greatly indebted to John Creighton for his efficient management of the conference. Further thanks are due to the contributors to the volume for their patience in rewriting their papers for publication. Figure 6.1 is a reproduction of fig. 7.1 from B. Cunliffe, *Wessex to 1000 AD* and is reprinted by permission of Addison Wesley Longman Ltd. Figure 6.2 appears courtesy of Cambridge University Press and is taken from J. C. Barrett, R. Bradley and M. Green, *Landscape, Monuments and Society* (1991). Figure 6.3 appears by permission of the Wiltshire Archaeological and Natural History Society; it is based upon the Ordnance Survey map, with the sanction of the Controller of the Stationery Office (Crown copyright reserved). Figure 7.1 appears by permission of the University of Michigan Press and is taken from C. Nicolet, *Space, Geography and Politics in the Roman Empire* (1991). Figure 8.1 appears with the permission of Alfred P. Smyth. Figures 11.3 and 11.4 were supplied by the Musée Archéologique of Nîmes and appear with the museum's permission. Every effort has been made to contact copyright holders and we apologise for any inadvertent omissions. Finally, we would like to thank Richard Stoneman for encouraging us initially to pursue the project and Rebecca Casey and others at Routledge for efficiently producing the volume.

Ray Laurence
University of Reading
Joanne Berry
The British School at Rome

1

INTRODUCTION

Ray Laurence

Cultural identity has become a prominent topic of discussion for both archaeologists and ancient historians (Webster and Cooper 1996; Graves-Brown *et al.* 1995; Dench 1995; Shennan 1989), which has drawn on the debates in anthropology, social theory and history (see, for example, Bentley 1989; Friedman 1994; Tonkin *et al.* 1989). The new-found interest in theory and interpretation has led to a fundamental questioning of the meaning of our evidence (see in particular Dench 1995; Cornell and Lomas forthcoming) and key concepts in the disciplines, for example Romanisation (see Webster and Cooper 1996). Both disciplines would appear to be altering the ways in which they conceive of the meaning of their objects of analysis, but in many cases these developments have seldom been communicated beyond the discipline in which they were originally defined (a notable exception is Webster and Cooper 1996) – hence we deliberately decided, at an early stage, to include contributions by both archaeologists and historians. The reasons for doing so were simple and should be obvious: the two groups of scholars had clearly become isolated through the definition of archaeologists as 'not historians' from the 1970s onwards and with the main concern of study for the discipline of Roman archaeology in the UK as Roman Britain and the western provinces. Similarly, ancient historians had lost touch with their archaeological colleagues and expressed little or no interest in the study of the western provinces and even less interest in Roman Britain. (This may be too simplistic and there are obvious exceptions to the general rule.)

To bring participants from the two disciplines together, two sessions of the Theoretical Roman Archaeology Conference in 1995 were given over to the topics of Romanisation and cultural identity, with a view to including both archaeologists and historians. However, the latter were discovered to be already booked to attend the Classical Association conference, held over the same weekend, so were in many cases absent from the discussion, but they were later invited to submit their contributions to the volume. (The lack of co-ordination and information exchange in the organisation of the two conferences in a way typifies the relationship between the two disciplines; depressingly, the same clash repeated itself in 1997.) The general principle of broadening the debate of cultural change is also reflected in the subject areas of the papers, so that the book includes the cultural meaning of the use of marble in Britain, field survey evidence from Sardinia, funerary inscriptions of gladiators and the use of landscape in the definition of identity, alongside the more traditional studies based on literary and archaeological sources. The wealth of material for the debate over the nature of cultural identity is vast. Currently we are seeing only a small fraction of the evidence and can look forward in the future to a greater integration of the material available, regardless of whether it is deemed to be 'archaeological' or 'historical'.

The papers in this volume draw on the tradition of both archaeology and ancient history to understand the process of change after Rome had come into contact with other cultures. Traditionally, this process of change has been known by the term 'Romanisation' and has its origins in the early twentieth century (Hingley 1996; Freeman 1996). However, it should be noted that Romanisation has been shown to be a modern construct, as Woolf and Grahame point out in Chapters 8 and 10, to describe the penetration of material culture that we characterise as Roman into the provinces and the material world of barbarian Europe. Often, the absence of Roman material culture from a region of say Britain is seen in terms of resistance to the colonialism of Rome (see the assessment of Clarke 1996). Elsewhere the presence of a Roman material culture in a provincial context is regarded as a sign of assimilation or acculturation. The view set up is always one in which there is a dichotomy of the Roman colonial power and the conquered natives. Such a view is shown to be oversimplistic by the papers in the volume, because the construction of identity is a matter that does not simply happen or is observed to be in a state of happening. Instead an emphasis should be placed on the individual's use and construction of identity (Giddens 1984). Nor should we see the use or adoption of Roman material culture simplistically revolving around the dichotomies of Roman and native, resistance and acceptance, etc. All these conceptions can be seen to be embedded within the rhetoric of European imperialism from the nineteenth and early twentieth centuries (Gellner 1983; Hobsbawm 1990). What we find in the Roman Empire is a situation of greater complexity, in which individual agents have far greater choice over how they construct or present their identity within the context of Roman colonialism.

Key to any understanding of cultural identity within the Roman Empire is a clear conception of how the Romans viewed themselves and what made them distinctly *Roman*. This has been seen to be problematic for most ancient historians. 'Roman' does not refer to a person's ethnicity, nation, linguistic group, or common descent, but refers directly to a common citizenship (Finley 1973, 47). This association of identity with citizenship has led numerous scholars to discuss Romanisation with reference to the extension of citizenship to the Italian allies in the context of the Social War of the first century BC (e.g. Crawford 1995). The reaction to Romanisation in the context of a grant of citizenship does not imply automatically an explanation of cultural change and the use of Roman material culture. The response to Rome even in Italy is varied, as Lomas shows in Chapter 5, in her discussion of the cities of Italy and urban development. Although all the free inhabitants of these cities were Roman citizens after the Social War, it is more difficult to see similar forms of cultural change in the fabric of their cities. Indeed, as I suggest below, there may well have been greater cultural value in maintaining a localised identity once all Italians had been granted the citizenship of Rome (see Dench 1995). Further, as Grahame argues in his analysis of Pompeian houses, the very concept of a *Roman* material culture could be in question, given that other aspects of identity as well as ethnicity, such as wealth or status, would have been emphasised through the deployment and manipulation of material culture.

Methodologically, the approaches to the evidence and the use of this evidence differ from earlier studies of either Romanisation or the production of identity. In many ways, the authors of the papers problematise the debate and point to the complexity of cultural change and the nature of identity in the Roman Empire. Braund concentrates on the self image of Rome in the provinces. To do this he focuses on the role of the governor and his entourage in a provincial setting. He argues that Rome and Romanness were presented to the inhabitants of the provinces through the actions of the governor – hence legislation was passed to control this image of Rome and to prevent the governor from abusing his power. Equally, Braund argues, the governor's identity or self was being tested in a unique context. As a governor he was placed in the dangerous position of holding absolute power which in the Roman Republic was associated with the rule of alien kings. It was for the governor's entourage to observe his actions; any that were seen as an abuse of power (e.g. the sack of Athens) would be viewed later as transgressive and unRoman. Normality in the provincial setting is clear: the governor acted justly and protected the provincials and can be seen to have been a key agent in the promotion of Roman cultural values, whilst accepting the presence of other cultural traditions. Such evidence in the source material points to a situation in which Rome recognised that cultural change was not of primary importance. What was crucial, though, was the political control of the conquered provinces.

A similar theme is pursued by van Dommelen in Chapter 3, in his paper based on field survey data from Sardinia. Rather than seeing the process of cultural change, in the aftermath of annexation, as a simple dichotomy between colonial power and native, the situation in Sardinia raises the issue of the presence of two colonial powers: Carthage and Rome. In the period following Roman conquest, 238 BC, the Sardinians did not adopt Roman forms of material culture but instead continued to adopt and import material that was distinctly Punic. In terms of control, we might read the situation of conquest as purely political, with little or no impact on the actual lives of the Sardinians. However, what we do find in the material record is a situation in which the use of material culture can be interpreted as a response to Roman conquest/ colonialism. Individual members of the local elite would appear to have chosen whether to co-operate and adopt Roman cultural forms or to continue as before to utilise their traditional cultural forms (Sardinian and Punic). This question of choice and the ability to be seen by the governor and his entourage as adopting a Roman identity may have been politically advantageous to the local elite. Thus van Dommelen replaces any notion of a dialectic or binary opposition of colonial power and native with a trilectic based on two colonial powers and a single native population. Inevitably with all forms of binary opposition – us: them, civilised: barbarian, etc. – there is inevitably an 'other' to be dealt with. Thus, to draw on concepts used in modern theoretical approaches to the city, we should abandon such simplistic binary oppositions in favour of positions of greater complexity that resist simplistic dualisms (Lefebvre 1991, 21–67; summarised in Soja 1996, 8–12). What we should remember here is that it was the interaction of the local elite with the governor's entourage that was the reality of direct contact between Roman and native in the provinces.

Following on from the Sardinian case study, Marshall undercuts the simplistic notions of cultural change that have characterised the dualism of civilised and barbarian in her study of Cyrene. Here she finds three defined identities: Roman, Greek and Libyan. These identities she points out are deployed to create the maximum cultural value, according to the context in which they are used. For example, as members of the Panhellenic league of the second-century AD, Cyrenaicans were consistently identified as Libyan. In contrast, the myth of Cyrene's foundation by Battus and the Cyrenaicans' subsequent history could be seen to emphasise their Greekness in opposition to the Libyans of the region to create a distinction and value for those who were not Libyan. However, to see this as a representation of cultural identity would be mistaken, since as Marshall points out the foundation myth found in both Callimachus and Pindar stresses the role of intermarriage between the Greek colonists (males) and the Libyan women. The existence of these two views of Cyrenaican identity as expressed via a mythology of city foundation would appear at first sight to be mutually exclusive. However, what is key is that this contradiction illustrates the flexibility of myths of foundation in the creation of identity and, moreover, how any cultural identity was constructed and that cultural identity cannot be simply read off as a given or 'objective' characteristic from our evidence.

The use of the urban landscape in shaping identity is at the fore of Lomas's treatment of city development in response to Roman imperialism in Italy. She shows how it is difficult if not impossible to generalise about the cultural development of towns in Italy in response to Roman conquest. She identifies as part of this response the development of the built environment, with particular emphasis on buildings for communal use, but she also notes that there is considerable regional variation that hinders us from seeing any general pattern in the evidence. However, it is clear that the pattern of variation cannot be established according to geographical factors (physical or economic); for example, Samnium and Sabinum are found to have had quite different responses to Roman conquest. The changes would appear to vary according to what had gone before and how individual cities renegotiated their relationship with Rome. Nowhere is this negotiation clearer than with reference to the cities with a Greek origin in southern Italy, which utilised the value of Greek culture at Rome to emphasise their own Greek origins locally, for example at Naples. This opens up the landscape of the city as a cultural artefact that can be used to express ideals of identity, not simply to the local community, but to visitors from further afield as well. However, the city forms only part of the picture: the rural landscape could equally be utilised to express ideals of power and ideology, as Petts points out in Chapter 6. Taking a region of Wessex that contains numerous prehistoric monuments, such as Silbury Hill, he addresses questions concerned with the use and cultural value of this landscape in the context of the Roman period. He demonstrates that the countryside cannot simply be viewed as an economic resource but was full of cultural meaning. Although there is considerable change in terms of agricultural practice and the building of a Roman road through the region, the major monuments from the past were respected, and towards the end of the period of Roman occupation they were reused for burial. Petts stresses that the value of the landscape and its cultural meaning would vary according to the individual viewer. Thus, in terms of cultural identity, we must bear in mind that there is no single way of reading the landscape or any other cultural object. All will depend upon what the viewer wishes to see or fears to see. Cultural identity can present an image of the inhabitants of a region, but that image is then reinterpreted by those viewing it, who need not be involved in the production of the image itself.

Such views of distinct cultures can be found in the accounts of Italy's geography by Strabo and others, as I show in Chapter 7. The bases for distinguishing these cultures for Strabo and other geographers were dress, customs, language and history. It is clear from the evidence that as part of the geographical project of describing or representing the known world Strabo made divisions of space according to his perception of ethnic groups. A similar division can also be found in the eleven Augustan regions of Italy, which associate some groups – for example the Ombrici – with the region of Umbria. This linkage between a distinct ethnic group and a defined territory can be shown to be an ancient construct. Thus these perceptions of ethnic groups in Italy should not be read literally as a description of the peoples of Italy, because the ethnic characteristics and their associated territories are given to the peoples of Italy by outsiders, such as Strabo. Instead, we should view the texts as a way in which the ancients characterised other peoples and created distinctions between regions and peoples in Italy and the Mediterranean.

The problems of linking an ethnic group with a territory are highlighted in Chapter 8 with reference to Roman Britain. The context here, as Woolf stresses, is quite different from the Roman Mediterranean, which was characterised by cities with small territories of 100–200 square miles; in contrast the city territories of Roman Britain were on average about 2,000 square miles in area. This leads into the question of the nature of the socio-political unit that controlled such a large territory. Clearly, a model of the city drawing on the

Mediterranean pattern would be inappropriate for Britain. Instead, Woolf suggests that, by drawing upon the social cultural patterning of early medieval Ireland, we are able to put forward an alternative model that stresses the clan and the chief as the basic socio-political units. Given Rome's use of the local aristocracy in the local government of the provinces, these units would have been incorporated into the government structure of the new province. The importance and significance of these social formations can be seen in the context of the contact between native chief and Roman governor, as defined in Braund's Chapter 2. Using the model from Ireland, Woolf argues that it would take only a small number of the elite to influence cultural change and the adoption of Roman culture. The principles of this he makes clear by reference to the survival of Romance languages in southern Wales. The elite can be clearly seen to have been Romanced, which had the knock-on effect of ensuring the linguistic survival of Romance elements in the generations that followed. Again, we see the elite making a choice to become more Roman, or what they perceived to be more Roman, as mediated to them by the governor of Britain and his entourage.

Often Roman Britain has been presented as very different from the rest of the Roman Empire. It lacks the great monumental buildings, seen so clearly in the Mediterranean. This has caused many archaeologists and historians to view Britain as simply different from the rest of the empire; after all, there are no surviving buildings to rival the Maison Carrée in southern France. This view is fundamentally questioned by Isserlin in Chapter 9. He points out that archaeology in Britain has failed to see the potential of the analysis of public architecture in connection with the development of the province. From his analysis of the importation of marble into the province of Britannia, Isserlin puts forward a powerful argument for the presence of large monumental building in the first two generations after the invasion of southern Britain. For example, he points out that the temple of Claudius at Colchester in terms of size is comparable to the Maison Carrée in southern France. The marble for such projects was imported and can be seen to have been prefabricated. What is clear is that in the pre-Antonine period marble was being imported into Britain from a variety of quarries in the Mediterranean. Local quarries also developed in response to the demand for this new building material, which should be seen as marking buildings as Roman. This use of marble, often neglected in the past in Roman Britain, needs to be placed in a contemporary context from the Mediterranean. We should not be deluded by comparing such early developments with say the use of marble in Lepcis Magna. Instead, Pompeii may offer a model of how marble was used during the late first century AD. The study of this material being conducted by Clayton Fant and Kate Welch should in the future provide a tightly dated Mediterranean comparison for Isserlin's work on Britain. In terms of cultural identity in Britain, the use of marble and the development of architectural style should not be seen as in any way related to what had gone before, and Isserlin rightly argues that they mark a quantum leap in terms of cultural change. However, whether the motivation for the use of marble came from the Roman governor or was a response to acts of the Roman governor is hard to define from the archaeological record itself.

The question of what is Roman culture comes out in several chapters, but is placed in the foreground in Grahame's attempt to distinguish a Roman identity in the houses of Pompeii. The house is seen as a highly individualised form that follows, but does not entirely conform to, the classic *atrium* and peristyle format. The presence of such courtyards and, in particular, the peristyle is more prominent in the larger houses, in which there is greater space and which by implication tend to be owned by those of higher status and greater wealth. In fact what Grahame finds is that the larger houses display a larger amount of segregation and by implication a greater division within the house that created an ordered spatial layout for its inhabitants, free and unfree. However, what he concludes is that many houses were simply too small to emulate the larger elements of the peristyle in particular and the *atrium* to a lesser extent. Therefore, it can be concluded that although Vitruvius points to the *atrium* and peristyle as the Italian cultural form of housing (Wallace-Hadrill 1997), this should be seen as an unintentional outcome of a development in housing that emphasised status and wealth divisions locally. What we have here is the local elite emphasising their status through the elaboration of their houses, and later these forms were incorporated into an identity that was seen to be a distinctly Italian private architectural formation to match the distinctly Italian public space – the forum. Thus the use of architecture in Italy, created for the purpose of emphasising a social identity, was incorporated into an invented tradition of Italianness. (On invented traditions see Hobsbawm and Ranger 1983.)

A major problem, already raised earlier and a theme running through many of the papers, is how individuals present their identity and how that identity is read by the wider community. This problem is raised in the last chapter by Hope, discussing the negotiation of identity by gladiators at Nîmes. Gladiators were perceived by Roman society as a group of people who were outside the normal bounds of the social system, seen as *infames* or 'other'. Equally, we can see the gladiator as a hero of the arena and a prominent icon of Roman popular culture (Funari 1993). In this context, Hope points out that the way in which gladiators were commemorated after their death by way of tombstones broadly reflects this ambivalent position. The tombstone can be seen as a vehicle for the commemoration of the individual, but also as a means by which identity could be renegotiated in death. It expresses the cultural and social alignment of the deceased. In the case of gladiators in Nîmes, we find an emphasis on their mobility and a stress on their ethnicity as Spanish, Gallic, Thracian, Greek and Arabian. This may have added to their novelty in the arena in life. But what is clear is that the epitaphs of gladiators are formulaic and correspond to other groups buried away from their place of origin, for example soldiers and ex-slaves who had become *augustales*. The gladiator's affiliation and commemoration in a cemetery containing other memorials to gladiators stress their homogeneity in death as in life and their exclusion from the rest of society. Not surprisingly, alongside their ethnicity, there is also an emphasis on their achievements in the arena as professional fighters. This example of how a specific group in society was commemorated in death raises questions over the negotiation of identity in death generally. It is the unique qualities of the individual that are emphasised, alongside the membership of a wider group of professionals, whether gladiators or soldiers. Such an emphasis on group identity would seem to be commemorated only by those who were not entirely accepted within the Roman social system. Through commemoration in death an individual could emphasise his social prominence within a social group such as the *augustales* or within a profession, for example gladiators. The viewer would have seen these memorials perhaps in a different way from that intended by the commemorator. The gladiators of Nîmes may have inadvertently reinforced their marginal status through their commemoration as gladiators rather than as individuals with a *familia*.

Throughout the papers in this volume we can see the manipulation of the cultural artefacts to create images that we may associate with ethnicities, identities and cultures. However, what seems to be crucial to any understanding of cultural identity is to remember that there would have been more than one way of reading an identity or self. Indeed, as can be seen from the papers in this volume, a person might present his or her self in a specific manner, however outsiders might read that image in a completely different manner. There can be no single reading, only multiple readings and rereadings at a later date. Such a view questions the objectivity of the process known as Romanisation, since people manipulate images to renegotiate their identity and power relations with strangers through the deployment of the material record. Such a view questions the supposedly 'objective' basis of material culture in simply reflecting what happened in the past (see Moore 1986). Similarly, the historical record displays the representation of identities and the attribution of identities to others, rather than simply describing how these people lived (see Dench 1995). What we see in both the archaeological and the historical record is a process whereby identity is a negotiable concept. The fact that both disciplines contribute in different ways to our understanding of cultural identity in the past should promote collaboration in this area between archaeologists and classicists.

However, before such a collaboration is possible, those involved in the two disciplines will have to reconstruct their own identities. To explain, archaeology over the last thirty years has very deliberately presented itself as not classics and not history – these disciplines could be described as 'other' to the discipline of archaeology. Characteristically, in dialogue with the others' source material (classical literature and epigraphy) this material is marginalised, misunderstood as description or simply best forgotten in favour of a more 'objective' archaeological record. It should be noted that for many ancient historians and classicists archaeology is also an 'other' which 'we do not do' and, in consequence, is misunderstood, its results belittled as of no interest. This is not true of all in the two disciplines, admittedly, and we are beginning to see an uneasy dialogue begin to take place. It is with this view in mind that the volume was produced to highlight how much we can learn from each 'other's' disciplines about a subject, cultural identity, that is recognised as central for all involved in the study of the Roman past.

Bibliography

Bentley, G. C. 1989. 'Ethnicity and practice', *Comparative Studies in Sociology and History* 29: 24–55.

Clarke, S. 1996. 'Acculturation and continuity: reassessing the significance of Romanisation in the hinterlands of Gloucester and Cirencester', in J. Webster and N. J. Cooper (eds) *Roman Imperialism. Post-colonial Perspectives*, Leicester: 71–84.

Cornell, T. and Lomas, K. forthcoming. *Gender and Ethnicity in Ancient Italy*, Accordia Specialist Studies in Italy 6, London.

Crawford, M. 1996. 'Italy and Rome from Sulla to Augustus', in A. K. Bowman, E. Champlin and A. Lintott (eds) *The Cambridge Ancient History* (second edition) 10, *The Augustan Empire*: 414–33.

Dench, E. 1995. *From Barbarians to New Men. Greek, Roman and Modern Perceptions of the Central Apennines*, Oxford.

Finley, M. I. 1973. *The Ancient Economy*, London.

Freeman, P. 1996. 'British imperialism and the Roman empire', in J. Webster and N. J. Cooper (eds) *Roman Imperialism. Post-colonial Perspectives*, Leicester: 19–34.

Friedman, J. 1994. *Cultural Identity and Global Process*, London.

Funari, P. P. A. 1993. 'Graphic caricature and the ethos of ordinary people at Pompeii', *Journal of European Archaeology* 1.2: 133–50.

Gellner, E. 1983. *Nations and Nationalism*, Oxford.

Giddens, A. 1984. *The Constitution of Society. Outline of the Theory of Structuration*, Cambridge.

Graves-Brown, P., Jones, S. and Gamble, C. 1995. *Cultural Identity and Archaeology. The Construction of European Communities*, London.

Hingley, R. 1996. 'The "legacy" of Rome: the rise, decline and fall of the theory of Romanisation', in J. Webster and N. J. Cooper (eds) *Roman Imperialism. Post-colonial Perspectives*, Leicester: 35–48.

Hobsbawm, E. J. 1990. *Nations and Nationalism since 1780. Programme, Myth, Reality*, Cambridge.

Hobsbawm, E. J. and Ranger, T. O. 1983. *The Invention of Tradition*, Cambridge.

Lefebvre, H. 1991. *The Production of Space*, Oxford.

Moore, H. 1986. *Space, Text and Gender*, Cambridge.

Soja, E. W. 1996. *Thirdspace. Journeys to Los Angeles and other Real-and-Imagined Places*, Oxford.

Tonkin, E., McDonald, M. and Chapman, M. 1989. *History and Ethnicity*, London.

Wallace-Hadrill, A. 1997 'Rethinking the Roman *atrium* house', in R. Laurence and A. Wallace-Hadrill (eds) *Domestic Space in the Roman World* (*JRA* Suppl. 22), Portsmouth: 219–40.

Webster, J. and Cooper, N. J. (eds) 1996. *Roman Imperialism. Post-colonial Perspectives*, Leicester.

2

COHORS

The governor and his entourage in the self-image of the Roman Republic

David Braund

I

It has long been understood, thanks not least to seminal studies by Brunt and Gruen, that an important facet of the Roman self-image under both Republic and Principate was that of the beneficent imperialist. The development of legislation against magistrates' abuse of power in the provinces was held up as but one proof of Roman commitment to just rule, whatever may have been the particular circumstances or aims of the drafting of such legislation (Lintott 1993, 97–110). Against the background of that legislation, particular cases of malad-ministration could be accommodated within the ideology of beneficence, for they could be conceived as exceptional deviations which somehow proved the general rule. In that sense, the prosecution of abusive governors may even have served a useful ideological purpose. For, given that Roman literature contains many expressions of anxiety about the propriety of Roman imperialism, and that Roman writers find no difficulty in constructing and presenting strong (and weak) critiques of Roman imperialism (Brunt 1978), the condemnation of abusive governors (both actual and potential) served to dispel, or at least to soothe, such imperialist anxieties as may have been felt at Rome. Such mis-governors functioned as scapegoats who bore away such blame as Romans might admit for their imperialism. The punishment of the unjust redeemed the empire as just in principle and in practice, within the limits of practicality (cf. Cicero, *Rep.* 3. 35–8). The abusive governor had failed not only himself but also the Roman community at large: in that sense, his exile from the community was an appropriate outcome of his prosecution. In short, the prosecution and condemnation of abusive governors may be included among the various justifi-cations of Roman imperialism and imperial administration: they seemed to show that there were limits to misrule and fixed much of what seemed negative in Roman imperialism upon individual abusive governors, not on the underpinning ideology of imperialism nor on the very system of governors itself.

For the individual in the Roman elite, governorship had become by Cicero's day (and perhaps always had been) a key test of character whose results were watched closely by peers and rivals in Roman society (Braund 1996). And of course accusations of maladministration against a governor also became an integral feature of the political game at Rome: many of Cicero's speeches, for example, are concerned with the affirmation or rebuttal of such charges. While the individual sought to demonstrate good character by passing the test of governorship, his enemies had an interest in characterising his governorship as a failure and proof of bad character. Accordingly, there was a prominent place in the discourse of prosecution and defence (not least in cases of maladministration) for the argument that charges laid were (or were not) simply the fruits of personal enmity, not the legitimate prosecution of an abusive governor (e.g. Cic. *Font.* 38; *Balb.* 11).

Since Roman ideology privileged the past, writers of the late Republic would look at earlier Roman imperialism as more just than that of the present. Cicero's judgement in the *De Officiis* was that Roman imperialism had once been more a *patrocinium*, a 'patronage': abuse had set in, he argued, when tyranny had set in at the centre of power in Rome too, particularly in the aftermath of Sulla (*De Off.* 2. 26–7; cf. Rich 1989). For Cicero there was an intimate relationship between the quality of Roman imperialism and the quality of Roman political life in general, a further indication, if one were needed, of the centrality of provincial activities to Roman social and political thought: once justice had been replaced by tyranny at Rome, tyrannical misrule would become the norm in the provinces too (cf. Juvenal, *Satires* 2 and 8 for an imperial perspective). In such ways Cicero could incorporate abusive governors into a much broader analysis of the Roman state, an analysis heavily charged with the concerns of the aftermath of Caesar's assassination, wherein monarchy was a central issue.

Sallust also sees an intimate relationship between tyrannical dominance in internal politics at Rome and tyrannical abuse in the provinces. However, whereas Cicero locates the onset of decline under Sulla, Sallust explains and presents the Jugurthine War as already symptomatic of the tyranny of the few at Rome. A centrepiece of that presentation is a speech which he attributes to the orator Memmius:

> It is not a matter of the misappropriation of treasury funds or of monies seized by force from our allies, which, though grave, are now familiar and reckoned as nothing. To the fiercest enemy has been betrayed the authority of the senate, has been betrayed your empire: at home and abroad the state has been put up for sale.
>
> (*Jugurthine War* 31. 25)

This view has no place for the patronal imperialism that Cicero imagined before Sulla (and Cicero had little time for Memmius: *Brutus* 136; *De Orat.* 2. 240, 267): abuse, argues Sallust's Memmius, was already well established by the end of the second century. And one may find such arguments still earlier in the second century, as in the fragments of the elder Cato, and even in the scanty survivals of discourse on foreign relations in the third century (see below on Ap. Claudius Caecus). Looking back to better days of old seems to have been an ever-present tendency at Rome, at least from the third century BC, in provincial administration as in all else.

Throughout, we must observe the centrality to the Roman self-image of external relations and foreign commitments. Indeed, not only at Rome but in other instances and in the broad field of national identity, it has long been recognised that 'self' tends to be understood in terms of and by contrast with 'other' (e.g. Smith 1991). Of course, the Roman self-image entailed not simply the conquest of others, but also the rule of others for their own good and even their inclusion within the Roman self, for example by the bestowal of citizenship and even by subsequent admission into the senate. At the same time, the Roman abroad (rather as the Spartan) was readily perceived by fellow Romans as at risk, not only physically but also morally: even the likes of the elder Africanus could be imagined as in moral danger (Astin 1978, 13–14). And abroad he was at risk not only from non-Romans but also from Romans, whose behaviour in the provinces might not be restrained by the norms that held sway at Rome, particularly where those Romans held positions of power. Richardson must be right to draw attention to the fact that not only provincials but also Romans in the provinces needed the protection of Roman law against the abuses of governors (Richardson 1986, 140; 1987).

II

The entourage of the governor (*cohors*) was a particular locus for such concerns. Not only had the governor personally chosen most of its members, but he also lived among his entourage and employed it for the conduct of public office, notably as a judicial court wherein he presided (Lintott 1993, 50–2). In the governor's entourage the fate of provincials was decided. To the provincials, a member of the governor's entourage was a mighty figure. At the same time, it was in his entourage that the governor was most on view to members of the Roman elite: the reports of the entourage would have a great bearing upon the reputation of the governor at Rome. Hence, no doubt, Caesar's attempt to discredit those who left his entourage and returned to Rome on the outbreak of controversial war in Gaul (*BG* 1. 39 with Braund 1996). Perhaps he recalled the early career of Marius, who had shone in a governor's entourage and then fallen out with him, returning to Rome as his opponent, full of criticism (e.g. Plut. *Marius* 7).

However, the privilege of inclusion within the entourage also put its members in the governor's power. And the youth of many of the entourage made corruption a particular concern: the entourage seemed to threaten the corruption of the young not only through the sexual abuse of power, particularly by the governor (as we shall see), but also through their early exposure to non-Roman customs and their premature power *vis-à-vis* provincials.

A fragment of a speech of Gaius Gracchus illustrates the supposed corruption of the young through exposure to non-Roman culture and, it seems, premature power (one could wish for more context):

> How great is the passion, and how great the intemperance, of young men I shall show you by one example. A few years since, a man was sent from Asia who had not held a magistracy but had been a young fellow there as legate. He was being carried in a litter. A herdsman came across him, one of the plebs of Venusia, and in jest, since he did not know who was being carried, he asked whether they were carrying a dead body. When the young man heard that, he ordered that his litter be put down and that the herdsman be beaten with the straps of the litter until he breathed his last.
>
> (*ap.* Gellius, *NA* 10. 3. 5)

Earthy encounters between the elite and the peasantry were the stuff of anecdote: like Pisistratus in a better known case, the elite should not take umbrage (*Ath. Pol.* 16. 6). The foreign (particularly Bithynian: cf. Catull. 10) litter was not only the focus of the joke, but also indicated the corruption of the young man, whose fault was both to use it and to react so badly to the herdsman's joke, which was itself an assertion of a traditionally sensible Italian perspective and sense of humour. We are left to wonder what sort of entourage the young man had experienced in Asia (in the implied narrative of the story, if not in reality).

We may also wonder about his character before his experience in Asia: he was perhaps not the sort of young man who should have been taken to Asia in the first place. Cicero reports with approval Scaevola's dusty dismissal of the avaricious Septumuleius of Anagnia, whose dubious character and greed are indicated by the statement that he had been rewarded for the head of Gaius Gracchus with its weight in gold:

> When he [*sc.* Septumuleius] asked that Scaevola might take him to Asia as a prefect, the latter replied, 'What do you want, madman? So vast is the number of bad citizens that I guarantee you this, that if you stay at Rome you will attain in a few years the greatest riches'.
>
> (Cicero, *De Oratore* 2. 269)

Selection of the entourage was one feature of a particular *cause célèbre*, about which both Gracchus and Scaevola must have known, namely the case of the entourage of Lucius Quinctius Flamininus, the elder brother of the 'liberator' of Greece, Titus. Our fullest version is provided by Livy, who chooses to focus his account of the censorship of M. Porcius Cato in 184 BC upon that particular case (Livy 39. 42. 5–44. 9 with Astin 1978, 79–80). We are told that Lucius was one of seven men ejected from the Senate by Cato and his colleague (L. Valerius Flaccus). So damning was Cato's speech against him that, in Livy's judgement, not even Titus could have saved him had Titus himself been censor. Livy may have read the speech: at least he knew a lot about it. For Livy states that harsh speeches of Cato (and of others) against the victims of his censorship were still extant in his day, including the speech against Lucius, which was by far the most damning (*Catonis et aliae quidem acerbae orationes exstant in eos ... longe gravissima in L. Quinctium oratio*: Livy, 39. 42. 6–7). Quotations from and allusions to speeches of the second and even third centuries BC are commonplace enough in the works particularly of Cicero and Aulus Gellius to confirm the currency of such works in the late Republic and well beyond into the second century AD and after: their impact upon the rhetoric of the late Republic is easily underestimated.

Livy reports a key element of Cato's denunciation of Lucius Quinctius Flamininus, the story of Philippus the Carthaginian and the murder of a Gallic deserter:

> Amongst other things Cato denounced him for leading Philippus the Carthaginian, a dear and noble prostitute, from Rome to Gaul in hope of huge rewards. Cato claimed that the boy often reproached the consul, while grossly teasing him, on the grounds that he had been brought from the midst of a gladiatorial show at Rome to sell his favours to his lover. Further, that when they happened to be dining and had already grown hot with wine, they received word at their banquet that a noble Boian had come as a deserter with his children and that he wanted to meet the consul in order to receive his good faith in person. And that when he had been brought into the tent and had begun to address the consul through an interpreter, Quinctius turned to the prostitute in the course of his address and asked, 'Since you left a gladiatorial show, do you want now to see this Gaul dying?' And when Philippus nodded assent (hardly in earnest), that at the prostitute's nod the consul with the drawn sword that was hanging above him first struck the Gaul on his head as he was speaking and then ran him through the side as he ran and besought the good faith of the Roman people and of those who were present.
>
> (Livy 39. 42. 8–12)

Livy's reported statement contains several strands of criticism. The principal line of attack is that Lucius had brought into disrepute the good faith (*fides*) not only of himself but of his entourage and, most important, of the Roman people (cf. Rich 1989). He had done so, ultimately, by killing the Gaul, who had come to him as a suppliant, not only on a whim and without reason but against the reasoned interests (and moral code) of the Roman state, according to which good faith was to be maintained and deserters accepted accordingly, not least to encourage others. His lack of reason is manifested in his abuse of power. And that abuse is located in a banquet, at which Lucius is drunk and in no condition to deal with public affairs: his lack of reason is explained by his drunkenness, at least in part. At the same time, his lack of reason is further illustrated by his inappropriate choice of the prostitute Philippus as a member of his entourage, not to mention the sexual incontinence that such a choice suggested. Further, as Cato seems to have stressed, Philippus had been attracted on campaign by allurements which were themselves improper: the gifts were doubtless to be gained from the dubious proceeds of Lucius' provincial regime. It was in that sense (if the text is right) that Philippus sold himself to his lover Lucius. Further, Lucius had plucked Philippus from a gladiatorial show at Rome to bring him on campaign: the prostitute's interest in such a show serves not only to confirm his turpidity, but also to facilitate the story of the murder of the Gaul. In committing the murder Lucius sought to turn his provincial campaign into a gladiatorial show, and in so doing debased another traditional field for the Roman expression of virtue, war itself. Throughout, Lucius behaved, according to Cato, without regard for the dignity and responsibility of his consular position. Instead, he obeyed a prostitute: Livy's word order stresses the reversal of roles (as perhaps did Cato's) by juxtaposing the two statuses, which could hardly be further apart in the Roman social order, at different ends of the scale, 'at the prostitute's nod the consul . . .' (*ad nutum scorti consulem* . . .: Livy 39. 42. 12). Of course, it is the consul's nod that should command. However, the consul's act remains his own direct responsibility, for the prostitute was joking (*cum is vixdum serio adnuisset* . . .: Livy 39. 42. 12): even he, it seems, had not imagined that the consul would abuse his power so outrageously, contrary to reason. Indeed, the Gaul too behaved with complete propriety in Roman terms, albeit a deserter, so that his murder by the consul is made to seem all the more appalling. Cato charges that in this nexus of ways Lucius has behaved in the disreputable fashion in which he had evidently conducted himself in his private life, despite his position as a consul of the Roman people.

The several strands of the story are each familiar enough, earlier in the Greek discourse of monarchy and tyranny (e.g. Hdt. 3. 80–2; Xen. *Hiero, Agesilaus, Cyropaedia*; Plato, *Republic, Gorgias*, etc.; Isocrates, *Evagoras* etc.). The abuse of power by tyrannical monarchs had long been a commonplace, abstracted in theory and instantiated in particular cases. And the irrationality of such abuse had been recognised as a key factor in any explanation of its causes. Murder, not least capricious and counterproductive murder, was incorporated as a regular feature. The banquet had long been established as a plausible location for instances of abuse, particularly by drunken monarchs. Moreover, tyrants were often imagined as surrounding themselves with the worst elements in society when they should have chosen the best, upon whom, instead, they preferred to prey. Such cronies were commonly thought even to be responsible for the misdeeds of their tyrannical 'masters', whom they were thought in reality not to serve but to manipulate to their own ends. Moreover, the tyrant was perceived as a consumer, expropriating his subjects for his own improper purposes, by contrast with the beneficent good king. He was seen as living an immoral life of luxury, which encompassed the gamut of excesses. And, of course, the condemnation of luxury seems to have been a key feature of Cato's social and political position, as, for example, in his *bon mot* that a city would find it hard to survive when a fish cost more than an ox there (Plut. *Cato Maior* 8. 2). In Cato's view luxury was bad for the community, no doubt because it was at once divisive and suggestive of tyranny, both inside the state and in its external relations (cf. Davidson 1993 on the association between luxury and tyranny in the Greek world).

Cato's denunciation of Lucius Quinctius Flamininus owes a heavy debt to Greek formulations of a monarchical discourse. As Gruen has recently stressed, we must abandon the familiar notion that Cato was in some crude sense an enemy of Hellenic culture (Gruen 1992, 52–83). Rather, Cato adopted and adapted Greek themes for telling use in a Roman context. The speech against Lucius is an instance of the development of Greek conceptions of monarchy into Roman thought and discourse on provincial governorship. In a sense it must be an early example of that development, if only in so far as Cato stands at the beginning of Roman prose literature in Latin and, further, in 184 Rome had only had overseas territorial responsibilities for less than a century. Yet, there are grounds for suspicion that, by Cato's day, that development may have been much more advanced than might first be thought.

In recent years scholars have come to take a far more sympathetic view than used to be fashionable of Heraclides Ponticus' description of Rome as 'a Greek city' late in the fourth century BC (Wiseman 1995, esp. 58). It is now fairly clear that archaic Rome was steeped in what we regard as Hellenic culture, not in some superficial way but even in some of its core institutions, beliefs and public buildings. The very historiography of Rome emerged in connected prose in a language and genre that were Greek (Wiseman 1994, 1–22). Since monarchy was so central a feature of Greek life and thought, from Homer onwards, it seems likely enough *a priori* that Rome had been exposed to and engaged with Greek conceptions of monarchy for centuries before Cato. Indeed, monarchy may have been the prevailing political regime in early Rome, for it was with regard to and ultimately in opposition to monarchy that the Roman Republic constructed its history and identity. At the same time, there are strong indications of Roman interaction with monarchs, such as the early Ptolemies (e.g. Braund 1984, esp. 34), and even philosophers whose concerns encompassed monarchy, such as Pythagoreans (e.g. Wiseman 1995, 58–9; cf. Cic. *De Sen.* 41 for the tradition). Perhaps the most famous instance from a perspective in the late Republic and after was Ap. Claudius Caecus' expression of hostility against Roman dealings with King Pyrrhus of Epirus in about 280 BC (*ORF*$_2$ 1, with Powell 1988, 136–9). Further, although western Sicily became the first territorial responsibility of the Roman state overseas in 241, Rome had been sending out armies under consuls for many years before that. Cato no doubt made a substantial contribution to the adaptation and application of Greek conceptions of monarchy to the position of the Roman governor and, further, to their formulation and presentation in Latin prose. However, he probably did so in a Rome whose elite was well acquainted with those ideas and, in all probability, well aware of their relevance to forms of monarchy (including that of consuls) both at Rome and in the provinces.

Yet, even a century after Cato, the application of Greek conceptions of monarchy to the position of a Roman governor seems to have required argument and explication. In 60 BC Cicero (in a treatise on provincial governorship addressed to his brother Quintus, praetorian governor of Asia) seems still to have felt a need to affirm the relevance of Greek thought on monarchy to Roman experience. Xenophon is given particular attention:

> how welcome, I ask you, must the courteousness of a praetor be in Asia, where so vast a multitude of citizens and allies, so many cities and communities concentrate their gaze upon the nod of a single man, where there is no succour for the oppressed, no facility for protest, no senate no popular assembly?! It must therefore ever be the privilege of some great man – and a man not only instinctively self-controlled, but also refined by learning and the study of all that is best in the arts – so to conduct himself in the possession of so vast a power that the absence of any other power may never be regretted by his subjects.
>
> The great Cyrus was portrayed by Xenophon not only in accord with historical truth, but as a model of just government, and the impressive dignity of his character is combined in that philosopher's description of him with a matchless courtesy. And indeed it was not without reason that our great Africanus did not often put those books out of his hands, for there is no duty belonging to a painstaking and fair-minded form of government that is omitted in them. And if Cyrus, destined as he was never to be a private citizen, so assiduously cultivated those qualities, how carefully, I ask, should they be preserved by those to whom supreme power is only given on the condition that it must be surrendered, and given too by those very laws to the observance of which those rulers must return?!
>
> And my personal opinion is that those who govern others must gauge their every act by this one test – the greatest possible happiness of the governed.
>
> (Cicero, *Letters to his brother Quintus* 1. 1. 22–4)

Cicero stresses the strongly monarchical position enjoyed by the provincial governor, albeit temporary and vulnerable to censure and subsequent prosecution. He offers the view, familiar in Greek thought, that the good ruler (whether king or governor) requires instinctive self-control honed by proper education: the key test of the goodness of the ruler is the benefit of those whom he rules. Elsewhere in this letter-cum-treatise Cicero draws attention to Plato, whose ideal of philosopher-kings accords very well with that position. But here it is Xenophon's *Cyropaedia* that is warmly recommended, an account of the development of an ideal ruler in the person of Cyrus the Great. Quietly, Cicero deals with the potential hostility that a Roman audience might have against Greek philosophy by indicating that the *Cyropaedia* was good enough for the younger Africanus, sacker of Carthage and very Roman friend of philosophers. Africanus, claims Cicero, had found the *Cyropaedia* to be of practical value in the daily exercise of supreme authority: the text and the ideas it presented had been adopted as part of Roman practice by the best of examples. At the same time, Cicero also dismisses the obvious objection – that Roman governors are not kings *stricto sensu* – by the telling observation that if a king may see fit to cultivate good government, though an absolute ruler, how much more valuable would such concern be for a Roman governor who would shortly abdicate his temporary monarchy and become subject to the rigours of the law.

If Cato had broken new ground by applying Greek ideas to the conduct of a Roman magistrate, Cicero evidently considered that he must break that ground again. Of course, Cicero was very well acquainted with the history of Rome in general and not least with the career of Cato, whose works he knew well: he even mentions Cato's denunciation of Lucius (*De Senectute* (alias *Cato Maior*) 42). Cicero's treatise constitutes a more overtly theoretical and formulated treatment of the relevance of monarchical thought to Roman governorship than anything we can find in the extant fragments of the elder Cato, but, for all that, there is something disingenuous in his approach to the subject. Not only Cato, but others too, had written a great deal on the theme before Cicero had even been born, as the various texts cited and quoted in the present discussion serve to illustrate. Perhaps Cicero sought to acknowledge as much by observing that Africanus had paid close attention to the *Cyropaedia*. However, there can have been little in Cicero's treatise that was startlingly new to the Roman elite: within a few years Philodemus of Gadara had produced a more philosophically developed treatise for his patron in the Roman elite, Piso (Dorandi 1982). It seems that the application of Greek thought to Roman practice had repeatedly to be justified across the centuries as Romans sought to negotiate (not least with regard to their own identity) the familiar conundrum constituted by the imbalance between their own present and practical power, on the one hand, and the Greek tradition of strength, especially of intellectual strength, on the other.

III

The line of Cato's attack upon Lucius for taking Philippus in his entourage seems to be replicated in his speech against M. Fulvius Nobilior, whom he had criticised for taking poets to his province. Cicero mentions the issue:

It was late, therefore, that poets were either recognised or accepted by our countrymen [*a nostris*]. Although it is stated in the *Origines* that banqueters used often to sing at feasts, accompanied by a piper, about the virtues of famous men, that there was no honour in this genre, even so, is declared by a speech of Cato, in which he denounced M. Nobilior on the grounds that he had taken poets into his province. As consul he had taken Ennius into Aetolia, as we know.

(Cicero, *Tusculan Disputations* 1. 3; cf. *Brutus* 75)

The passage deserves close attention. Cicero's point is that no honour was accorded to laudatory poetry sung at feasts although the practice was customary. Cicero seems to have chosen Cato as an authority particularly because Cato affirms the practice in the *Origines* and could also be taken to criticise it in his speech against Nobilior, though it is not so much Ennius (still less laudatory poetry) but the taking of poets by a governor into his province that is identified as the issue in Cato's attack upon Nobilior. One can only agree with Gruen that there is no sign whatsoever of Catonian anti-Hellenism here, though neither do I see any indication that Nobilior's fault was an attempt to revive an obsolete practice of laudatory verse scorned in better days (*pace* Gruen 1992, 71–2; where also note *aut* at Gellius, *NA* 11. 2. 5). Cato seems actually to have favoured the practice (as Gruen 1992, 71 acknowledges; cf. also Wiseman 1994, 31–2). I suggest that the governor's choice of entourage was the issue: Nobilior's selection of Ennius and perhaps others of poetic inclinations offered Cato a line of attack that was to become familiar and may well have been familiar enough already.

If that is right, Cato's denunciation of Nobilior's taking of poets into his province may be seen as another manifestation of the sort of attack that he made against Lucius Quinctius Flamininus, namely a criticism of a governor by the criticism of his choice of entourage. It was appropriate in such a context that Cato should mention poets in general: poets were out of place on campaign, as were prostitutes, whoever the poets (or prostitutes) might be. It may be a consequence of these charges against Nobilior that Ennius included within his *Annales* (Book 7, *ap.* Gellius, *NA* 12. 4) a treatment of friendship between unequals, where the superior figure is a consul in the field and the lesser an upright member of his entourage (cf. Habinek 1990, 173–4, where much is cautiously inferred). Certainly, Gellius tells us that in those verses L. Aelius Stilo (lived *c.* 150–90 BC) considered that Ennius was writing about himself (Gellius, *NA* 12. 4. 4). Be that as it may, there can be no real doubt that in the elder Cato's day the composition of a magistrate's entourage was a well recognised concern. And it is tempting further to speculate that Cato had also made something of Nobilior's conduct at banquets (complete, perhaps, with poets: Ennius presumably dined with Nobilior and performed), rather as he did in his attack upon Lucius Flamininus: it is at least coincidental that Cicero mentions Cato's attack on Nobilior over Ennius in the same passage as he recalls Cato's evidence on songs at banquets in the *Origines*.

19

IV

It seems that there was already a well established Roman discourse on governorship by the time that Gaius Gracchus delivered a speech before the people on his return from his quaestorship in Sardinia. As with Cato's treatment of Lucius Flamininus, the issues in Gracchus' speech centred upon banquet conduct and upon sexual and financial probity, or so extant fragments of the speech seem to indicate. Gracchus of course asserts his own good conduct in provincial office:

> I behaved in the province as I thought to be in your interests, not for personal gain. With me there was no drinking-shop, no boys of great beauty attended me and at my banquets your sons' honour was safer than at headquarters . . . I behaved in the province in such a way that no one could truly claim that I took a penny (or more) in gifts or that anyone was caused expense by my actions. For two years I was in the province: if any tart entered my house or if anyone's little slave was seduced for me, then consider me the basest and most depraved of all mankind. Since I conducted myself so purely where their slaves were concerned, you can see how you may suppose me to have lived among your sons . . . And so, Quirites, when I set out for Rome, I brought back empty the money belts which I had taken out full of silver. Others, who had taken out amphoras full of wine, brought them home brimming with silver.
>
> (*ap*. Gellius, *NA* 15.12)

It is a pity that so little has survived of Cato's assertion of his own propriety whether as consul in Spain or as legate in Aetolia: the few extant fragments permit at most the suggestion that Gracchus may have drawn heavily upon Cato for his account of his good conduct in Sardinia (*ORF*² 8. 21–55 (Spain), 132–3 (Aetolia)).

Again, Cato seems to have identified the entourage as a central issue, here as a mark of his good conduct in Spain. For, according to Plutarch, when Cato distributed the spoils of military success widely among his soldiers, he stated that it was better that many of the Romans should go home with silver than that a few should return with gold (cf. Sall. *BJ* 8. 2 and 30–1 on few/many). Plutarch adds that Cato said that none of the booty came to him except what he ate or drank (*Cato Maior* 10. 4). The few in question were evidently the consul's immediate entourage (Astin 1978, 53).

After Cato and probably Gracchus, but still in the second century BC, Lucilius had mentioned a praetor's entourage, evidently in satirical vein (*ut praetoris cohors et Nostius dixit aruspex*). The fragment is usually ascribed to the second book of Lucilius, a satire which featured a robust treatment of T. Albucius' prosecution of a praetorian governor of Asia (Q. Mucius Scaevola) on the charge of extortion, apparently in 119 BC. Moreover, that satire became quite famous. Cicero and Catullus seem to have known it and to have used it in their own treatments of the activities of the governor's entourage, as I have argued elsewhere (Braund 1997 on Catullus 10 and Cic. *Verr.* 2. 3. 28). Horace certainly used it (*Serm.* 1. 7 with Du Quesnay 1984), while well into the Principate Persius and Juvenal could still expect their audiences to catch an allusion to that satire (Pers. 1. 115; Juv. 1. 154).

Again, therefore, in his treatise for Quintus, Cicero does nothing new in substance when he draws attention to the importance of the entourage to the image and reputation of the governor (here, as in Lucilius, a governor of Asia):

> As to those whom you wanted to be with you . . . , who are usually called, as it were, the 'cohort' of the praetor [*qui quasi ex cohorte praetoris appellari solent*], we must take responsibility not only for their every deed, but also for their every utterance. But you have with you men whom you may easily hold dear when they act rightly, and whom you may very easily check when they show insufficient concern for your reputation – men among whom, when you were inexperienced, your generosity may have been open to abuse . . . Now let your third year display the same integrity as your previous years, if not an integrity more cautious and more diligent. May your ears have the reputation of hearing what they do hear, not false imagined whispers prompted by gain. May your signet ring not be some bauble but an embodiment of you yourself, not a servant of another's will but the witness of your own. Let your assistant [*accensus*] hold the position that our ancestors wanted for him, who treated the post not as a form of beneficence but as one of work and trouble and did not readily confer it upon anyone but their own freedmen, whom they controlled very much as if they were slaves. Let your lictor be the dispenser not of his own but of your clemency: let those rods and axes present the symbols more of status than of power. Finally, let it be known to the whole province that you hold most dear the lives, children, reputation and property of all those over whom you preside.
>
> (Cicero, *Letters to his brother Quintus* 1. 1. 12–13; cf. Tac. *Agr.* 19)

Here Cicero addresses key issues raised in Cato's denunciation of Lucius Flamininus and in the other cases adduced above. The choice of an entourage is of the first importance. Where Cato denounces Lucius' choice of Philippus, Cicero praises his brother's choices. Further, power must stay with the governor: Cicero stresses that it is for the governor to command his entourage, not (as Cato suggests of Lucius) vice versa. And greed is also a central concern: the entourage must be no more corrupt than the governor himself. Members of the entourage must not act like a Philippus, set on 'gifts', whether from the governor himself or from those seeking to reach the governor through his entourage. Hence one way of praising a governor for his control of his entourage was to imagine the complaints of a greedy and disgruntled entourage, as we find in the poetry of Catullus (Braund 1997). Power is not to be paraded and abused, but to be played down: so far from being a murderer the governor is to be a protector of life, status and property, upholding the standards of the imagined past when Romans were Romans, in dealing with foreigners as in the proper conduct of society and politics at Rome itself.

Further, the Roman self-image as a beneficent imperial power (self-criticism notwithstanding) came to be broadly accepted among provincials themselves, even among provincials who asserted the value of their own cultural heritage. That acceptance is both a cause and a symptom of the success of the Roman Empire in incorporating a range of other, non-Roman, cultural identities, which in turn helps to account for the paucity of revolts against Roman power in the provinces. For all its concern with legal status and for all the capacity of Romans to differentiate culturally, the Roman Empire did not require individuals or even communities to adopt a distinctly Roman identity to the exclusion of all other identities. Local identities survived and flourished under the Roman Empire, whether individual, communal, regional or supra-regional: the most striking example of the latter is perhaps the trenchant Hellenism of the empire, particularly that of the second and third centuries AD.

Pausanias offers a convenient example of the willingness even of champions of Hellenic culture to accommodate the most appalling Roman imperialist outrages as in some sense exceptional. He explains Sulla's sack of Athens in 86 BC in a manner that amounts to an affirmation of the virtues of Roman rule and the Roman identity. In part, for Pausanias, Sulla's sack was the fault of Athens itself: the city had chosen to throw in its lot with Mithridates, who is described as a 'king of the barbarians around the Euxine Sea', with no mention of the Greek cities of the region which formed so much of Mithridates' empire (1. 20. 4). Athens had chosen the side of the barbarian king, we are told, because the *demos* – and the dregs of the *demos* at that – had willed it so (1. 20. 5). In other words, an enemy within (the dregs) had conspired with an enemy without (Mithridates, the king of distant barbarians) against the best interests of Athens. Pausanias does not seek directly to excuse the cruelty of Sulla that followed, but his introductory presentation of Athens' conduct amounts to a plea in mitigation. Remarkably, Pausanias then pronounces Sulla's conduct as untypical of Roman imperialism as being 'not appropriate to a Roman' (1. 20. 7; cf. Ziolkowski 1993, 85, defending Sulla).

Pausanias' treatment of Sulla's sack of Athens offers a reconciliation of the tension in Roman imperial identity along the lines found in Cicero, as we saw at the outset of this chapter. In accepting and affirming the benefits of Roman rule in general and in principle (which, of course, not all chose to do) Romans and provincials both had to develop strategies which enabled them to accommodate or at least to account for the particular instances of Roman imperial malpractice and exploitation, whether minor or gross, which occurred in everyday experience. Each case had its own attendant circumstances, but the favoured strategy in accounting for such instances was akin to that employed by Pausanias in dealing with Sulla. The bad governor was a rogue exception, it could be claimed, whose exceptional example served to highlight the dangers of imperialism, for governor as well as for governed, and to validate the otherwise high quality of Roman imperial administration (see further Swain 1996, esp. 240). Finally, it is worth pausing to observe that the very fact that provincials could come to share so benign a perspective on Roman rule with their imperial masters further indicates the extent to which the Roman Empire was so very coherent, both despite and because of the variety of identities which it embraced. After all, the governor of a province in the Greek east under the Principate might prove on closer examination to be not only a Roman but also a Greek (Millar 1964, 184–90 remains very valuable; cf. now in general Swain 1996).

Bibliography

Astin, A. E. 1978, *Cato the Censor* (Oxford).

Braund, D. C. 1984, *Rome and the Friendly King* (London).

Braund, D. C. 1996, *Ruling Roman Britain. Kings, Queens, Governors and Emperors* (London).

Braund, D. C. 1997, 'The politics of Catullus 10 Memmius, Caesar and the Bithynians', *Hermathena*, 158: 45–57.

Brunt, P. A. 1978, '*Laus imperii*', in P. D. A. Garnsey and C. R. Whittaker (eds) *Imperialism in the Ancient World* (Cambridge): 159–91.

Davidson, J. 1993, 'Fish, sex and revolution in Athens', *CQ* 43: 53–66.

Dorandi, T. 1982, *Filodemo. Il buon re secondo Omero* (Naples).

Du Quesnay, I. M. Le M. 1984, 'Horace and Maecenas: the propaganda value of *Sermones* 1' in T. Woodman and D. West (eds) *Poetry and Politics in the Age of Augustus* (Cambridge): 19–58.

Gruen, E. S. 1992, *Culture and National Identity in Republican Rome* (London).

Habinek, T. N. 1990, 'Towards a history of friendly advice: the politics of candor in Cicero's *De Amicitia*' in M. C. Nussbaum (ed.) *The Poetics of Therapy* (Edmonton): 165–85.

Lintott, A. W. 1993, *Imperium Romanum. Politics and Administration* (London).

Millar, F. 1964, *A Study of Cassius Dio* (Oxford).

Powell, J. G. F. 1988, *Cicero: Cato Maior, De Senectute* (Cambridge).

Rich, J. W. 1989, 'Patronage and international relations in the Roman republic' in A. Wallace-Hadrill (ed.) *Patronage in Ancient Society* (London): 117–36.

Richardson, J. S. 1986, *Hispaniae. Spain and the Development of Roman Imperialism, 218–82 BC* (Cambridge).

Richardson, J. S. 1987, 'The purpose of the *lex Calpurnia de repetundis*', *JRS* 77: 1–12.

Smith, A. D. 1991, *National Identity* (London).

Swain, S. 1996, *Hellenism and Empire. Language, Classicism and Power in the Greek World, AD 50–250* (Oxford).

Wiseman, T. P. 1994, *Historiography and Imagination. Eight Essays on Roman Culture* (Exeter).

Wiseman, T. P. 1995, *Remus, a Roman Myth* (Cambridge).

Ziolkowski, A. 1993, '*Urbs direpta*, or how the Romans sacked cities' in J. Rich and G. Shipley (eds) *War and Society in the Roman World* (London): 69–91.

3

PUNIC PERSISTENCE

Colonialism and cultural identities in Roman Sardinia

Peter van Dommelen

The Roman conquest of Punic Sardinia

The island of Sardinia became part of the Roman world following the end of the First Punic War. Although Carthage had lost the struggle for Sicily and had been forced to give up all claims to that island in the peace treaty of 241 BC, Sardinia remained in Carthaginian hands. However, when internal conflicts and widespread mercenary revolts in North Africa and Sardinia had further weakened Carthage, Rome seized the occasion and occupied Sardinia in 238 BC. Later the islands of Corsica and Sardinia were annexed by Rome in 227 BC with the creation of the *provincia* of Sardinia and Corsica.

The Roman occupation of Sardinia was easy to accomplish, since the mercenary revolts had already overcome the Carthaginian garrisons. However, the establishment of Roman authority over the entire island was achieved only in the long term and was certainly not completed in 227 BC. Whereas the mountainous interior of Sardinia would long remain reputed for numerous small uprisings and frequent attacks of Roman troops – who did not succeed in formally pacifying the region before AD 19 – Roman authority was seriously challenged by the inhabitants of both the plains and the upland regions. Although these areas had initially offered little or no resistance to Roman rule, the landed gentry of west central Sardinia openly sided with Carthage during the Second Punic War. In 215 BC, when Hannibal was raiding southern Italy, they headed a large revolt, backed by Carthaginian troops and armed tribes from the mountainous interior. This revolt was put down with difficulty by the Roman garrison and their hastily assembled reinforcements. Until the end of the Second Punic War, in 201 BC, Roman troops were stationed permanently in Sardinia to secure the loyalty of the island (Meloni 1975, 7–66).

Before the Roman occupation of the island, Sardinia had been an integral part of the Carthaginian territories around the western Mediterranean from the later sixth century BC: the southern half of the island in particular had already participated actively in the Phoenician commercial networks across the Mediterranean in the seventh and sixth centuries BC and had become closely related to the North African hinterland of the city of Carthage. The Roman take-over of Sardinia in 238 BC represented a sharp break with the Punic and Semitic orientation of (southern) Sardinia as the Italian peninsula instead of, the much nearer, North African coast became the principal point of reference. Although Roman undertakings in Sardinia after 238 have been described in detail by several (Roman) historians writing about the Punic Wars, these sources hardly give any insight into what was happening in Sardinia at this time. The import-ance of Sardinia as a supplier of grain and as a strategic naval base for both Romans and Carthaginians is repeatedly stressed and the revolt in 215 BC is extensively covered by Livy (XXIII. 32–41 *passim*) but none of these sources goes beyond the description of mere events.

The period after 238 BC must nevertheless have been of crucial importance for Sardinia, as it was during this period that the island was gradually incorporated in the Roman world. In order to understand this period of 'Romanisation', it is necessary to examine which developments and processes took place on the island; how the inhabitants coped with the newly established Roman domination; and how they viewed their traditional relations with North Africa and the newly imposed ties with the Italian peninsula. Although the widely used term 'Romanisation' might suggest otherwise, the developments of this period are likely to have differed significantly from the 'processes of Romanisation' taking place elsewhere at other moments, because, in Sardinia, the changes in identity and the speed of change were largely determined by the particular historical and political circumstances of the western Mediterranean in the third and second centuries BC, in the context of opposition between Romans and Carthaginians. If we take apart the 'processes of Romanisation' and examine them as a series of specific local developments, we may be able to highlight the particularities of the processes of Romanisation in west central Sardinia. At the same time, a number of crucial concepts can be distinguished, which may provide a fruitful basis for comparison with other regions and periods.

One such concept is that of *cultural identity*, which enables people to group themselves together and set themselves apart from others: it is through the construction of a cultural identity that people can place themselves as well as others in the world. And if the world changes, cultural identities must of necessity change as well: cultural identity can therefore be understood in terms of 'practice' or as a process which is closely related to the 'constitution of mean-ingful worlds' (Friedman 1992, 837). Cultural identity represents a particularly useful means of exploring periods of change such as those of 'Romanisation', which forced people to redefine their position in the context of the larger 'Roman world' using elements from both the past situation and the new con-stellation (cf. Friedman 1992, 853–6). A further crucial concept, which may also serve as a basis of comparison, is that of *colonialism*.[1] Although this term covers a vast range of situations which are characterised by different colonial intentions and correspondingly different local responses, it does bring out the essential characteristics of the situation. These essential characteristics were the presence of one or more groups of foreign people in a region at some distance from their place of origin (the 'colonisers') and the existence of asymmetrical socio-economic relationships of domination or exploitation between the colonising groups and the inhabitants of the colonised region (Prochaska 1990, 6–11). Irrespective of the specific characteristics of each case, cultural as well as personal identities invariably play a major part in colonial situations, as both the colonisers and the colonised must (re)define their position in the new colonial situation (cf. Marcus 1992, 313).

Studying issues of cultural identity or analysing the colonial situation of Sardinia has long suffered from a dearth of suitable data, as the literary sources generally gloss over the local situations in Sardinia. This lack of relevance in specific local contexts is only partially compensated for by the epigraphic evidence. The archaeological data, however, have an enormous potential for overcoming the histories of events documented by the literary sources: despite its general bias towards the major cities and their monuments, archaeology has already contributed much to a better understanding of local developments (cf. Zucca 1985). It is, however, most of all the recent adoption of rural and regional perspectives in Sardinian archaeology that allows studies of mid- to long-term developments – the Braudelian *conjonctures* – which may shed light on issues of regional organisation and identity (Vismara 1990, 46–7).

Taking the two notions of cultural identity and colonialism as starting points, I shall focus on the region of west central Sardinia and look into the development of rural settlement during the third and second centuries BC, i.e. just before and after the Roman take-over of Sardinia. By paying particular attention to the role of material culture as a means of constructing local and regional identities in a colonial situation, I intend to explore the relationship between the Roman authorities and the local population of west central Sardinia, examining how the socio-economic structures of this specific context were transformed and how people responded to these changes and coped with Roman colonialism.

Roman domination and Punic settlement in west central Sardinia

The region of west central Sardinia (Fig. 3.1) is dominated by the large Campidano plain which stretches across the island from Karales (modern Cagliari) on the south-east coast to Tharros on the central west coast. The main feature of the central west coast is the shallow Gulf of Oristano, which is bordered by an extensive strip of wetlands, known as the Arborèa, and farther east the coast and associated wetland give way to the slightly higher ground of the Campidano (Fig. 3.2). In the interior of the region the Campidano plain is flanked by the steep and inaccessible Iglesiente mountain range in the south and the fertile marl hills of the Marmilla to the north.

27

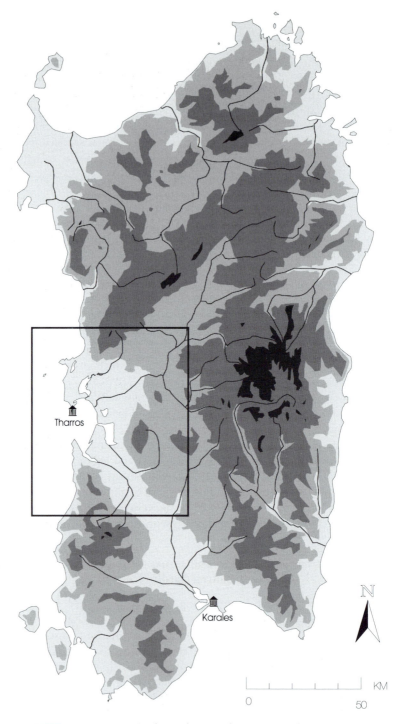

Figure 3.1 Sardinia, showing the west central region

0–100–400–1000>
(m above sea level)

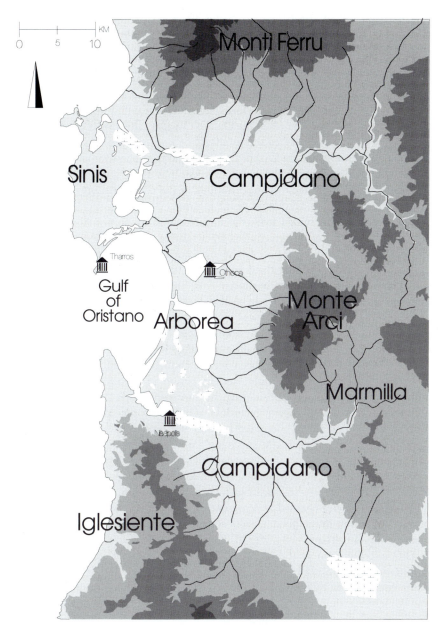

Figure 3.2 The principal landscapes of west central Sardinia as reconstructed for the later first millennium BC

0–100–300–700> (m above sea level)

Many characteristics of both urban and rural settlement in this region (Fig. 3.3) date back to the Carthaginian period and in some cases to the preceding centuries of Phoenician colonisation, while in the interior of the region numerous sites have indigenous Iron Age predecessors. For example, the Phoenician origins of Tharros, the only urban settlement of the region, are revealed by its typically Phoenician location on a narrow peninsula with access to both the open sea and the Gulf of Oristano. Two minor towns named Othoca and Neapolis are late Phoenician and early Carthaginian foundations respectively. They are located on the eastern and southern shores of the Gulf of Oristano, the former on an isolated sandy knoll amidst the marshes and ponds of the northern Arborèa and the latter on the higher grounds of the Campidano plain along the lagoons and fens of the southern Arborèa. Dispersed rural settlement has been attested throughout the entire region, with major concentrations in the coastal Arborèa and on the northern fringe of the Campidano in the interior.

The archaeological record from the first centuries of Roman domination in Sardinia is paradoxically characterised by a relative *absence* of Roman material culture; its most striking aspect is the markedly Punic nature of the archaeological record from the later third and second centuries BC, i.e. until well after the establishment of Roman authority over the island. This was recognised long ago and much ink has already been spilt on discussions and explanations of these remarkable phenomena. It was suggested that Sardinia represented a peripheral region within the expanding Roman state, thus dismissing the Sardinian situation as a case of 'failed Romanisation' (e.g. Sirago 1992, 243–7); but the causes of this failure have not been well accounted for. More generally, the archaeological record of the early Roman period in Sardinia has been dealt with in terms of *persistence*, considering the numerous Punic features that can be identified in the archaeological record as relics of the preceding Carthaginian domination, which simply persisted beyond the limits of that phase into the Roman period. In this view, the 'surviving' Punic elements represented isolated, perhaps more or less casual, phenomena which at best could be indicative of the limited survival of an otherwise debased Punic culture which had lost its vitality (e.g. Zucca 1985, 95). As the use of such terms as 'substratum' shows, these Punic manifestations were regarded as representing a secondary aspect of this period, because according to the documentary sources Sardinia should display a Roman identity (e.g. Tronchetti 1984, 245–6).

This interpretation of the archaeological record from the period of Roman domination in Sardinia has more recently been criticised for depreciating the Punic contribution to the Roman period. In particular, it has been shown that the Punic dimension of the archaeological record from that period represents much more than mere isolated relics of an otherwise obsolete culture: the Punic evidence dating from the later third century BC and afterwards unmistakably demonstrates the *vitality* of the Punic culture in a wide range of aspects of social and economic life under the Roman Republic in Sardinia (Bondì 1990).

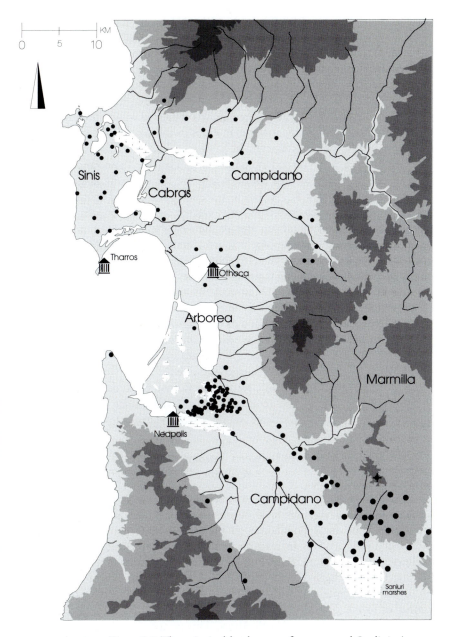

Figure 3.3 The principal landscapes of west central Sardinia (reconstructed situation in the later first millennium BC), showing urban and rural settlement in the third and second centuries BC (after Artudi and Perra 1994; Barreca 1986; Zucca 1987; Nieddu and Zucca 1991; cf. Tore and Stiglitz 1994). The crossed dots in the Campidano plain and Marmilla hills respectively indicate the location of the Bidd'e Cresia necropolis and the Genna Maria sanctuary

In west central Sardinia the city of Tharros demonstrates this particularly well, with the compelling evidence of the *tophet*, an open-air sanctuary, where the cremated remains of young children and animals were buried and related rituals were performed. These sanctuaries, which are generally interpreted in terms of the communal identity of the city, represent a typical as well as unique aspect of the major Phoenician and Carthaginian cities in the central Mediterranean (see Gras *et al.* 1991 for an overview). In Sardinia, in all cases where stratigraphic excavations have been carried out, including Tharros, these sanctuaries have been shown to have remained continuously and unchangedly in use until well into the second century BC. As late as the end of the second century, a temple with typically Punic characteristics was erected on the acropolis of Tharros. In the same period the built-up area of the city was enlarged but the existing layout of streets and building-blocks was maintained (Bondì 1987). Epigraphic evidence, often in Punic language, has shown that Tharros (as well as other major cities) was administered along Carthaginian lines, with a local council chaired by two magistrates named *suffetes* (Mastino 1985, 69–76).

The significance of this alternative interpretation is that it not only emphasises continuity with the preceding period of Carthaginian domination but also draws attention to new and original achievements of Punic culture in Sardinia under Roman rule. It also shows that after 238 BC Sardinia had not lost all contact with North Africa but had somehow managed, despite the Punic Wars, to maintain its ties with that region: most Punic features of Roman Sardinia can be paralleled in North Africa, which had remained under Carthaginian domination until 146 BC, when the city of Carthage was destroyed (Mastino 1985).

Cultural identities between Roman colonialism and local resistance

In a slightly different vein, the representation of early Roman Sardinia as characterised by a vigorous local Punic culture has been suggested to denote *resistance* of the local population to the Roman colonisation of the island (Mastino 1985, 48–50). In reaction to negative interpretations of local Punic traditions demonstrating the incapacity of the local population to adopt Roman culture, there has been an attempt to represent the persistence of Punic culture positively in competition with but essentially equal to the dominant, colonial culture of Rome: a mode of interpretation that follows from the interpretation of local cultures in Roman North Africa. This perspective of the coexistence of local Punic traditions alongside the dominant Roman culture enables 'une vision double de la réalité unique' of the colonial situation of early Roman Sardinia, instead of the conventional one-sided colonialist view (Bénabou 1976, 18). This effectively means that the history of (early) Roman Sardinia should not be written exclusively in Roman terms (as in e.g. Meloni 1975) but should clear an equal space for the local Punic culture of this period (as described by Barreca 1986, 43–52): these histories should no longer be kept separate but need to be integrated into a unified and multifaceted whole (Vismara 1990; cf. Bénabou 1976, 15). Interpreting the local Punic traditions of Roman Sardinia in terms of cultural resistance is in keeping with the frequent acts of armed resistance in the mountainous interior of Sardinia. Such a representation of the continuing use of Punic material culture in the Campidano plain may also provide a proper background to the violent large-scale rebellion of 215 BC in the Campidano plain of west central Sardinia (see below).

From a more general point of view, the criticism of conventional representations of persisting Punic traditions in Roman Sardinia as outlined above corresponds closely to critical comments about other archaeological, historical and anthropological studies of colonial situations. Partial representations from the point of view of the colonialist with a total neglect of the part played by local colonised people in colonial situations may therefore, by and large, be expected to have been overcome (cf. Thomas 1994, 33–44). Archaeologists too, including those working in the Mediterranean, have become aware of their siding with colonising Romans and Greeks (e.g. Sheldon 1982; Whitehouse and Wilkins 1989).

The alternative interpretations put forward both in the Sardinian situation and elsewhere, however, have more recently come under fire: anthropologists in particular have commented on the *dualist* nature of these conceptions of colonial situations, which are often reduced to a relatively simple binary opposition between colonisers and colonised, whose respective communities are usually *a priori* regarded as unified groups without contradictions or internal conflicts of interest (cf. Stoler 1989, 134–9). This notion of colonialism is rooted in a holistic interpretation of culture as a well defined and clear-cut entity (or 'system'). It effectively reduces colonialism to a mere confrontation between two independent and separate cultures, in which the colonising one often inevitably, in an almost 'natural' way, prevails over the colonised 'native' one. As a consequence, it usually is an accepted *assumption* that colonisers impose their culture on the colonised. It also means that the nature and intensity of the relationship between the colonisers and the colonised generally provide the point of departure for the study of a colonial society, rather than attention being paid to the actual relationships between the colonisers and the colonised (Thébert 1978, 76–80; cf. Pels 1993, 9–10).

While the critical remarks on simplified dualist representations of colonial situations assert that 'the colonizing process itself is rarely a simple dialectic of domination and resistance', it is nevertheless also clear that 'the power structure of colonialism is everywhere clearly laid down' (Comaroff and Comaroff 1989, 291); the above comments should therefore not be understood as a denial of domination and exploitation of colonised regions and their inhabitants. Instead, I intend to explore the complex, ambiguous and 'murky' dimensions of colonial situations, recognising that neither colonisers nor colonised constitute neatly defined groups and emphasising that any colonial society is made up of a range of social groups with different intentions and interests. As a consequence, below the manifest opposition between colonisers and colonised some groups may co-operate across the colonialist divide, while others can even be excluded by both sides (cf. Stoler 1989, 139–55; Prochaska 1990, 135–79). It is therefore not an exaggeration to characterise a colonial situation as 'a congeries of activities and a conjunction of outcomes that, though related and at times coordinated, were usually diffuse, disorganized and even contradictory' (Dirks 1992, 7). If these social groups and their relations with each other are to be recentred as the object of study in colonial societies, together with the various social and cultural identities constructed along these lines, it is necessary to adopt a theoretical perspective in which human agency plays a central part within a wider context of structural conditions. Pierre Bourdieu's concepts of practice and *habitus* provide an obvious framework for examining and reflecting on colonialism in terms of *local practice* (Thomas 1994, 58–61; see Bourdieu 1977, 1992). Accepting that '*co-presence* and its material mediations are the point from which an understanding of colonial situations should start' (Pels 1993, 6), it is significant that Bourdieu's theory of practice integrates situations of everyday practice and co-presence with relations of power and exploitation – which are usually an all too evident feature of colonial society, and are thought of as 'embodied' social structures which are both reproduced and transformed in daily social practice (cf. Pels 1993, 11–15).

Punic tradition and Roman rule in west central Sardinia

The city of Tharros is the only urban centre in the region, which as a whole is characterised by a dispersed pattern of rural settlement. The landscape in west central Sardinia (Fig. 3.3) features the following elements: two non-urban central places, Othoca and Neapolis; a number of rural sanctuaries, mostly in reused prehistoric *nuraghi*;[2] and above all a large number of dispersed small to medium-sized settlement sites, often in association with small cemeteries. Nearly all of these sites are known from surface finds only, as excavations are rare in this region: neither Othoca nor Neapolis has been excavated systematically (Zucca 1987; Nieddu and Zucca 1991), only one of the sanctuaries has been excavated (Lilliu 1993a), and very few of the rural settlement sites have been explored in depth. Over a century of professional archaeological activity has nevertheless accumulated a wealth of data across the entire region, which has partially been made accessible in published surveys of Punic and Roman finds (e.g. Zucca 1987, 115–47). Within the region, the area of the southern Arborèa and adjoining tracts of the Campidano plain have been studied more intensively, as they appear to occupy an important place at the junction of the Campidano plain and the Arborèa wetlands with access to both the Gulf of Oristano and the near Marmilla hills. The presence of the town of Neapolis in the area would seem to confirm this impression.

The southern Arborèa and contiguous Campidano (Fig. 3.4) are dominated by the roughly parallel courses of the Riu Mannu and Riu Mògoro rivers, which

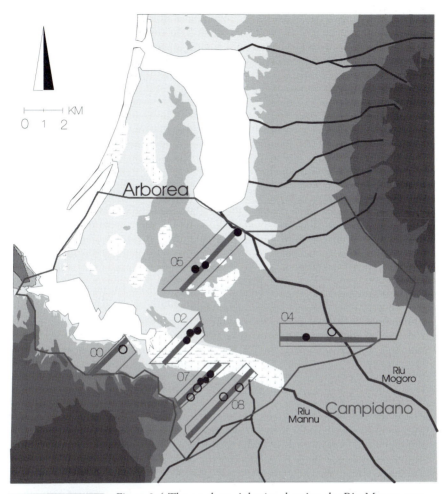

Figure 3.4 The southern Arborèa, showing the Riu Mannu estuary key area with the six transects examined until 1994 (Nos. 00, 02, 04, 05, 07, 08) and the respective sample grids that have been intensively surveyed. The symbols in the transects indicate the sites located by the survey dating from the Punic–Roman (○) period, including those occupied during the third and second centuries BC (●)

enter the area through the central Campidano and flow into the San Giovanni and Sassu lagoons respectively. The southern and eastern stretches of the area consist of the higher ground of the Campidano, which is dominated by heavy and often very coarsely textured soils, occasionally interspersed with basalt outcrops. The most significant element of the area is the elongated sandy rise of Terralba between the two rivers, which is slightly higher than the bordering stream valleys and the extensive wetlands of swamps and dunes to the west of it. It is made up of aeolian sands on which light soils have developed, while its clayey subsoil has given rise to several freshwater bogs (*pauli*).

In this area, systematic and intensive field surveying by the Riu Mannu survey project of Leiden University has confirmed the supposition that the southern Arborèa was an important rural district in Punic and Roman times. The Riu Mannu survey project has not covered the entire area of the southern Arborèa, which measures some 160 km². Instead, a representative sample of systematically and probabilistically defined transects has been examined intensively, in which various types of easily distinguishable sites (settlements, cemeteries, etc.) have been located and much less marked distribution patterns of *off-site* surface finds have been documented. In the six transects examined until 1994, sixteen sites dating from the Punic or Roman period have been located on the intensively surveyed sample grid (Annis *et al.* 1995). Ten of these were occupied during most, if not all of the third and second centuries BC (Fig. 3.4). Seven of them are associated with the light sandy soils of the Terralba rise between the Riu Mannu and Riu Mògoro, being located either on top of the rise itself or on its lower slopes in the proximity of the marshy banks of the meandering lower Riu Mannu. The remaining three sites are located south of the Riu Mannu on the higher ground of the Campidano along a minor torrent.

All these sites have been surveyed in great detail and have yielded ample materials for further consideration. With the exception of two sites which are of a clearly different type, the remaining eight sites have yielded comparable assemblages of numerous roof tiles, large storage jars (*dolia*), various types of transport amphorae, all sorts of utilitarian and kitchen ware, including cooking stands (so-called *salvacenere* or *tabuna*), and fine ware. These sites measure between 3,000 and 4,000 m² with the exception of two significantly larger ones of about 1 ha. In combination with the abundant presence of roof tiles and some construction stone, these finds identify the sites as moderately sized settlement sites probably made of mudbrick walls on stone pediments and covered with tiled roofs; they are likely to have been inhabited permanently. Given their storage facilities and locations, they can be interpreted as 'farms' involved in agricultural or pastoral activities of various kinds (cf. Leveau *et al.* 1993, 42–4). In some cases a so-called 'halo' of off-site finds has been documented around the site (Fig. 3.5), which may suggest that the fields immediately surrounding the farms were intensively cultivated (Hayes 1991; cf. Alcock *et al.* 1994). All the sites were established in the Carthaginian period, most of them in the fourth century and some already in the later fifth century BC. Two farms may have been abandoned in the later third or perhaps in the early second century BC, i.e. during the first years of the Roman occupation, but the others remained inhabited throughout most, if not all of the second century BC. By that date, all sites but one were abandoned. Only one farm in the surveyed sample, therefore, remained continuously inhabited from the Carthaginian period until well into the Roman imperial period (and one more was apparently reoccupied

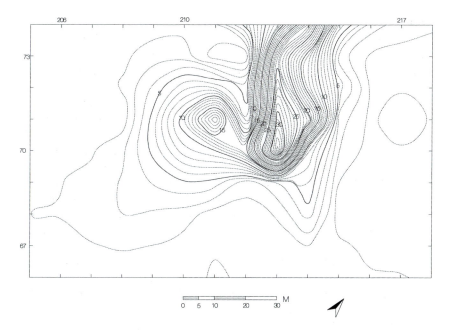

Figure 3.5 The distribution of pottery surface finds at and around a minor Punic farm in the Santa Chiara area: both the site itself and the surrounding *off-site* finds can be distinguished (cf. Fig. 3.6). The densities (in fragments per m²) have been interpolated from a 10 × 10 m collection grid (see Annis *et al.* 1995)

by the second century AD). The two other sites have provisionally been interpreted as a small cemetery and a small subsidiary building or shed (see Fig. 3.6).

Detailed study of the finds, 90 per cent of which consisted of pottery, at the Leiden Institute of Pottery Technology has shown that the vast majority of the pottery was produced locally. This does not necessarily imply that all items were made at each site but indicates rather that they were produced in the area of the Riu Mannu estuary (see Annis *et al.* 1993/4, 37–41). Imported materials occurred in only two categories: the commercial transport amphorae and fine ware. The latter category even consisted almost exclusively of imports, usually so-called 'Attic' and 'Campanian' Black Glaze ware. The majority of the amphorae were locally produced Punic transport amphorae but there were a number of non-local fabrics, which points to their importation from elsewhere. Other shapes include the so-called Graeco-Italic ones. The actual provenance of both Black Glaze pottery and amphorae still remains difficult to establish. These imports nevertheless show that the inhabitants of the sites had access to international trading networks, presumably through Neapolis or Tharros.

The results of the representative Riu Mannu sample transects can be compared with those of extensive amateur surface collections on the Terralba

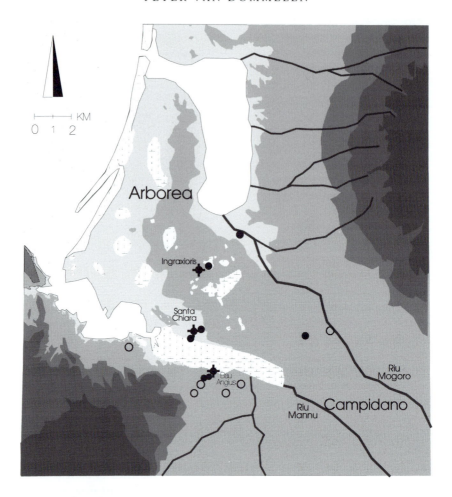

Figure 3.6 The southern Arborèa, showing the late Punic and early Roman Republican farms located by the Riu Mannu survey

0–5–50–100–300>
(m above sea level)

rise, where 124 Punic and Roman sites, both settlements and cemeteries, were identified in an area of approximately 32 km² (Fig. 3.7).[3] These remarkably high figures have now been confirmed by the even slightly higher estimated site density of about 5.5 sites per km² of the Riu Mannu survey sample for the Terralba rise. Most of the 110 settlement sites inhabited during the third and second centuries BC appear to be roughly comparable to those documented by the Riu Mannu survey.

The Riu Mannu survey has confirmed the relative absence of typically Roman products from the third or second century BC in the area of the southern

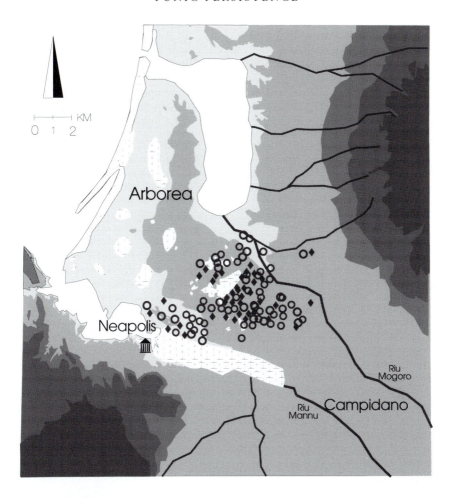

Figure 3.7 The southern Arborèa, showing the Punic and Roman sites which have been located by extensive amateur fieldwork (after Artudi and Perra 1994). The sites marked by a diamond (♦) were abandoned by the first century BC

0–5–50–100–300>
(m above sea level)

Arborèa. Of the locally produced pottery, which makes up the overwhelming majority of the ceramic assemblages of the farms that have been examined, all types closely adhere to Punic models. This holds for both common kitchen and utilitarian ware and for commercial amphorae. The shapes produced are not only those already current before 238 BC (e.g. amphorae of Bartoloni's type *Forma D*) but also later neo-Punic ones that came in vogue during the second century (e.g. amphorae of the Maña D type, Bartoloni's *Forma E*). All Roman materials invariably are imports, mostly Campanian Black Glaze table ware (the Campana A variety being the most common), and occasionally amphorae (Graeco-Italic as

39

well as Dressel 1 types). In the Riu Mannu sample there is one conspicuous exception to this picture, where a significantly larger quantity and variety of Roman imports have been found. This farm, located in the middle of the Terralba rise at a place called Ingraxioris (Fig. 3.6), is not only the largest one found (about 1 ha) but also the only one which remained inhabited until well into the Roman imperial period. With regard to the period under consideration, it has yielded not only the usual assemblage of locally produced Punic-style amphorae and kitchen ware but also numerous imports from the Italian mainland (Campana A and B table ware, Dressel 1 amphorae) and other regions under Roman authority (Graeco-Italic and Massaliote amphorae), including Sardinia itself (stamped *bacili* from Tharros and Sardinian Black Glaze table ware (from Karales?)).

Elsewhere in west central Sardinia a similar picture appears to emerge from the published evidence of the inland central Campidano. In particular in the area between the Sanluri marshes and the Marmilla hills eighteen settlements and eleven cemeteries have been located, which have generically been characterised as 'Roman' (Fig. 3.3; Paderi 1982a). Excavation of the cemetery at Bidd'e Cresia, which was continuously used from the fourth century BC until the fourth century AD, has shown that the burials datable in the third and second centuries BC were almost exclusively accompanied by locally made Punic objects. Several burials, moreover, attest a burial rite with a distinctly Punic character (enchytrismos burial in a reused Punic amphora), although simple trench burials were the norm (Paderi 1982b). Typically Roman graves (*alla cappuccina* – tombs covered with standing tiles) and cremation burials, both associated with locally made Roman *ceramica comune* and imported *sigillata*, occur only from the first century BC onwards (Paderi 1982c).

Colonial categories and local identities in west central Sardinia

Considering the results of the Riu Mannu survey, it is clear that the overall picture of Sardinia during the first centuries of Roman domination is generally confirmed. The rural evidence appears to correspond quite closely to the urban situation of Tharros: Punic traditions did not merely 'persist' but were also renewed, significantly along neo-Punic lines. As in the case of Tharros, this points strongly to continuity of contacts with (neo-Punic) North Africa, where, despite the Punic Wars, Carthage and its African territories passed through a period of substantial development and prosperity (Lancel 1995, 142–72, 269–88).

The intensive surface collections and the detailed studies of the finds of the Riu Mannu survey, however, at the same time allow the available data to be viewed from a slightly different angle. The Riu Mannu survey evidence for the rural southern Arborèa in particular suggests that the theoretical considerations about ambiguous colonial categories and complex or even 'murky' colonial situations may be highly relevant to the archaeological record of the early Roman period. Subtle differences and variations as well as certain constants in the archaeological record have become visible which can be related to different strategies of the inhabitants in the densely inhabited southern Arborèa. In the sample transects of the Riu Mannu survey, the differences primarily are in terms of imported ware from the Italian peninsula and from several other regions under Roman rule. Whereas the inhabitants of most farms in the sample transects received very few Black Glaze cups and only occasional imported amphorae, the inhabitants of the farm at Ingraxioris obtained a far greater number and variety of Roman imports. This might at first sight be ascribed to a relative scarcity of these objects, which meant that only the inhabitants of the largest farm were able to acquire them in substantial numbers. But at a farm on the southern bank of the Riu Mannu at Bau Angius (Fig. 3.6), which has yielded a functionally similar assemblage of material culture and appears to have been of roughly the same size, virtually no imported fine ware or amphorae have been found amidst the abundant remains of locally produced Punic and neo-Punic pottery. It would make more sense, therefore, to attribute these differences to a conscious choice made by the inhabitants of the farm in the face of changing political and economic conditions after 238 BC. One such change was the increasing importance of Karales, a naval base of the Roman fleet. This city had become the principal political and economic centre of Sardinia at the expense of other Punic cities such as Tharros, which was cut off from its Punic trading contacts across the western Mediterranean (Tronchetti 1984, 252). While the inhabitants of all the farms continued to receive large quantities of locally manufactured Punic-style pottery, only those at Ingraxioris apparently responded positively to the new situation and established contact with Karales to participate in Roman trading networks. The others evidently were unable to do so, perhaps out of loyalty to their landlord, or were simply reluctant to abandon established traditions. From Livy's account of the armed rebellion in 215 BC (XXIII. 40. 1–41. 7) it is clear that many landowners in west central Sardinia were of Punic origin and sided with Carthage during the Second Punic War (Meloni 1975, 54–61). The large farm at Bau Angius illustrates this situation well: the virtual absence of imports contrasts with the presence of several neo-Punic (second-century) amphorae, which show that the inhabitants of the farm did maintain contact with the outside world but evidently avoided Roman imports.

In the central Campidano (Fig. 3.3), the published evidence of the Sanluri district suggests a similar picture: within one community, Bidd'e Cresia, various burial practices were followed, one of which was of a distinctly Punic character (*enchytrismos* – burials in Punic amphorae), while most were indeterminate trench burials. Clearly Roman innovations (*alla cappuccina* burials and cremations with Roman grave goods) only occur much later. The inhabitants of the nearby settlement, one or perhaps a number of farms, apparently were unable or reluctant to abandon their traditional burial rites or to commemorate the dead with objects that were not in the traditional Punic style. A similar phenomenon can be observed in the nearby rural sanctuary dedicated to Demeter and Tanit, which was established in the ruins of the *nuraghe* of Genna Maria (Villanovaforru) in the fourth century BC. One of the most common offerings made was that of oil lamps, which were dropped in the central pit of the former courtyard of the *nuraghe* (Lilliu 1993a, 15–18). While coins attest the continuity of the sanctuary, remarkably few imported Italian Black Glaze lamps have been found,[4] none of them antedating the second half of the second century BC (Lilliu 1993b, 43–5). Several dozen coarse locally made lamps, however, were offered in the same period, which demonstrates their association with other finds. In this case, too, it was evidently felt inappropriate to use explicitly 'foreign' Roman objects in the rituals which were of a markedly local Punic character (Lilliu 1993a, 19).

These forms of practice which 'avoided' Roman imports from the Italian mainland and instead show a strong preference for Punic-style products can be seen to be acts of resistance to Roman domination, which can best be labelled 'cultural resistance'. Although reluctance to depart from the established tradition can hardly be regarded as an act of resistance, clinging to tradition does contribute to the development of a 'counter-hegemonic' discourse (Keesing 1994). The Riu Mannu survey evidence has also shown, however, that the situation in west central Sardinia under the Roman Republic cannot be reduced to a clear-cut opposition between supporters of Rome and supporters of Carthage. In the sample transects of the southern Arborèa, the two largest farms at Ingraxioris and Bau Angius can perhaps be cited as exemplifying the two sides of the colonial divide, and the other minor farms can all be situated at intermediate positions between the two extremes. These observations can be interpreted as representing a range of positions taken by various social and economic groups, who followed slightly different strategies for coping with the colonial situation and, thus, contributed to a complex set of socio-economic structures in the region. The strategy adopted may have been determined by these structures, which for example made it difficult for certain people to obtain Roman imports. Many people, in particular peasants, are furthermore likely to have been guided by local tradition. Yet certain choices made in the face of the colonial situation must also have led people to prefer Punic-style products. It is significant in this respect that no Roman-style utilitarian ware (Roman *ceramica comune*) was produced locally before roughly the (later) first century BC. Such choices can safely be interpreted in terms of cultural identities. In the particular case of the southern Arborèa, a clear sense of a Punic cultural identity referring to the earlier period of Carthaginian domination was constructed in the later third century. It held out during the entire second century BC. But, if the construction of a cultural identity was a considered response to the new structures imposed on west central Sardinia, the Punic identity is likely to have been emphasised in different ways among different socio-economic groups.

These various socio-economic positions and related responses correspond closely to the political and economic structures imposed on Sardinia by the

Roman authorities. When Sardinia (together with Corsica) was formally annexed as a *provincia* in 227 BC, all land had been confiscated by the Roman state as *ager publicus* and a fixed tribute, the *stipendium*, had been imposed on the *provincia* as a whole. Moreover, a tithe (*decima*) was collected from all grain that was produced. More important was the well tried Roman policy to maintain local elites in power: the *ager publicus* was leased out directly either to the former Sardinian landowners or to Roman *publicani*, who speculated in state-owned land.[5] Both groups in turn rented it out to the local population, who in the end had to hand over a substantial rent (*vectigal*) on top of the *stipendium* and tithe (Meloni 1987, 221–3). As a consequence, former landowners who agreed to collaborate with the Roman authorities could maintain their local patronage network and socio-economic position. At the same time, small peasants could bypass these local structures and turn to the Roman *publicani* in order to rent land. The inhabitants of the farm at Ingraxioris can perhaps be identified as such former landowners who had decided to lease their land back from the Roman provincial authorities, whereas the various small farms must have rented their land from either local landowners or *publicani*.

Conclusion:
Roman colonial reorganisation and local resistance

Roman colonisation in west central Sardinia clearly was primarily a process of economic exploitation through taxes and rents; migration and cultural assimilation played only a secondary part. Nevertheless, the consequences of these colonial policies were considerable, particularly in the longer run. In west central Sardinia the previously thriving countryside began to decline under Roman rule; in the end (i.e. by the first century BC), many minor farms and some of the larger ones were abandoned. In the southern Arborèa the effects were particularly strong: extensive amateur collections indicate a reduction of about 35 per cent of rural settlement (cf. Fig. 3.7), a figure which is supported by the results of the representative sample examined by the Riu Mannu survey. Whereas under Carthaginian domination city and country were closely related, Roman rule led moreover to an ever-increasing divide between city and country. This was a direct consequence of the Roman policy, which was directed towards the urban centres and left the countryside in the hands of the local elites (Sirago 1992, 243–4). This development can best be regarded in Braudelian terms as the dominant *conjoncture* of Sardinia during the first centuries of Roman rule, which constituted the wider context for both colonising Romans and colonised Sardinians in the (re)definition of their own positions.

The construction of a strong sense of being Punic (or perhaps rather Sardinian?) has been shown to have been a general response to the changes of this period. But within the conditions imposed by the Roman administration, people acted differently according to the possibilities and alternatives that were open to them: former landowners could go along with the Roman authorities but this option was not available to tenants. Their conduct can perhaps be understood in terms of prevailing traditions, although even these peasants must have faced certain choices in the new colonial situation. It seems plausible that former landowners could either play down their Punic identity or instead cultivate it. While some accommodated Roman policies, others developed a strategy of cultural resistance against Roman authority, which at one point, in 215 BC, was transformed into armed rebellion. Most peasants, however, had few options: some gave up their farm at an early stage (the late third century BC), while others continued as best they could, occasionally obtaining Roman imports but by and large holding on to the local Punic traditions. It remains doubtful whether the conduct of these peasants can be termed 'resistance', as it was to a large extent determined by the prevailing social and economic conditions. By sticking to Punic traditions in their daily practice, however, they contributed to the preservation of these, thus (unconsciously) supporting the more deliberate practice of cultural resistance of their former landowners (cf. Comaroff and Comaroff 1991, 27–32). The virtual absence of imported Roman objects in funerary and ritual contexts as shown at Bidd'e Cresia (Sanluri) and Genna Maria (Villanovaforru) (see above) further demonstrates the existence of a strong Punic cultural identity which excluded Roman material culture.

Interpreting the persistence of local Punic traditions under Roman rule as an instance of 'silent resistance' offers a convincing explanation of the armed uprising of 215 BC in the Campidano plain of west central Sardinia. This violent and massive rebellion has often been regarded as an isolated event, presumably closely related to the ongoing Second Punic War (Barreca 1986, 45). From the perspective outlined above, however, the armed revolt was intimately tied to, and even grounded in, the cultural resistance which was widespread in the plains and coastal areas; the event of 215 BC was therefore not just an event related to other events of the Second Punic War but can actually be interpreted as an extraordinary as well as integral manifestation of a wider current of inarticulate resistance in west central Sardinia (cf. Keesing 1992, 213–17).

This case study of west central Sardinia under the Roman Republic thus provides a fine example of the nuanced many-faceted nature of colonial situations, as it clearly demonstrates that their *réalité unique* presents several points of view instead of only one or two (*contra* Bénabou 1976, 18). It is also clear, however, that such a variety of perspectives, experiences and responses dissolves neither colonial power structures of domination and exploitation nor the resistance of the colonised. In west central Sardinia, Roman domination was present both militarily (the crushing of the rebellion of 215 BC) and economically (the heavy taxes), and the Riu Mannu survey evidence has unambiguously exposed its consequences of decline and isolation in the rural southern Arborèa. The construction of a well developed notion of Punic cultural identity within this framework proved to be quite successful, as it enabled the region to preserve its distinct character for a considerable period. That Punic cultural identity was also understood as such is tellingly demonstrated by Cicero, who as late as 54 BC in his defence of M. Aemilius Scaurus, the corrupt ex-governor of Sardinia, could still convincingly depict the Sardinians as 'sons of Africa' (19, 45: *Africa ipsa parens illa Sardiniae*).

Acknowledgements

This chapter reports part of a wider study of colonialism in west central Sardinia during the first millennium BC which is supported financially by the Netherlands Foundation for Scientific Research (NWO). The Riu Mannu survey project is an initiative of the Department of Archaeology of Leiden University. Earlier versions were read in 1995 at the Theoretical Roman Archaeology sessions of the Roman Archaeology Conference in Reading and at a staff seminar of the Department of Archaeology of Leiden University. I am indebted to my colleagues of the Riu Mannu survey project, Dr M. Beatrice Annis and Dr Pieter van de Velde, as well as to Antoine Mienties and Jan Slofstra, whose critical comments have much contributed to this chapter.

Notes

1 The term 'imperialism' is avoided (particularly in the context of the Roman Republic), as the notion is not well defined and appears to represent only a specific instance of colonialism (cf. Doyle 1986, 45). The term 'colonialism' is not used in any 'technical' sense of the Latin term *colonia* as a settlement of Roman citizens, unless explicitly stated.
2 Dry stone-walled towers dating from the middle and late Bronze Age, which have been found mostly to have been continuously inhabited until the later Iron Age.
3 These have been described in several unpublished essays by Gino Artudi and Sandro Perra, from Terralba (one of which has now been published in a local magazine: Artudi and Perra 1994).
4 Only eight oil lamps have been identified as Roman Republican, as compared with 194 items which could be ascribed to the imperial period.
5 *Ager publicus* could also be rented out directly to individual Roman citizens or collectively to groups of them when a *colonia* (in the technical Roman sense of the word) was founded. Neither of these practices was common in Sardinia, where only one fully fledged *colonia* (Turris Libisonis Colonia Iulia, modern Porto Torres in the north of Sardinia) was founded and only one other town (Colonia Augusta Iulia Uselis) was raised to colonial rank. As both names clearly show, these are of Augustan date (Meloni 1987, 203–31).

Bibliography

Alcock, S., Cherry, J. and Davis, J. (1994), 'Intensive survey, agricultural practice and the classical landscape of Greece', in I. Morris (ed.) *Classical Greece: Ancient Histories and Modern Archaeologies*, New Directions in Archaeology, Cambridge: Cambridge University Press, 137–70.

Annis, M. B., van Dommelen, P. and van de Velde, P. (1993/4), 'The *Riu Mannu* survey project in west central Sardinia: a first interim report', *Newsletter of the Department of Pottery Technology* 11/12: 31–44.

Annis, M.B., van Dommelen, P. and van de Velde, P. (1995), 'Rural settlement and socio-political organization: the *Riu Mannu* survey project in Sardinia', *BABesch* 70: 133–52.

Artudi, G. and Perra, S. (1994), 'Gli insediamenti punico-romani nel territorio di Terralba', *Terralba ieri e oggi* 8, 16: 32–8.

Barreca, F. (1986), *La civiltà fenicio-punica in Sardegna*, Sardegna Archeologica Studi e monumenti 3, Sassari: Carlo Delfino Editori.

Bénabou, M. (1976), *La Résistance africaine à la romanisation*, Paris: Maspéro.

Bondì, S. F. (1987), 'La dominazione cartaginese', in *Dalle origini alla fine dell'età bizantina*, Storia dei Sardi e della Sardegna, Milan: Jaca Book, 173–203.

Bondì, S. F. (1990), 'La cultura punica nella Sardegna romana: un fenomeno di sopravvivenza?', in A. Mastino (ed.) *L'Africa romana 7* (Atti del convegno di studio, Sassari, 15–17 dicembre 1989), Sassari: Edizioni Gallizzi, 457–64.

Bourdieu, P. (1977), *Outline of a Theory of Practice*, Cambridge: Cambridge University Press.

Bourdieu, P. (1992), *The Logic of Practice*, Cambridge: Polity Press.

Comaroff, J. and Comaroff, J. (1989), 'The colonization of consciousness in South Africa', *Economy and Society* 18: 267–96.

Comaroff, J. and Comaroff, J. (1991), *Of Revelation and Revolution. Christianity, Colonialism and Consciousness in South Africa*, Chicago: University of Chicago Press.

Dirks, N. (1992), 'Introduction: colonialism and culture', in N. Dirks (ed.) *Colonialism and Culture*, Comparative Studies in Society and History series, Ann Arbor: University of Michigan Press, 1–25.

Doyle, M. (1986), *Empires*, Ithaca: Cornell University Press.

Friedman, J. (1992), 'The past in the future: history and the politics of identity', *American Anthropologist* 94: 837–59.

Gras, M., Rouillard, P. and Teixidor, J. (1991), 'The Phoenicians and death', *Berytus* 39: 127–76.

Hayes, P. (1991), 'Models for the distribution of pottery around former agricultural settlements', in A. Schofield (ed.) *Interpreting Artefact Scatters. Contributions to Ploughzone Archaeology*, Oxford: Oxbow Books, 81–92.

Keesing, R. (1992), *Custom and Confrontation. The Kwaio Struggle for Cultural Autonomy*, Chicago: University of Chicago Press.

Keesing, R. (1994), 'Colonial and counter-colonial discourse in Melanesia', *Critique of Anthropology* 14, 1: 41–58.

Lancel, S. (1995), *Carthage. A History*, Oxford: Blackwell.

Leveau, Ph., Sillières, P. and Vallat, J.-P. (1993), *Campagnes de la Méditeranée romaine*, Bibliothèque d'Archéologie, Paris: Hachette.

Lilliu, C. (1993a), 'Un culto di età punico-romana al nuraghe Genna Maria di Villanovaforru', in *Genna Maria* II,1: *Il deposito votivo del mastio e del cortile*, Cagliari: Università degli Studi di Cagliari–Comune di Villanovaforru, 11–39.

Lilliu, C. (1993b), 'Lucerne tardo-ellenistiche e tardo-repubblicane', in *Genna Maria* II,1: *Il deposito votivo del mastio e del cortile*, Cagliari: Università degli Studi di Cagliari–Comune di Villanovaforru, 43–105.

Marcus, G. (1992), 'Past, present and emergent identities: requirements for ethnographies of late twentieth-century modernity worldwide', in S. Lash and J. Friedman (eds) *Modernity and Identity*, Oxford: Blackwell, 309–30.

Mastino, A. (1985), 'Le relazioni tra Africa e Sardegna in età romana: inventario preliminare', in A. Mastino (ed.) *L'Africa romana* 2 (Atti del convegno di studio, Sassari, 14–16 dicembre 1984), Sassari: Edizioni Gallizzi, 27–92.

Meloni, P. (1975), *La Sardegna romana*, Sassari: Chiarella.

Meloni, P. (1987), 'La Sardegna e la repubblica romana', in *Dalle origini alla fine dell'età bizantina*, Storia dei Sardi e della Sardegna 1, Milan: Jaca Book, 213–34.

Nieddu, G. and Zucca, R. (1991), *Othoca. Una città sulla laguna*, Oristano: S'Alvure.

Paderi, M. C. (1982a), 'L'età romana', in *Ricerche archeologiche nel territorio di Sanluri*, Sanluri: Comune di Sanluri–Soprintendenza Archeologica per le province di Cagliari e Oristano, 59–62.

Paderi, M. C. (1982b), 'La necropoli di Bidd'e Cresia e le tombe puniche', in *Ricerche archeologiche nel territorio di Sanluri*, Sanluri: Comune di Sanluri–Soprintendenza Archeologica per le province di Cagliari e Oristano, 49–51.

Paderi, M. C. (1982c), 'Bidd'e Cresia: sepolture e corredi di età romana', in *Ricerche archeologiche nel territorio di Sanluri*, Sanluri: Comune di Sanluri–Soprintendenza Archeologica per le province di Cagliari e Oristano, 67–80.

Pels, P. (1993), 'Critical matters: interactions between missionaries and Waluguru in colonial Tanganyika, 1930–1961' (Ph.D. thesis, University of Amsterdam), Amsterdam.

Prochaska, D. (1990), *Making Algeria French. Colonialism in Bône, 1870–1920*, Cambridge: Cambridge University Press.

Sheldon, R. (1982), 'Romanizzazione, acculturazione e resistenza: problemi concettuali nella storia del Nordafrica', *Dialoghi di Archeologia* 4, 1: 102–6.

Sirago, V. (1992), 'Aspetti coloniali dell'occupazione romana in Sardegna', in *Sardinia antiqua. Studi in onore di Piero Meloni in occasione del suo settantesimo compleanno*, Cagliari: Edizioni della Torre, 239–53.

Stoler, A. (1989), 'Rethinking colonial categories: European communities and the boundaries of rule', *Comparative Studies in Society and History* 31: 134–61.

Thébert, Y. (1978), 'Romanisation et déromanisation en Afrique: histoire décolonisée ou histoire inversée?', *Annales ESC* 33: 65–82.

Thomas, N. (1994), *Colonialism's Culture. Anthropology, Travel and Government*, Cambridge: Cambridge University Press.

Tore, G. and Stiglitz, A. (1994), 'Urbanizzazione e territorio: considerazioni sulla colonizzazione fenicio-punica in Sardegna', 1 'L'urbanizzazione e lo spazio urbano', 2 'Lo spazio rurale: parametri geografici e indicatori territoriali', in A. Mastino and P. Ruggeri (eds) *L'Africa romana* 10 (Atti del convegno di studio, Oristano, 11–13 dicembre 1992), Sassari: Editrice Archivio Fotografico Sardo, 779–808.

Tronchetti, C. (1984), 'The cities of Roman Sardinia', in M. Balmuth and R. Rowland, Jr (eds) *Studies in Sardinian Archaeology*, Ann Arbor: University of Michigan Press, 237–83.

Vismara, C. (1990), 'Sopravvivenze puniche e persistenze indigene nel Nord Africa ed in Sardegna in età romana. Introduzione', in A. Mastino (ed.) *L'Africa romana* 7 (Atti del convegno di studio, Sassari, 15–17 dicembre 1989), Sassari: Edizioni Gallizzi, 39–47.

Whitehouse, R. and Wilkins, J. (1989), 'Greeks and natives in south-east Italy:

approaches to the archaeological evidence', in T. Champion (ed.) *Centre and Periphery. Comparative studies in Archaeology*, One World Archaeology series 11, London: Unwin Hyman, 102–26.

Zucca, R. (1985), 'I rapporti tra l'*Africa* e la *Sardinia* alla luce dei documenti archeologici. Nota preliminare' in A. Mastino (ed.) *L'Africa romana* 2 (Atti del convegno di studio, Sassari, 14–16 dicembre 1984), Sassari: Edizioni Gallizzi, 93–104.

Zucca, R. (1987), *Neapolis e il suo territorio*, Oristano: S'Alvure.

4

CONSTRUCTING THE SELF AND THE OTHER IN CYRENAICA

Eireann Marshall

Several recent works have focused on the construction of identity through the definition of an other. Hall has examined how the Greeks, and in particular the Athenians, defined their self by inventing the barbarian other (Hall 1989, 1–2). To Hartog, the barbarian in Herodotus functions like a mirror which reflects the Greek norms of his readers in reverse (Hartog 1992, 5–6). The other is, therefore, defined through the self because it is the reverse self. Conversely, the other serves to unite a group, or a number of groups, because it defines the group's self, and, in other words, defines who the group is. The invention of the Persians as barbarians united Greece because, as others, they allowed the Greeks to develop a common self (Hall 1989, 1–2; Cartledge 1993, 39). Through the construction of the barbarian, the Greeks erected an 'us–them' boundary which separated Greece from all others and marked out Greekness (Cartledge 1993, 11).

In a context where the self and the other interact closely, however, the boundaries dividing the self and the other can shift (Dench 1995, 11). Relations between neighbouring groups can be fluid in the sense that these groups can be hostile to one another or, at different times, can be allied to one another. In these circumstances the same group can be defined as both other and a part of the self. Dench has shown, for example, how the Romans perceived the Sabines both as their others and as integral to their identity (Dench 1995, 85–91).

In Cyrenaica, hostility between Cyrenaicans and Libyans gave rise to Libyans being constructed as other. However, conflicts also occurred between Cyrenaican cities, and in these circumstances the Cyrenaicans could ally themselves to Libyans against one another. In these cases, some Cyrenaicans would construct a common identity with the Libyans. In other words, the Cyrenaicans defined their identity by constructing the Libyans in opposition to themselves and by constructing the Libyans as a part of the Cyrenaican self. The construction of the Libyan in these contrasting ways allowed the Cyrenaicans to express their multifaceted identity.

In this chapter, I will examine how the Libyans were constructed as the other, both by the Cyrenaicans and by other Greeks. I will then proceed to consider how the Libyans were incorporated into the Cyrenaican self and will conclude by exploring the ways in which the self and other are constructed.

Libyans in the works of non-Cyrenaican authors

The Libyan tribes with whom the Cyrenaicans came into contact were both numerous and diverse in character. Ancient sources describe a number of large tribes bordering Cyrenaica, such as the Garamantes, Marmaridae, Macae and Nasamones, as well as several smaller, more assimilated tribes living in Cyrenaica, such as the Asbystae and Auchisae. The difficulty in examining how the Cyrenaicans constructed these Libyans lies in the fact that there are very few extant Cyrenaican texts. Therefore, in order to gain a more complete picture of the way in which the Cyrenaicans viewed the Libyans, it is necessary to examine the works of other Greek writers. Three of the most important representations of the Libyans are given by Herodotus, Diodorus and Strabo, who, though writing at different times, tend to characterise the Libyans in similar ways. To differing degrees, these three authors represent some Libyans as barbaric and others as almost civilised.

Herodotus' characterisation of the Libyans is complex in that he both characterises them as barbarian and attributes Greek customs to them. Herodotus claims that the *aegis* derives from the clothing of Libyan women and that Libyan women exported the custom of crying at religious festivals to Greece (Herodotus 4. 189). Herodotus, in addition, draws parallels between the Libyans and the Greeks by writing that the two groups bury their dead in the same way (Herodotus 4. 190; see also 3. 38). However, he concurrently characterises the Libyans as barbarians. Several tribes are represented as being promiscuous; for example, the females of the Gindanes advertise the number of lovers they have by wearing leather anklets given to them by their lovers (Herodotus 4. 176, 4. 172, 4. 180; see also Hall 1989, 201; Cartledge 1993, 71). Herodotus, furthermore, constructs some Libyans as barbarian by describing them as bestial; the Ausoi are said to copulate like flocks and herds (Herodotus 4. 180, 4. 183, see also 1. 203; Hall 1989, 126; Williams 1990, 184).

Herodotus does not characterise particular groups of Libyans as either wholly civilised or barbarian. He does represent the Libyans living in the desert as more marginal than the other Libyans and credits them with stranger customs than the others. Herodotus says, for example, that the Atlantes do not dream and that the Atarantes do not use names (Herodotus 4. 184). Furthermore, some desert Libyans, such as the Garamantes, eschew regular interaction with outsiders (Herodotus 4. 174; see also 4. 196; Agatharchides, *Periplus of the Erithraean Sea*, ed. Huntingford, 18; see also Smith 1990, 24). Conversely, the nomads are represented as being more influenced by the Greeks. The Asbystae, who lived near Cyrene, and the Auchisae in particular are said to imitate Cyrenaican customs (Herodotus 4. 170–1). However, while the nomads are more civilised than the desert Libyans, they are also constructed as barbarian; they are, for example, the only Libyans whom Herodotus defines as barbarian through their promiscuity. Furthermore, the nomads are characterised as barbarian in similar ways to the desert Libyans; both the nomadic Ausoi and the desert Garamantes are represented as bestial (Herodotus 4. 180, 4. 183).

Diodorus' treatment of Libyans is both more general and less ambivalent than Herodotus'. He makes a much stronger contrast between Libyans, whom he characterises as barbarians, and others who are almost civilised. In other words, while the farmers and nomads are described as having kings and leading semi-civilised lives, the desert Libyans are characterised as completely barbaric (Diodorus 3. 49). The criteria that Diodorus uses to represent desert Libyans as barbarians are similar to those Herodotus uses to define the Libyans in general as barbaric. Diodorus' depiction of the clothing of the desert Libyans matches the clothing which Herodotus attributes to the Libyan women in general (Herodotus 4. 189). But unlike Herodotus, who does not pass any judgement on the clothing, Diodorus explicitly characterises these goatskin mantles as barbaric (Diodorus 3. 49). Furthermore, Diodorus defines the desert Libyans as savage by saying that they attack everything they see and that they have no justice (Diodorus 3. 49). Herodotus, on the other hand, does not describe the desert Libyans as hostile and even goes so far as to say that the Garamantes do not know how to defend themselves (Herodotus 4. 174).

Like Diodorus, Strabo represents the desert Libyans as barbaric, and contrasts them with other, more civilised Libyans. Strabo constructs a polarity between coastal and desert Libya. While the desert is said to be thinly populated by people who live in a savage fashion, the coast is urban, prosperous and densely populated (Strabo 2. 5. 33, 17. 3. 1, 17. 3. 24). Strabo emphasises that the coastal region is civilised, and opposed to the desert, by saying that Rome rules the best parts of the *oikoumene* and that only coastal Libya is a part of the Roman Empire (Strabo 17. 3. 24). In making this opposition between the coast and the desert, Strabo contrasts the uncivilised desert Libyans with the Cyrenaicans, as well as with other agricultural Libyans living on the coast.

Herodotus, Diodorus and Strabo, to different extents, construct some Libyans as barbarian and others as almost civilised. Herodotus' treatment of the Libyans is more complex in that he does not characterise any particular group as wholly civilised or as wholly barbaric. While Herodotus constructs the desert Libyans as marginal, Strabo and Diodorus, more specifically, represent them as wholly barbaric and contrast them with the Cyrenaicans and other more civilised Libyans. The construction of the desert-dwelling Libyans as barbarians renders them the 'others' of the readers of the Greek authors. In other words, the representations of these barbarian Libyans in both Herodotus and in Diodorus and Strabo constitute the reversal of these readers' norms. In representing Libyan customs as barbaric, these authors, conversely, help to represent the readers' norms as Greek (Hall 1989, 1–2; Hartog 1992, 5–6; Cartledge 1993, 56–8).

Conversely, those Libyans who are represented as civilised or semi-civilised are, to a certain extent, incorporated into the Greek norm.

The fact that the desert Libyans are constructed as the Cyrenaican other by non-Cyrenaican authors while other Libyans are, to an extent, incorporated into the Cyrenaican self does not, however, necessarily mean that they were so perceived by the Cyrenaicans themselves. However, by examining the relationship between the Libyans and Cyrenaicans one can see how the construction of the Libyans by outsiders, to a certain extent, matches the construction of Libyans by the Cyrenaicans themselves. In particular, it will be seen that the Cyrenaicans made a similar dual representation of Libyans as both civilised and barbarian.

Cyrenaicans and the Libyan other

The Cyrenaicans came into conflict with Libyans throughout their history, which may suggest that the Cyrenaicans would have constructed the Libyans in opposition to themselves, just as non-Cyrenaican authors tended to do. Most of the wars fought between the Cyrenaicans and Libyans have gone unrecorded and existing evidence is scant. Herodotus says that Libyans fought against Cyrene at Irasa after Battus II issued land grants which encroached on the Libyans' territory (Herodotus 4. 159). Thucydides and Pausanias describe Libyans attacking the Cyrenaican city Euhesperides in 414 and 404 respectively (Thucydides 7. 50; Pausanias 4. 26). In the Augustan period the Cyrenaicans fought a protracted series of battles against southern Libyans, notably the Nasamones and Marmaridae. The seriousness of the threat posed by these Libyans at the time can be gauged by the fact that the Cyrenaicans appealed to Rome for help. Cassius Dio says that the Legio III Augusta was sent to quell the desert Libyans (Cassius Dio 55. 10A. 1). The Romans did not subdue these Libyans with any ease; the proconsul for Africa, L. Cornelius Lentulus, was ambushed by Libyans (Eusthatius 209–10) and it was not until AD 6–7 that P. Sulpicius Quirinius finally defeated the Libyans (Florus 2. 31).

It would appear that the majority of these conflicts were fought against the Libyans living in the desert, south of Cyrenaica (Laronde 1990, 176). The way in which the Cyrenaicans evoked their past during times of conflict with these Libyans suggests that the threat posed by the southern Libyans reinforced Cyrenaican identity. An inscription erected in the *agora* at Cyrene during the Augustan period, which commemorates peace in the Marmaric war, refers to Cyrene as the city of the descendants of Battus (*SEG* 9. 63). In this inscription the suppression of the desert Libyans is celebrated with a reminder of Cyrene's founding father and an appeal to the city's past. The inscription recreates Cyrene's history and identity; it also re-erects the ideological boundaries separating the city from the southern Libyans. Early in the fourth century BC, five Cyrenaican *strategoi* commemorated the defeat of the Macae and Nasamones by dedicating a tenth of their booty to Apollo (*SEG* 9. 77). Apollo is central to the foundation of Cyrene, as constructed in both historical and mythological terms; he gives the oracle which instructs Battus to found the city and his hierogamy with the eponymous nymph Cyrene is represented as symbolic of the birth of the city (Herodotus 150, 155; Diodorus 8. 29; Pindar 4. 5–8, 9. 5–8; Callimachus, *Hymn to Apollo* 90–2). As a result, Apollo is central to the fabric of Cyrenaica throughout its history. Cyrene's most important intramural sanctuary, the sanctuary of Apollo, is located in the place where the god consummated his love for the nymph Cyrene and where the Theran settlers first arrived at Cyrene; and the eponymous priesthood of Apollo is the city's most important priesthood (Herodotus 4. 158; Callimachus, *Hymn to Apollo* 90–2; Apollonius Rhodius 2. 505; Chamoux 1953, 268; Stucchi 1975, 117; Ensoli 1990, 157–71). Therefore, by making a dedication to Apollo, these *strategoi* represent the defeat of the Libyans as central to Cyrenaican identity. Diodorus and Pausanias, similarly, describe the defeat of the Libyans as necessary to the colonisation of Cyrene. Pausanias says that Chronus helped Battus found Cyrene and defeat the neighbouring Libyans (Pausanias 3. 14. 3). According to Diodorus, the oracle given to Battus foretold that Battus would rule over Libya after he had defeated the barbarians (Diodorus 8. 29). Strabo, perhaps in response to the Marmaric war, writes that Cyrenaica is prosperous partly because it produced men who had shown courage in defeating the Libyans (Strabo 17. 3. 21). These authors and the Cyrenaicans themselves represent Cyrenaican existence as dependent on the defeat of the Libyans.

Accordingly, the reduction of the Libyans gave new impetus to Cyrenaican identity. As a result, it is likely that the Cyrenaicans constructed the desert Libyans, in particular, as their other. Hall has shown how, in Athens, the concept of the barbarian was developed at a time when the Greek world was threatened by Persia (Hall 1989, 60; Cartledge 1993, 39). Dench has more recently demonstrated that the Oscans were constructed as barbarians because of the threat they posed to the Greeks in southern Italy (Dench 1995, 11). When the existence of an ethnic group may depend on the reduction of another group, it defines itself in opposition to the group with which it is in conflict. A group does so by projecting qualities viewed as opposite to the ones it embodies on to the threatening group. (Lippmann 1922, 148; Hall 1989, 60, 103, 121; Dench 1995, 23). It seems likely that the Cyrenaicans constructed the desert Libyans as their other by emphasising the non-agricultural, non-urban life style of the southern Libyans, since these characteristics opposed those which were representative of Cyrenaica. Since the Libyans posed such a threat to the Cyrenaicans, it seems likely that the Cyrenaicans constructed them as savage, dangerous and lawless in much the same way as the aforementioned authors. Synesius, a Cyrenaican who lived in the fourth and fifth centuries AD, provides a late but useful testimony to the way in which the Cyrenaicans constructed the desert Libyans as their other. According to Synesius, the Libyans who inhabit the desert region live far from towns, roads and commerce; they are perceived to be ignorant of the sea and to be immoral (*The Letters of Synesius*, ed. Fitzgerald, 243–7). In his construction of the southern Libyans, Synesius focuses on the same characteristics as Diodorus and Strabo. These Libyans are constructed as non-urban, isolated from other people and unjust.

Libyans incorporated into the Cyrenaican self

While the Cyrenaicans constructed the southern Libyans as their other, they also developed a common identity with the neighbouring Libyans. This may be explained by the fact that the Cyrenaicans were not in a constant state of conflict with all the Libyans (Laronde 1990, 173). According to tradition, the Cyrenaicans had had a close relationship with neighbouring Libyans since the foundation of Cyrene, traditionally dated 631 BC. Herodotus says that it was the Libyans who led the Theran settlers from Aziris to the site of Cyrene (Herodotus 4. 157; Parisi Presicce 1994, 85). While the early history of the colony is uncertain, the Libyans probably helped the Cyrenaeans when they first arrived in Libya. White has suggested that, since the Cyrenaeans had undergone difficult times in Aziris, they would need the assistance of the Libyans with their first harvests, in terms of both manpower and expertise (White 1987, 76). This hypothesis is supported by the fact that colonisers in other parts of the ancient world, such as southern Italy, depended on the manpower provided by natives (Guzzo 1990, 140).

Cyrene continued to have a close relationship with the Libyan tribes into the Roman period. An inscription from the first century BC honouring a Cyrenaean for his services both to the cities in Cyrenaica and to Libyan tribes testifies to a bond forged between the Cyrenaicans and the Libyans (*SEG* 20. 29; see also Reynolds 1987, 380). While the Libyans dwelling in Cyrenaica lived in tribes in the Greek and Hellenistic periods, by the Roman era many had become sedentary and integrated within Cyrenaican towns and cities, perhaps because of the need to produce surplus corn (Reynolds 1987, 379–83). Reynolds has suggested that the *ochloi* mentioned in a first-century inscription from Taucheira are a group of non-citizen Libyans who lived within that city (*Archeologia Classica* 25–6 [1973–4] 622 ff.; Reynolds 1987, 379). Two inscriptions from El Gubba and Hmeda, villages outside Cyrene and Ptolemais respectively, consist of a list of names among which there are a notable number of Libyan names (El Gubba, SEG 9. 348; the Hmeda inscription is unpublished; Reynolds 1987, 380; Laronde 1990, 178–9). While this may indicate that a considerable number of Libyans lived in villages of this sort, it is difficult to identify Libyans on the basis of their names, since Cyrenaicans frequently used Libyan names (Reynolds 1987, 380; Laronde 1990, 178). Carrhotos, the charioteer who drove the quadriga owned by Arcesilas IV to victory in the Pythian games in 462 BC, provides an early example of a Cyrenaican who bore a Libyan name (Pindar 5. 26). While the scholiast to Pindar's fifth Pythian ode says that Carrhotos is an indigenous name, Carrhotos had to be Greek in order to compete in the Panhellenic games (Chamoux 1953, 174 n. 7).

Libyans could become fully integrated within Cyrenaican cities through inter-marriage with Cyrenaicans. Intermarriage between the two populations had probably occurred since the foundation of Cyrene, since the Theran settlers would have needed to supplement their population with Libyan women. In the fourth century BC Ptolemy Soter's *Diagramma* enabled children of Cyrenaican fathers and Libyan mothers to be citizens (*SEG* 9. 1, 2–3). By enacting this edict, the Cyrenaicans, or at least Ptolemy Soter, allowed Libyans to be incorporated into the Cyrenaican self and allowed the boundaries dividing the Libyans from the Cyrenaicans to be fluid. However, since the children of Cyrenaican women and Libyan men were not granted citizenship, some boundaries separating the two populations remained intact. On the other hand, as Laronde has indicated, this edict permitted the children of Libyan women from Catabathmus to Automalax, the whole of Libya stretching from Egypt to Tripolitania, to be Cyrenaican citizens (Laronde 1990, 178). This seems to suggest that the Cyrenaicans intermarried not only with Libyans dwelling in Cyrenaica but also with those living outside. It appears that the Cyrenaicans allowed even desert Libyans to be incorporated in their self, and that they did not construct distinct boundaries separating themselves from the desert Libyans.

Just as the Cyrenaicans did not use citizenship to distinguish themselves from Libyans, so they did not, apparently, represent themselves as physiologically different from Libyans. Art historians, notably Rosenbaum, have shown that many Cyrenaican portraits have somatic features which resemble those of modern Libyans (Rosenbaum 1960, 21 ff.; Bacchielli 1987, 471; Chamoux 1953, 48). Therefore, it would appear that these statues, while they may not record the actual features of the sitters, represent Cyrenaicans as looking like Libyans. However, even if these physical characteristics have been identified as Libyan by modern historians, it does not necessarily follow that the Cyrenaicans themselves identified them as Libyan or that the Cyrenaicans consciously represented themselves as Libyan. Indeed, Susan Walker has published a series of portraits, identified as members of the Julio-Claudian dynasty, which bear the same 'Libyan features' (Walker 1994, 181–2). Since the Cyrenaicans represented Romans with 'Libyan features', it can be seen that they did not characterise such features as distinctly Libyan, as opposed to Cyrenaican or Roman. Therefore, even if the Cyrenaicans apparently represented themselves as looking like Libyans, they seem to have done so unconsciously. However, while they did not consciously construct a bond with Libyans, the Cyrenaicans did not construct themselves as distinct from Libyans either. The fact that they did not identify certain physical characteristics as Libyan, as opposed to Cyrenaican, suggests that they did not use physiognomy as a criterion for constructing the Libyans as other. In other words, they did not construct Libyans as inherently and 'biologically' different from themselves and as such could incorporate Libyans into their collective self (see Thompson 1989, 12–20; Dench 1995, 46.) Owing to the intermarriage between Libyans and Cyrenaicans, it would not be surprising if Cyrenaicans inherited Libyan characteristics. Portraits are, however, stylised and not exact representations of the sitters. The Cyrenaicans, therefore, could have constructed themselves as being physically distinct from the Libyans but they did not. Furthermore, portraits are likely to have represented members of the elite, which suggests that the Cyrenaicans did not perceive Libyan physiognomy in a negative light.

Since the Libyans were integrated within their cities, the Cyrenaicans asserted bonds between themselves and the Libyans. In other words, the Cyrenaicans incorporated the Libyans within the Cyrenaican self. As will be seen, they did so by constructing a common past and by adopting Libyan symbols to represent them.

In his *Hymn to Apollo* Callimachus incorporates the Libyans into Cyrene's foundation myth. He describes the Theran settlers celebrating the first Carneian festival in front of Apollo and Cyrene and a group of adoring Libyan women (Callimachus, *Hymn to Apollo* 85–6). Pindar ends his ninth Pythian ode with the marriage of the daughter of Libyan Antaeus to the Cyrenaican Alexidamus (Pindar, Pythian 9. 125). As Dougherty has already suggested, Pindar weaves this marriage into the principal theme of the ode, namely the marriage between Apollo and Cyrene, which Pindar represents as a metaphor of the colonisation of Cyrene (Dougherty 1993, 151–2; see also Calame 1990, 302–4). By comparing the two marriages, he integrates the marriage between Libyans and Cyrenaicans into the colonisation myths of Cyrene. The foundation of the city in these accounts contrasts with those given by Diodorus and Pausanias. The foundation of the city, according to Callimachus and Pindar, was conditional not on the reduction of the Libyans but on the intermarriage with Libyan women. Libyans in the works of these authors are an integral part of the foundation and are instrumental to its success.

The Cyrenaicans represented themselves with symbols which were emblematic of Libya, which seems further to suggest that they incorporated the Libyans into their self-definition. The Cyrenaicans did not worship Ammon, the god of the oasis of Siwa, in the same way as the Libyans, in that they conflated him with Zeus (Bacchielli 1987, 477–8; Fabbricotti 1987, 232–3). Zeus Ammon was, however, associated with Libya both by the Cyrenaicans and by other Greeks. The god was represented on Cyrenaican coinage throughout its history (Jenkins 1974, 30). Pausanias, in addition, relates that Cyrene dedicated a chariot bearing Ammon at Delphi (Pausanias 10. 13. 5–6). By using Ammon as a collective symbol the Cyrenaicans advertised a Libyan aspect of their identity.

Silphium offered another image redolent of Libya. The plant frequently appears on Cyrenaican coins in the Greek and Hellenistic periods (Robinson 1927, pl. XIX). Although the plant was not used on Cyrenaican coins in the Roman period, it, to some extent, remained emblematic of Cyrenaica even when it became extinct (Strabo 17. 3. 22; Pliny the Elder 22. 100). Silphium is represented next to Battus on a figured capital of the House of Jason Magnus, near the *agora* of Cyrene (Stucchi 1967, 112–13). Pliny says that silphium first grew after a heavy rainfall seven years before the foundation of Cyrene, the same year in which the Therans first settled in Libya, in Aziris (Pliny the Elder 19. 41; Theophrastus 6. 3. 3). Silphium, in other words, is made to coincide with the arrival of the Cyrenaicans, which suggests that the Cyrenaicans may have appropriated the plant as their own. Although silphium was associated with Cyrenaica, the plant was not cultivated by the Cyrenaicans but grew wild south of Cyrenaica (Strabo 17. 3. 20; Chamoux 1953, 137, 1985, 165–72; Parisi Presicce 1994, 86–7). Libyans, furthermore, were responsible for the collection of silphium (Aristophanes fr. 528 Teubner=FHG II. 166). By using silphium as an emblem the Cyrenaicans appropriated a plant peculiar to Libya and symbolic of Libya.

The goddess Libya was used by the Cyrenaicans as a representative symbol both on coins and on dedications in Panhellenic sanctuaries. Pausanias describes a dedication the Cyrenaeans made at Delphi which consisted of a chariot bearing Battus, Cyrene and Libya (Pausanias 10. 15. 6). Although Herodotus says that the Greeks view the goddess Libya as a native goddess, it is uncertain whether she was an indigenous deity appropriated by the Cyrenaicans or whether she was invented by them (Herodotus 4. 46; Catani 1987, 385–6). Libya is associated with the Egyptians and Bablyonians by virtue of being the daughter of Epaphus and the mother of Belus (Diodorus 1. 28; Pausanias 4. 23. 10; Nonnus 3. 284–99). Whether she is an indigenous goddess or not is less important than the fact that the Cyrenaicans represented her as a native goddess. Libya is characterised by corkscrew curls and a leather mantle, both of which are clearly identified in a British Museum relief from the Antonine period (BM Reg. No. 61 11–27 30; Huskinson 1975, 31–2; Catani 1987, 387). Apollonius describes Libyan nymphs wearing goatskins from the neck downwards and around the waist and back (Apollonius 4. 147). Reliefs recently studied by Fabbricotti and Bacchielli depict deities wearing the same apparel (Fabbricotti 1987, 221–2; Bacchielli 1994, 45–57). These appear to be the same goatskin mantles which Herodotus says Libyan women wear and which Diodorus attributes to southern Libyans (Herodotus 4. 189; Diodorus 3. 49, 8. 29; Strabo 17. 3. 7). The Cyrenaicans, in other words, represented the goddess Libya as resembling a Libyan woman. Since the personification of the Libyan continent is represented as being Libyan, the goddess Libya not only locates the Cyrenaicans geographically but also associates them with Libyan customs.

The Cyrenaicans also asserted a bond with the Libyans through charioteering, a skill for which both the Libyans and the Cyrenaicans were famous. Cyrene's excellence in charioteering is extolled by Pindar in his fourth and fifth Pythian Odes written in commemoration of the Delphic victory of Arcesilas IV in 462 BC. In these odes Pindar refers to Cyrene as the 'chariot racing city' and praises Cyrene's mastery of charioteering (Pindar, Pythian 4. 7–8; see also Pythian 9. 4, 4. 17–18). Cyrenaica's prowess in driving chariots extended into the Roman period, when, Strabo says, the province grew strong because of its horses (Strabo 17. 3. 21). The Cyrenaicans themselves took pride in their horse-racing success. Callimachus is quoted by Strabo as saying that his homeland is famous for its horses (Callimachus fr. 716=Strabo 17. 3. 21). Herodotus and Strabo write that the Libyans, and in particular the Asbystae, who were neighbours of Cyrene, were masters of the quadriga and of horse breeding (Herodotus 4. 170; Strabo 17. 3. 19). Herodotus mentions that the southern Libyans as well as the nomads ride quadrigas and says that the Libyans taught the Greeks to use the four-horse chariot (Herodotus 4. 183, 189). The Cyrenaicans not only assimilated Libyan skills but also attributed their skills to the Libyans. Pausanias writes that an Olympic victor from Cyrenaica, Theochrestus, dedicated a chariot on which an inscription recorded that he bred his horses after the traditional Libyan custom (Pausanias 6. 12. 7). The way in which the Cyrenaicans were associated with Libyans through charioteering is evident by the extent to which Cyrenaican horses and charioteers are referred to as Libyan both by themselves and by other Greeks. Sophocles in his *Electra* says that Libyans are masters of the yoke (Sophocles, *Electra* 702). Since the Libyans described by Sophocles are competing at Delphi, it is clear that he is actually referring to Cyrenaicans. Callimachus in his epinician ode to Sosibius, victor at Isthmia, refers to Asbystian horses hearing the sound of the axle (Callimachus fr. 384). Therefore, through their success in horse racing, the Cyrenaicans were associated with the Libyans, both by themselves and by other Greeks.

Factors contributing to the construction of Libyans

The Cyrenaicans represented the Libyans in contrasting ways, both as their other and as a part of the Cyrenaican self. This suggests that the construction of an outside group is not necessarily coherent. The same outside group can be represented in different ways according to the nature of the relationship between the two groups and the context in which that relationship is expressed.

To a certain extent, the Libyans were constructed in different ways because the Cyrenaicans had different relations with different Libyans. As has been seen, the Libyans fought mainly against the southern Libyan tribes, including the Macae, Nasamones and Marmaridae, and were friendly with the neighbouring tribes. The closeness of the relationship between the Cyrenaicans and the Asbystae is evident from the fact that this tribe is described by Herodotus as the most Hellenised Libyans and by the way in which Cyrenaicans substituted the term 'Asbystaean' for 'Libyan' (Herodotus 4. 170). Callimachus writes that Battus brought Apollo Carneios to the 'Asbystaean land' (Callimachus, Hymn to Apollo 2. 76). He also refers to Lake Tritonis, which is not close to the Asbystae, as Asbystaean Trito (Callimachus fr. 37). Although it is possible that Callimachus uses this term in order to appear more erudite, it is equally clear that Callimachus chose to use the name of the Asbystae and not that of any other tribe in place of Libya.

The bond between the Cyrenaicans and the neighbouring Libyans is likely to have been reinforced by the fact that the southern Libyans posed a threat to both groups. As Laronde has indicated, conflicts between Cyrenaicans and Libyans should be characterised as conflicts not between Greeks and natives but between agriculturalists and pastoralists (Laronde 1953, 173). The defeat of the desert Libyans in the Marmaric war may have induced the Libyans living in Cyrenaica to move into towns and as a consequence develop closer links with the Cyrenaicans (Reynolds 1987, 383). Faced with a common enemy, the Cyrenaicans and the neighbouring Libyans could construct themselves as belonging to one another.

The ambivalent construction of the Libyans is due not only to differing relations with Libyans but also to the fact that the relationship between Cyrenaican cities was not static but fluid. The same Libyans could be allies and enemies at different times. This is most clear in the examples in which the Cyrenaicans used the Libyans in their fights against one other. Herodotus mentions that the brothers of Arcesilas II founded Barca after arguing with the king and induced the Libyans to break off their alliance with Cyrene (Herodotus 4. 160). According to Diodorus in 322 BC, Thibron struck an alliance with Barca and Euhesperides on the basis that he would reduce the neighbouring Libyans (Diodorus 18. 9. 5). Cyrene, in its desire to defeat Thibron, forged an alliance with Libyans and Carthaginians and fought against Barca and Euhesperides, who remained loyal to Thibron (Diodorus 18. 20. 3, 21. 4; Arrian, *FGrH* 156. 9, 16–19; Justin 13. 6. 8). The Barcaeans and Euhesperidans, presumably, stayed with Thibron because they wanted to subdue the Libyans. The Cyrenaeans were able to exploit the enmity between these Cyrenaican cities and the Libyans by making an alliance with the Libyans against the latter two cities. Plutarch says that, in 88–81 BC, Aretaphila plotted with the Libyan Anabus in order to get rid of her husband, the tyrant Nicocrates (Plutarch, *De Mul. Vir.* 19). Just as in the previous examples, Cyrenaicans made alliances with Libyans in their conflicts with one another. (See Dench 1995, 12–13.) Thucydides relates, furthermore, that the Athenians, who were hostile to Tarentum, struck alliances with the Metapontines and Messapians (Thucydides 7. 33. 3–4, 6. 34. 4–5, 6. 94. 2; Robinson 1990, 264–5).

Since the relationship between the Cyrenaicans and Libyans was variable, the representation of the Libyans was similarly variable. When allied to the Libyans, the Cyrenaicans probably forged bonds with them and incorporated them into the Cyrenaican self. Conversely, the Libyans were probably constructed as others when in conflict with the Cyrenaicans. Given that the Libyans could be allied with one Cyrenaican city against another, Libyans could be constructed as both 'us' and 'them' simultaneously. Dench has recently given a similar explanation to the contrasting representations of the Sabines in Roman literature; the Sabines were perceived as austere and upright on the one hand and wealthy and decadent on the other (Dench 1995, 85–91). The change in perception, according to Dench, resulted from a change in the relationship between the Romans and Sabines. When the Sabines posed a threat to Rome they were constructed along similar lines to other enemies, notably the Persians in fifth-century Athens; upon conquest, when the Sabines were no longer threatening, the

Romans represented the Sabines as the uncorrupted peasants the Romans had ceased to be (Dench 1995, 91).

The representation of the Libyans is also dependent on the context in which Cyrenaican identity is being expressed. In a Panhellenic context, Cyrene was frequently associated with a Libyan identity by both the Cyrenaicans themselves and other Greeks. Dionysius relates that a certain Mnaseas 'the Libyan' won the Olympic hoplite race in 456 (Dionysius of Halicarnassus 11. 84). Similarly, Pausanias refers to the Cyrenaican treasury at Delphi as the treasury of the Libyans of Cyrene (Pausanias 6. 19. 10). It has already been shown, furthermore, that the Cyrenaican dedications at Delphi emphasise Libyan connections (Pausanias 10. 13. 5–6, 10. 15. 6). To a certain extent the Cyrenaicans are referred to as Libyans because they lived in that continent. This is made clear by Pausanias when he refers to Cyrene as the 'Greek city in Libya' (Pausanias 10. 13. 5–6); Libya is mentioned here purely for geographical purposes. However, cultural connections with Libya are also expressed, as has been shown by the way in which the charioteer Theochrestus emphasised that his horses were bred according to Libyan traditions (Pausanias 6. 12. 7). The context in which Cyrenaican identity is expressed through the coinage similarly extends beyond Cyrenaica. On their coins, just as in the Panhellenic dedications, the Cyrenaicans adopted symbols, such as Ammon and Libya, which associated them with Libyans. When Cyrenaican identity is expressed in the context of the Greek world as a whole, the Cyrenaicans are associated with Libyans, in both geographical and cultural terms. This connection with Libya allowed the Cyrenaicans to emphasise their overall distinctness from other Greek cities; it also allowed other Greeks to view themselves as different from the Cyrenaicans. Context, therefore, determines whether the Libyans are incorporated into the Cyrenaican self.

Finally, the representation of Libyans is determined by the environment which the various Libyans inhabit. Libya is divided by outside ethnographers and by the Cyrenaicans themselves into distinct regions, each associated with a particular environment and mode of living. Strabo describes the coastal region of Libya as fertile and well watered by lakes and rivers (Strabo 17. 3. 5). It is this region which is subjected to Rome and in which agriculture is practised, perhaps in part because of the quality of the soil. The interior of Libya, on the other hand, consists of a desert in which there is only a scattering of dwellings (Strabo 17. 3. 1). In contrast to the sedentary, urban coast, this desert region is occupied solely by pastoralists, perhaps partly because of the poor land. The quality of land determines whether Libyans practise agriculture and live in cities and consequently whether they are civilised or not. Desert Libyans, in other words, are made others by the environment they occupy, just as coastal Libyans are incorporated into the Cyrenaican self by the environment they inhabit. Synesius constructs the southern Libyans in a similar way. These Libyans are 'other' because their environment does not allow them to know the sea or live in towns (*The Letters of Synesius*, ed. Fitzgerald 243–7). The construction of Libyans by these means, however, is not static. Ptolemy Soter's *Diagramma* allowed intermarriage between

Cyrenaicans and all Libyans, so that the integration of southern Libyans into a Cyrenaican context was possible. Libyans could, in other words, change habitat and be perceived in different ways accordingly (see Williams 1990, 181).

Conclusion

The Cyrenaican perceptions of Libyans were not static or objective. The Libyans were constructed both as others and integral to the Cyrenaican self. The contrasting representations of the Libyans resulted from a diverging relationship between the Cyrenaicans and the Libyans. The Cyrenaicans could ally themselves with the Libyans against other Libyans or against other Cyrenaicans. One cannot, therefore, categorise the relationship between them as simply Greek versus native or Greek versus barbarian, since the barriers dividing the Cyrenaicans and Libyans were in flux. The Cyrenaicans constructed the Libyans as other because of the threat which the Libyans posed. The construction of the Libyan 'other' allowed the Cyrenaicans to develop a common self in contrast to a common 'other'. In other words, the Libyan 'other' united the citizens of each individual city and united the Cyrenaican cities amongst themselves. Since the relations between the Greek cities could also be hostile and relations with the Libyans amicable, the impetus to the construction of the Libyan other was not always there. Cyrenaican cities struck alliances with Libyans when fighting against other Cyrenaicans or other Libyans. In such cases there was an impetus to forge a common identity with the Libyans. The construction of common identity incorporated the Libyans within the Cyrenaican self and allowed the Cyrenaicans to cement alliances with Libyans. The representation of the Libyans also changed according to the context in which Cyrenaican identity was expressed. In a Panhellenic context the Cyrenaicans referred to themselves, and were referred to by others, as Libyans. By forging themselves as Libyans the Cyrenaicans could differentiate themselves from other Greeks and could define their Greek identity more precisely. The differing construction of Libyans enabled the Cyrenaicans to construct their own identity in different ways. By defining themselves in contrast to Libyans, the Cyrenaicans could forge a Cyrenaican or Greek identity. Conversely, by developing a common Libyan identity, the Cyrenaicans could define themselves in contrast to other Greeks. Since ethnic groups each have various overlapping identities, by constructing outside groups in different ways they can express those different identities (Light 1981, 70–73; Hall 1989, 6–7). Constructing the Libyans as their other and as a part of their self enabled the Cyrenaicans to express their plurality of identities.

Bibliography

Bacchielli, L. (1987) 'La scultura Libya in Cirenaica e la variabilità delle risposte al contatto culturale greco-romano', *Quaderni di Archeologia della Libia* 12: 459–88.

Bacchielli, L. (1994) 'Un santuario di frontiera fra polis e chora' in J. Reynolds (ed.) *Cyrenaican Archaeology*, Libyan Studies 25: 45–59.

Calame, C. (1990) 'Narrating the foundation of a city: the symbolic birth of Cyrene' in L. Edmunds (ed.) *Approaches to Greek Myth*, Baltimore.

Cartledge, P. (1993) *The Greeks*, Oxford.

Catani, E. (1987) 'Per un iconografia di Libya in età romana', *Quaderni di Archeologia della Libia* 12: 385–402.

Chamoux, F. (1953) *Cyrène sous la monarchie des Battiades*, Bibliotèque des écoles françaises d'Athènes, Paris.

Chamoux, F. (1985) 'Du silphion' in G. Barker, J. Lloyd and Reynolds (eds) *Cyrenaica in Antiquity*, Oxford.

Dench, E. (1995) *From Barbarians to New Men. Greek, Roman and Modern Perceptions of Peoples from the Central Appenines*, Oxford.

Descoeudres, J. P. ed. (1990) *Greek Colonists and Native Populations. Proceedings of the First Australian Congress of Classical Archaeology*, Oxford.

Dougherty, C. (1993) *The Poetics of Colonization. From City to Text in Archaic Greece*, Oxford.

Ensoli, S. (1990) 'Notizie sulla campagna di scavi del 1987 sulla Terrazza della Myrtusa a Cirene' in *Atti dei convegni Lincei. Giornata Lincea sull' archeologia cirenaica, Roma 3 novembre 1987*: 157–71.

Fabbricotti, E. (1987) 'Divinità greche e divinità libie in rilievi di età ellenistica', *Quaderni di Archeologia della Libia* 12: 221–44.

Guzzo, P. G. (1990) 'Myths and archaeology in south Italy' in Descouedres (1990): 131–41.

Hall, E. (1989) *Inventing the Barbarian. Greek Self-definition through Tragedy*, Oxford, 60, 103.

Hartog, F. (1992) *The Mirror of Herodotus. The Representation of the Other in the Writing of History*, Berkeley, Cal.

Huskinson, J. (1975) *Roman Sculpture from Cyrenaica in the British Museum*, London.

Jenkins, G. K. (1974) 'Some ancient coins of Libya', *Society for Libyan Studies Fifth Annual Report (1973–4)*: 29–34.

Laronde, A. (1990) 'Greeks and Libyans in Cyrenaica' in Descoeudres (1990): 169–180.

Light, L. (1981) 'Ethnic succession', in C.F. Keyes (ed.) *Ethnic Change*, London, 54–86.

Lippmann, W. (1922) *Public Opinion*, New York.

Parisi Presicce, C. (1994) 'La dea con il silphio e l'iconographia di Panakeia a Cirene' in J. Reynolds (ed.) *Cyrenaican Archaeology*, Libyan Studies 25: 85–100.

Reynolds, J. (1987) 'Libyans and Greeks in rural Cyrenaica', *Quaderni di Archeologia della Libia* 12: 379–84.

Robinson, E. G. D. (1990) 'Between Greek and native: the Xenon group' in Descoeudres (1990): 251–65.

Robinson, E. S. G. (1927) *A Catalogue of the Greek Coins in the British Museum*, London.

Rosenbaum, E (1960) *A Catalague of Cyrenaican Portrait Sculpture*, London.

Smith, B. (1990) 'Greece and European colonization of the Pacific' in Descoeudres (1990): 19–30.

Stucchi, S. (1967) *Cirene 1957–67. Un decennio di attività*, Rome.

Stucchi, S. (1975) *Architettura Cirenaica*, Rome.

Thompson, L. (1989) *Romans and Blacks*, London.

Walker, S. (1994) 'The imperial family as seen at Cyrene' in J. Reynolds (ed.) *Cyrenaican Archaeology, Libyan Studies* 25: 167–84.

White, D. (1987) 'Demeter Libyssa: her Cyrenaean cult in light of the recent excavations', *Quaderni di Archeologia della Libia* 12: 67–84.

Williams, M. (1990) 'The colonization of Australia – an aboriginal perspective' in Descoeudres (1990): 181–9.

5

ROMAN IMPERIALISM AND THE CITY IN ITALY

Kathryn Lomas

The city occupied a highly privileged position in the Roman world, and was recognised even in antiquity as one of the central features of Roman imperialism. It was the preferred form of social, political and administrative organisation throughout the empire. In those regions, particularly in the western provinces, where there were no indigenous cities or only a low level of urban development, Roman conquest was rapidly followed by a programme of urbanisation, pursued either by direct imposition or by indirect encouragement. As such, urbanisation went hand-in-hand with Roman conquest and acculturation, and was an integral part of Roman imperial expansion. Indeed, Tacitus makes a clear correlation between urban life, Roman conquest and civilisation, as does Strabo. The consensus of ancient authors was that, as a general point, civilised people lived in cities, and, more specifically, so did those who had adopted a Roman way of life (Strabo, *Geog.* 4. 1. 5; Tac. *Agric.* 21, *Germ.* 16, *Hist.* 4. 64). Tacitus overtly connects this Romanocentric (and Hellenocentric) viewpoint with imperial expansion by his assertion that the Germans looked down upon urban life, seeing it as the chief symptom of servitude to Rome (Tac. *Hist.* 4. 64). To some extent he even endorses this view himself, describing the adoption of urban amenities by the British as a symbol of slavery and corruption (Tac. *Agr.* 21). The tight control maintained by Rome over both the process of city foundation and the assignment of legal status to cities under Roman law further emphasises the close relationship between urbanism and Roman imperialism. Ultimately, in the Roman Empire, a city was a city because the senate (or later, the emperor) had decreed as much, and new foundations or existing cities which changed their status had the framework of their civic existence determined for them in the form of detailed charters drawn up by Roman commissioners. The relationship between urbanisation, imperialism and acculturation is not, however, a straightforward one. The processes at work are highly complex, and any understanding of them must include both the direct and overtly imperialist imposition of urbanisation, most graphically seen in Roman programmes of colonisation, and the more indirect processes of acculturation within existing cities.

As with so many aspects of Roman expansion, the connection between urban development and imperialism appears first, and is most fully developed, in Italy. By the middle of the third century BC, Roman power had been extended to cover the whole of Italy south of the Po valley, bringing Rome into contact with a variety of urban structures at varying stages of development, and also with the substantially non-urbanised population of the Apennines and Calabria. These included types of cities whose disparate nature reflected the differing cultures which produced them – for instance the Greek *poleis* of southern Italy, the indigenous (but Greek-influenced) cities of Etruria and Campania, and the emerging urban settlements of Apulia. By the end of the first century BC, however, many of these regional differences in levels of urban settlement had disappeared and regionalised urban cultures were being eroded. Undoubtedly the growing political and cultural domination of Rome was an influential factor in this process of homogenisation, but the relationship between Romanisation and urban change is a complex one. A simple diagnosis of 'Romanisation' is insufficient, not least because it ignores changes both in indigenous cultures and in the idea of what it meant to be Roman. The reign of Augustus, for instance, was characterised by the emergence of a more uniform urban culture through-out Italy and arguably throughout much of the western Mediterranean – a development which reflects both the political and social changes inherent in the Augustan regime and the evolution of a new and more coherent notion of *Romanitas*. This chapter will address two particular aspects of this process, namely the different patterns of urbanisation in Italy and some of the ways in which changes in them can be traced, and the extent to which changes in urban topography can be used as an indicator of levels of acculturation, and the social dynamics behind it.

Patterns of urbanisation

Urban development can be divided into two distinctly opposed categories, which tend to split along geographical as well as typological lines. Indigenous development of urban centres was very much a phenomenon of lowland Italy – regions such as Campania, Latium, Etruria and Apulia, with a small amount of development on the Adriatic coast. Appennine Italy did not have an indigenous urban culture, partly as a result of its cultural traditions and partly because this highly mountainous region does not lend itself to supporting large concentrations of population. The Oscan peoples traditionally conducted their political assemblies and legal business at religious sanctuaries which provided a focus for the religious, economic and political life of the population, but which were not centres of habitation (Salmon 1965, 77–100; Dench 1995). By the end of the second century BC, however, the resilient culture of this region, and of the Samnites in particular, had given an added twist to the lack of urban settlement. Rome had fought three bitter wars against the Samnites for domination of central Italy, a fourth (the Pyrrhic war), in which the Samnites had substantially assisted

Rome's enemies, and finally the Hannibalic war, during which many of Rome's Samnite allies defected to Hannibal. After each successive defeat, Rome gradually chipped away at both Samnite culture and Samnite political structures by constricting the powers of the Samnite League (Salmon 1965, 277–9, 291–2) and by increasing pressure towards urbanisation. For instance, it is possible that the Caudini, inhabitants of the upland fringes of Campania, were prised away from the league after the Pyrrhic war and were persuaded into abandoning indigenous political structures in favour of urbanisation (Salmon 1965, 278; Dench 1995). The process was reinforced by a programme of colonisation and enforced movement of population which had the effect, amongst other things, of diluting Oscan culture. Beneventum, founded in 268 BC, replaced a preceding Samnite settlement with a substantial Romanised city (Livy 9. 27. 14, *Per.* 15), while a mass resettlement programme in 180 BC replaced the inhabitants of part of Samnium with Apuan Ligurians, giving rise to the curiously named community of Ligures Baebiani (Livy 40. 38; Brunt 1971, 197; Patterson 1988).

The principal phase of urbanisation in Samnium occurred after the final suppression of the region during the Social War. The indigenous Samnite sanctuaries were abandoned during the early first century BC and the population was reorganised into Roman *municipia* as part of the general overhaul of administration occasioned by extension of the Roman franchise. These had the status of independent cities by legal definition and most of them rapidly acquired the culture and physical structures of a Romanised urban community. The sharpness of this rupture is clear at many sanctuaries, but particularly at Pietrabbondante, probably the site of the assembly of the Samnite League. During the second century the site flourished, with a lavish reconstruction of the sanctuary and the addition of a large temple and theatre and numerous inscriptions relating to dedications or new building (Poccetti 1979; Strazzulla and De Marco 1982). Immediately after the Social War it was abandoned, and the only subsequent sign of use is the mausoleum of the *gens* Socellia, a prominent family from the nearby city of Bovianum (Strazulla and De Marco 1982). This example is repeated throughout Samnium. The elite families which had escaped the war and the subsequent Sullan proscriptions, or which had gained their status during this period of instability, moved their base of operations to the new Roman *municipia* (Patterson 1991, 149–57). Interestingly, the behaviour of the Samnite rebels in the early stages of the war suggests that some of the Oscan peoples were seeking to adapt urbanism to their own culture and needs. Diodorus' description of the capital of the federation of rebel states, Italica, points to a city planned along Roman lines, but with the strong intention of subverting the conventions of Roman urban culture by turning them against Rome. Paelignian Corfinium, the site of the new capital, was to be rebuilt to include a forum, and a senate house to accommodate an assembly based on the Roman senate (Diod. 37. 2. 4). Coinage issued by the new confederacy carried subversive images such as the Italic bull goring the Roman wolf (Sydenham 1952: Nos. 619–21, 628, 640–1).

The difficulties of generalising are amply illustrated by the contrast between patterns of urbanisation in Samnium and those in the neighbouring territory of the Sabines – a region very similar in climate and geography but very different in its political history. The Sabines had acquired *civitas sine suffragio* in 290 BC, and full Roman citizenship in 268 (Livy, *Per.* 11; Vell. Pat. 1. 14. 6–7; Cic. *Balb.* 13) and thus had a long history as part of the Roman state, remaining loyal throughout most of the wars of the third to the first centuries BC. Given the closeness of the legal and political relationship, a rapid development of urban communities would be expected, but in fact it was not the case (Strabo, *Geog.* 5. 3. 1). The key centres of Reate and Trebula Mutuesca did not attain municipal status until the Augustan period (*CIL* 11. 4677). This is reflected in patterns of building. Before the Augustan era, the main buildings on the site of Trebula were sanctuaries dedicated to Angitia and Feronia, and it was only with the grant of municipal status *c.* 27 BC that a Roman city was laid out, with fortifications, public buildings and a monumentalised forum (Evans 1939; Coarelli 1982, 16–22). In this case, therefore, we have a rather different relationship between urbanisation and Roman domination. Rather than corresponding to an obvious assertion of Roman strength, urbanisation is a function of the political changes inherent in the grant of municipal status.

Changes in urban topography 200 BC–AD 14

One possible means of gaining insight into the processes of acculturation and the impact of Roman power on communities in Italy is to examine changes in topography, and in particular of those aspects which most closely reflect the political vision and cultural aspirations of the elite, namely the patterns of public building. The use of urban space to reflect social and cultural values is something which is recognised in ancient literature as early as the fourth century BC. Plato and Aristotle express views on the optimum layout for an ideal city, although ultimately both take the view that the essential character of a city lies in its citizens, not in its structures (Plato, *Laws* 778–9; Arist. *Pol.* 1330a34–1331b18). Pausanias (10. 4. 1) expresses surprise at the lack of monumental structures such as a theatre, *agora* and fountain house at the Phocian *polis* of Panopaeus, and in so doing reveals that the status of cities was increasingly judged by the level, and forms, of monumentalisation and of public buildings. Vitruvius, in *De Architectura*, is not just concerned to describe the architecture and construction techniques of particular types of building, but to describe the ideal Augustan city and its structure (Vitruv. *Arch.* 1. Pref.), thus demonstrating the extent to which urban form was bound up with cultural and political identity in the Augustan world.

The evidence for the topography of individual Italian cities is, inevitably, far from complete, but despite the distortions caused by patterns of survival and excavation, it nevertheless shows some very clear trends, particularly relating to the early Principate. There is a distinct move towards the 'standardisation' of the amenities and public buildings of a city which seems to correspond broadly to the preoccupations of Pausanias and Vitruvius, and which may well reflect a new vision of both Roman identity and urbanism. Regional differences are not eradicated, but the idiom in which they are expressed is increasingly that of Roman urban culture.

Even in the earlier history of Roman Italy, however, there are graphic examples of the drastic impact that Rome could have on indigenous urban cultures. In the south-east of Italy, urban sites have a very regional form which is entirely distinct from that of Graeco-Roman cities (Lomas 1993). It is characterised by the enclosure of large areas of land within massive fortifications and a less nucleated pattern of land use within the enclosure than is the case in the Roman city. By the fourth century BC, many of these sites had a nucleus of monumental buildings, frequently decorated with architectural terracottas in the style of the western Greek colonies and arranged in some sort of systematic fashion. Areas of habitation, however, were dispersed throughout the urban area, interspersed with open land, probably cultivated or used as pasturage. Cemeteries were not located outside the walls, as in Roman cities. Instead, groups of burials were associated with nuclei of houses, a pattern which suggests a strong gentilicial element in the social structure of these settlements. Elements of this type of structure cut across ethnic boundaries. The Greek colony of Tarentum was notable for the fact that it allowed burials inside the city walls, in defiance of the usual Greek and Roman custom (Lomas 1993, 72–4; Lo Porto 1971, 79–81), and other Greek cities caused comment in ancient literature because of the large area of land enclosed by their walls, relative to the actual area inhabited (Livy 24. 3–1–3).

The impact of Rome was felt in two phases by these settlements. During the initial conquest of the south-east, in the fourth century BC, a number of Messapic sites, such as Monte Sannace, Cavallino and Gravina were simply destroyed by the Romans as they moved south, and were either abandoned or, as in the case of Gravina, reoccupied by small Roman settlements or villas (Pancrazzi *et al.* 1979; De Iuliis and Ciancia 1989; Small 1991). The second phase, and the one which represents a distinct change in urban identity from Greek or Messapic to Roman, dates to the early second century BC. In the aftermath of the Punic wars, a number of these cities abandoned their traditional patterns of land use and urban space in favour of a nucleated, Romanised, city. At Herdonia, for instance, a dispersed settlement of Messapic type contracts into a compact city arranged around a forum in the north-east corner of the site (Greco 1980). At Metapontum a similar process takes place, with much of the urban area of the Greek city being abandoned and occupation being concentrated into one section of it, the so-called Roman 'castrum' (D'Andria 1975). Given that these cities were both hostile to Rome during much of the Hannibalic war (Livy 26. 39, 27. 1, 15–16, 51, App. *Hann.* 35, 48), it is highly likely that this represents a quite deliberate effort at suppressing the indigenous population and imposing urban culture of a Roman variety. As in Samnium, the way in which cities develop, and the changes in the culture which underlies the process, are products of a phase of overt Roman imperialism and increasingly close control of a region with a recent history of resistance.

Given that there is no corroborative evidence from literature or inscriptions to tell us what was going on inside these cities and to put the archaeological material in context, it is possible to identify only the broadest changes. There is little insight into the possible political and social changes which underlay them. In another context, however, we do have some additional evidence for the impetus behind changes in urban topography. The cities of Campania, again a region with a strong tradition of urban life which antedated the Roman conquest by several centuries (Frederiksen 1984), undergo changes in the decades after the Social War which are best explained in terms of acculturation and response to Roman policy. In this case, the impetus seems to come from within the cities themselves – from a pro-Roman elite, rather than being imposed by Rome itself. The result is very similar, however, in that it involves the transformation of certain key aspects of the urban landscape to reflect a more Romanised identity. At Pompeii the first stage of the large-scale reorganisation of the area around the forum has a clear political context in that it relates to the new identity of the city as a Roman colony, and one which was dominated by the needs and wishes of the incoming colonists (Laurence 1994, 20–7; Cic. *Sull.* 60–2).

In other parts of Campania evidence is less plentiful than at Pompeii, so detailed charting of changes in urban topography is not possible. One pattern which is documented from Campania, southern Latium and the borders of Samnium is an emphasis on the rebuilding of city walls and fortifications (Gabba 1971; Frederiksen 1976). This is not, as one might expect, done for pragmatic reasons – to strengthen defences or repair damage caused during the Social War by the campaigns of Sulla – but apparently as a cultural statement. Many of these cities were not building anew, but were replacing existing walls and gateways constructed in the polygonal masonry characteristic of second-century building in the Oscan areas of Italy with ones which used the Roman technique of *opus quadratum* and which adopted a Romanised form, with monumental gateways and turrets at regular intervals (Gabba 1971; Poccetti 1988). A number of cities constructed gateways which seem to have functioned purely as monumental entrances, and which do not have any apparent sign that they were designed to be closed off with gates. A number of inscriptions relating to wall-building, such as those at Fundi (*CIL* 10. 6233–5, 6238–9), indicate that the majority of this type of construction was funded by the cities concerned and was carried out by municipal magistrates – in other words, that the motivation came from within the municipal elite, not as direct pressure from Rome. A similar cluster of republican amphitheatres in Campania has been explained as the result of a first generation of Campanian senators who chose a specifically Roman building type as their favoured form of euergetism (Welch 1994, 67–9). However, without much hard evidence of the benefactors or details of their backgrounds and careers, it is difficult to do more than speculate. As Welch points out, the earliest amphitheatres were clustered in a region with a long tradition of gladiatorial games. It is possible that the impetus towards permanent amphitheatres was most marked in Campania because they related to an important element of local culture, namely gladiatorial displays, and arose out of the interplay between this and the Romanising agenda of the new colonists and the rising class of Campanian senators.

The largest body of data on changes in the chronology and distribution of major types of public building belongs, however to the later Republic and the first two centuries of the Principate. The relevant material has been collected by Hélène Jouffroy (Jouffroy 1986) and is a fascinating, if complex, body of data. Given that the information is drawn from a disparate collection of sources – archaeological, epigraphic and literary – there are obvious methodological problems. Archaeological dating is in many cases an inexact science, particularly in the case of early excavations, and there are cases where the dating of a particular building may be in doubt. There is also the vexed question of the epigraphic habit. The most frequent source of detail about the circumstances behind a building project and the identity of the benefactor are inscriptions, and this inevitably raises the question of whether perceived patterns of building are being distorted by the chronological clustering of inscriptions in the first and second centuries AD. In fact, this pattern is less marked in the distribution of building inscriptions than it is in the case of some other types of text, most notably epitaphs, and is therefore less likely to distort the picture. There is also the corrective effect of evidence drawn from other sources. While literary references to building activity are less frequent, and archaeological attestation provides less circumstantial detail, they do at least mean that the pattern is less open to distortion by the chronology of epigraphic production. There is also the question of multiple building phases on the same site and of duplication of amenities. It would seem logical, given the enormous outlay involved in building something the size of a theatre or temple, that, once a city had such a construction, there would be no need to build another. In fact there is plentiful evidence of duplication of amenities or of successive large-scale reconstructions and modifications of existing structures. (For the difficulties of interpreting inscriptions of this type, see Thomas and Witschel 1992.) There are, therefore, numerous methodological questions raised by this evidence, but nevertheless it is illuminating to examine it in the light of the relationship between urban development and Roman political and cultural imperialism.

Even a cursory glance at the material reveals a marked change in patterns of construction in the early Empire. Whereas Republican building was heavily biased towards the construction and maintenance of walls, towers and gateways – comprising both the defences of the city and a powerful statement of identity – and towards temples, imperial construction had very different priorities (Jouffroy 1986: 16–58). The construction and embellishment of temples still flourished, stimulated to a great extent by the establishment of the imperial cult. A large number of the temple constructions, and particularly those which were new rather than additions and repairs to existing sanctuaries, were dedicated to various manifestations of the cult of Augustus. A shrine to the *gens* Julia containing statues of Augustus was established at Bovillae on his death in AD 14 (Tac. *Ann.* 2. 41. 1; Suet. *Aug.* 2) and at Ferentum an Augusteum with statues was constructed, again in the last years of his reign or under Tiberius (*CIL* 11. 7431, *AE* 1911, 184). Elsewhere, there are cult buildings of the Lares Augusti (*Eph. Epig.* 9. 679; *CIL* 5. 18, 10. 3757), and to Salus Augusti (*CIL* 11. 361), Concordia Augusta (Johnson 1933) and Fortuna Augusta (*CIL* 10. 820), as well as the frequent combination of Roma and Augustus (*CIL* 10. 6305, 14. 73, 353, 4642, *AE* 1898, 79). Others, such as the extensive rebuilding of the temple of Apollo at Cumae, were restorations of the damage caused by the civil war.

Structures relating to defences were much less numerous, and were closely related to imperial patronage and activity, as were triumphal and commemorative arches. Many were constructed as part of imperial road-building programmes, or in commemoration of military events, and carried inscriptions to make this clear. Examples include arches at Brundisium (Dio 51. 19. 1), Ariminum (*CIL* 11. 365) and Ticinum (*CIL* 5. 6416) dedicated to Augustus, and arches at Spoletium (*CIL* 11. 4776–7), Bergamum, Ravenna (*CIL* 11. 5) and Pisa (*CIL* 11. 1421) dedicated to other members of his family. Most are dedicated by senatorial decree, although a few are set up by municipalities in recognition of imperial benefactions, or are connected with the foundation of a colony. City walls were still repaired or replaced by the council or magistrates of cities, but they also tended to drift into the sphere of imperial benefactions, for instance at Saepinum, Fanum Fortunae, Ravenna and Laus Pompeia (Jouffroy 1986, 63–6).

A whole series of new building types became prominent in the cities of early imperial Italy. Some have a connection with the systematisation of administrative structures in newly founded colonies, or newly enfranchised *municipia*. There is an upsurge of interest in the construction of basilicas and curiae, both of which housed important functions of civic government. Baths were also a popular structure during the early Empire. During the Republic their distribution had been very localised, and was confined mainly to Campania. The reasons are not entirely clear, but the prevalence of Campanian bath buildings must surely be rooted in the indigenous culture of the region. Many structures antedate the crucial period of acculturation after the Social War, and the tradition of baths as part of Campanian culture was of long standing. One of the factors behind Hannibal's defeat was said to have been the demoralising effect on his army of exposure to hot baths and other luxurious aspects of Campanian culture during the winter of 215 BC (Livy 23. 18). During the Julio-Claudian period they become very widespread (Jouffroy 1986, 52–3, 93–6) and remain a popular building type throughout the early Empire.

The main field of expansion, however, is in the construction of what Jouffroy terms *édifices de spectacle* – primarily theatres and amphitheatres, but including a small number of circuses (Jouffroy 1986, 96–105). Here the break with earlier patterns of public building is most marked, and there is also a very pronounced identification with Augustus. Theatres had not been a high priority in Republican Italy as a whole, although Campania is a notable exception to this pattern (Frézouls 1983). Particularly in the second century BC, Campania was an exception to the rule on several fronts. The number of bath buildings here which antedated the Social War is much higher than in other regions, and this was the only region of Italy where there was a significant number of pre-Augustan stone theatre buildings (Jouffroy 1986, 53–8; Frézouls 1983). It is only with the Augustan period that theatres are constructed in any significant number, and, as the figures show, that number was considerably large, given that a theatre was a building which represented a major outlay of resources either by a state or by an individual. In contrast, amphitheatres are the only major building type which was not prominent in the Augustan period. Here there is an increase in numbers of this type of construction in the second half of the first century AD, and the building of baths and amphitheatres is the major form of construction activity in the second century AD. In point of fact, the very notion of a special building for games and wild beast shows was a relatively new one in the reign of Augustus, although there are regions of Italy, notably Campania, where amphitheatres develop earlier (Welch 1994). One of the earliest examples to be actually described as an *amphitheatrum* was built at the Augustan colony of Luceria in Apulia (Welch 1994, 61) and was dedicated to the emperor and the *genius coloniae*. As Vitruvius makes clear, the assumption at this date was still that the forum of a city would be adapted for such events, using temporary wooden partitions and seating, and his description of the design for an Italian forum explicitly takes into account the need to be able to set up these structures (Vitruv. *Arch.* 5. 1. 2).

What is indicated by these figures for building activity is that there was a significant amount of urban change and renewal going on in the early Principate. Some of it can be accounted for by the very extensive programmes of colonisation which took place during the civil wars and the early years of Augustus' reign, but this is not the whole explanation. Even with administrative buildings, there is no easy correlation between patterns of colonisation and construction. The sort of development found at Pompeii, where the entire forum is reorganised around Roman administrative buildings in the aftermath of the Sullan colonisation and during the reign of Augustus (Laurence 1994, 20–7), is not necessarily the only pattern for this type of building.

Other types of structure are closely connected with the Augustan period, and with the figure of Augustus himself. Temples of Roma or of the imperial cult in its various manifestations are the obvious example, but theatres also seem to have an imperial connection. They were buildings which lent themselves perfectly to embodying Augustus' vision of an ordered society, as set out in the *Lex Julia Theatralis* (Rawson 1987), and many examples were pointedly ornamented with Augustan motifs and statues of the imperial family (Bejor 1979; Gros 1994). The example at Minturnae was constructed so as to incorporate a monumental precinct containing the *capitolium* of the fourth-century colony and a new temple to Concordia Augusta, which was itself the most conspicuous building in the forum. The overwhelming impression is of a major change in urban culture and the way it was used to express identity. The diminution of regional peculiarities of urban structure point to a stronger centralising influence, but, at the same time, the source of this impetus towards a more cohesive urban culture is open to question.

Urbanism and acculturation in Italy

While the circumstances of some phases of urban change in Italy are very obviously linked with a moment of overt Roman imperialism, the processes underlying other developments are less clear. During the third and second centuries BC, and in post-Social War Samnium, the transformation in settlement patterns and urban topography is clearly linked with the exercise of Roman power, but during the first century BC and the first century AD the driving force comes much more from the local communities of Italy.

The exceptions to this general assertion are the colonies, particularly those founded by Augustus, who made political capital out of his generosity to new colonies (Suet. *Aug.* 46; Keppie 1983, 114–22). Close control over the topographical form of cities is borne out by Vitruvius, who describes his work on the forum at Fanum Fortunae (Vitruv. *Arch.* 5. 1. 6–10; Gaggiotti *et al.* 1980, 207–9). His plan for the basilica was deliberately intended to maximise the visual impact of the shrine of the imperial cult which it contained by placing the columns so that the cult statue was visible from outside the building. The shrine was not only to be a conspicuous part of the basilica, however, but was to have a clear line of sight over the forum, so that the public business of the city was conducted under the gaze of the image of the emperor. Even when the emperor was not the prime mover, there could be strong links between private initiatives, civic identity and the emperor. The amphitheatre at Luceria was built by L. Vecilius Campanus (*AE* 1937, 64), clearly highly placed in the hierarchy of the colonists sent there (he was military tribune, *praefectus fabrum* and *duumvir* of the colony), who paid for it *sua pecunia*. It was thus a private benefaction, but concern for civic identity and the connection of this with the emperor is underscored by the last line of the text – *in honor. imp. Caesaris Augusti coloniaeque Luceriae* ('in honour of the emperor Caesar Augustus and the colony of Luceria'). A dedication using a very similar form of words is found at Beneventum, referring to the shrine of Caesar built by P. Veidius Pollio (*CIL* 9. 1556).

Elsewhere, however, the connection between urban transformation and direct Roman influence is less clear. The amount of direct imperial patronage for public building in Italy is relatively small, and mostly concerns large public works – items such as roads or aqueducts, which required finance and organisational ability beyond the scope of the individual *municipium*. Despite evidence of imperial planning for at least one colony, Vitruvius stresses that public building is the responsibility of the municipal magistrates (Vitruv. *Arch.* 5. 1), and this is borne out by surviving municipal and colonial charters. The *Lex Genetiva Julia* places emphasis on the responsibility of the magistrates for a large number of tasks relating to the upkeep of the fabric of the city. Amongst other things, it was the duty of the magistrates to ensure that adequate seating was constructed for citizens and visitors at games and to ensure that restrictions on the demolition of buildings within the city were upheld. The use of public space by magistrates and their access to the water supply of the city was regulated, and they were forbidden to use land owned by the *colonia* for private gain (*Lex Gen. Jul.* 73–81, 99–101; Crawford 1996, 403–5, 408–9). According to the *Lex Tarentina*, magistrates were also empowered to spend some of the money accruing to the municipal treasury from fines on either games or buildings, but the form of the benefaction was left to their own discretion (Crawford 1996, 307–8). What is difficult to trace is the relationship between indirect Roman influence and local benefactions. Zanker (1988) has documented in detail the way in which an ideological agenda set by Augustus gradually and indirectly filtered down through major monuments and artistic works and into popular iconography, becoming modified along the way. The actions generating a particular type of urban development or cultural change may have come from the local elite, but the impetus for the action may have come from another source, in which case the actual promoter of change can be very difficult to identify. In any case, where the impetus to change is coming from a source at one remove from the benefactors who actually enable it, the process becomes a dialogue between the central authority and the local elites, a fact which can in itself modify the process of change by adapting the central agenda to the needs and wishes of the local community and its elite.

Interestingly, there seems to be little connection between large-scale benefaction in the form of public building and social promotion. Some senators clearly felt a strong attachment to their native city (Cicero and Pliny being the two most prominent examples) and demonstrated it by paying for buildings as well as other forms of munificence, but the body of surviving building inscriptions contains surprisingly few senators. There have been attempts to explain this by postulating that only first-generation municipal senators retained strong links with their native community, and that their descendants were simply absorbed into the Roman elite (Whittaker 1994), but this is unsatisfactory. The converse is also true, that there is no close link between the municipal families which gained senatorial status and those which were prominent municipal benefactors. Given this, and the emphasis on municipal magistrates as controllers of public building in the charter of Urso, it is more likely that public building was simply not the outlet chosen by senators for their generosity. Pliny's principal investment in bricks and mortar at Comum, for instance, was a bath built as a testamentary bequest. His other noteworthy benefactions were in the form of endowments for various worthy schemes such as payment of a schoolteacher and the creation of an alimentary scheme (*CIL* 5. 5262). It is possible that senatorial benefactions of all types were prompted not so much by local contacts and patriotism, but by the formal legal position of *Patronus* of the community, which carried well defined obligations (Plin. *Epist* 4. 1). As is so often the case, Samnium is something of an exception to this pattern. Here a significant number of Samnite families who espoused the cause of urbanisation enthusiastically and whose euergetic activity equipped the new cities with Roman amenities found their way into the senate (Patterson 1991), but this is not replicated in other regions. Whatever the motive for large-scale building, on either a public or a private basis, it was not, apparently, social and political mobility in the wider Roman context, and on this basis it is probable that patterns of public building in municipal Italy are reflecting the world view of the municipal elite, not that of the senatorial class or the emperor.

A more important motivation for urban change may have been status and competition within local and regional hierarchies of communities. This process of peer polity interaction has been used to good effect by archaeologists as a tool for explaining cultural change, but literary evidence for it is more elusive. A revealing example, however, is an incident related by Tacitus (*Hist.* 2. 21). During the build-up to the first battle of Cremona in AD 69, Aulus Caecina attacked the nearby city of Placentia and burnt down the amphitheatre, presumably a wooden one, which was situated outside the city walls. Tacitus comments that this caused great outrage amongst the citizens because it was one of the largest and finest amphitheatres in Italy. Moreover, the destruction was assumed to be the work of people from other cities in the region who had taken advantage of turbulent events to smuggle in wood and set fire to it. The strong implication here is that the size and elegance of the public buildings were a major element in establishing the status of a city in the local hierarchy, and that status could be undermined if the building was compromised or destroyed. It also implies that surreptitious attacks on structures by neighbouring cities were not unknown, in an attempt to achieve precisely this effect. Corroborative evidence for buildings as prestige objects can be found in some inscriptions, for example *CIL* 11. 3614, in which a public building project at Caere – the proposed construction of a meeting house for the *Augustales* – is approved by the patron of the city on the grounds that it will enhance civic status. More generally, the imperial cult seems to have been used to express this competitive instinct between cities (Zanker 1988, 302–7).

An exhaustive exploration of the links between urbanism, imperialism and acculturation is well beyond the scope of a single chapter, particularly if due consideration is to be given to issues such as local adaptation or the subversion of aspects of Roman culture, but some possibilities can be suggested. First, it is clear that there were points in the history of Republican Italy when Roman norms of urban life were forcibly imposed on regions such as Samnium and south-east Italy, obliterating indigenous communities, whether urban or not, in an overtly imperialist gesture. In the period between the Social War and the death of Augustus, the widespread transformation of the urban landscape of Italy must be regarded as a form of cultural imperialism on the part of Rome, and of Augustus in particular, but it arose out of complex interactions between Rome and the municipalities, and equally complex social and cultural interactions with the cities of Italy. Even where the context is that of colonisation, as at Pompeii in the 80s BC, the changes in the urban landscape seem to happen by a process of interaction and negotiation over the years after the foundation of the colony. The origins of this urban transformation, whether it is regarded as Romanisation or 'Augustanisation', cannot be traced to direct imposition by the centre. The increasing absorption of Italians into the Roman elite points to a possible route of transmission of Roman norms through benefactions by senators of municipal origin, but the epigraphic evidence indicates that this was not necessarily the major force behind these developments. Roman forms of urban life seem to have been adopted voluntarily by the municipal elites as an idiom for expressing civic identity, to some extent in the early first century BC, but overwhelmingly in the aftermath of the civil wars, when a whole new range of building types, many relating to the imperial cult, were introduced. The comparative topographical similarity attained by Italian cities during the Augustan era may point to the emergence of a new and more coherent sense of *Romanitas*, partly but not entirely centring on the figure of Augustus himself. This was not, however, a single monolithic entity, but was used as a vehicle to express local aspirations. As such, it was open to interpretation and adaptation by individual communities and the evolution of regional variations on the central theme. In particular it became a means by which cities could establish their status within a local hierarchy.

In terms of the wider debate about the nature of acculturation in the Roman Empire and its relation to imperialism, the history of the Italian city makes a fascinating case study. Many aspects of Roman behaviour in the provinces had their roots in the conquest and acculturation of Italy, and urbanisation is no exception. Throughout the western empire, we can see an analogous process to that which is found in Italy. Existing cities are transformed into suitably Roman form, either by direct action – colonisation, viritane settlement of Roman veterans or piecemeal Roman benefaction – or indirectly, by the application of a mixture of pressure and persuasion to the local elites. In each case, there are many ambiguities and compromises as Roman influence is modified by dialogue with the indigenous population and its culture. Where Italy differs is in the extent of pre-Roman urbanisation and in its intense ethnic and cultural diversity, presenting a more complex scenario but, by this very complexity, giving a deeper insight into the development of the city as an instrument of Roman control and acculturation from the beginning of Roman expansion.

Bibliography

Bejor, G. 1979 'L'edificio teatrale nell'urbanizzazione Augustea', *Athenaeum* 57: 126–38.

Brunt, P. A. 1971 *Italian Manpower, 225 BC–AD 14*. Oxford.

Cavallino, I. 1968 *Scavi e ricerche 1964–7*. Galantine.

Coarelli, F. 1982 *Lazio*, Guide archeologiche Laterza. Bari.

Crawford, M. H. (ed.) 1996 *Roman Statutes*, BICS Supplement 64. London.

D'Andria, F. 1975 'Metaponto Romana', *Atti di 15° convegno di studi sulla Magna Grecia*: 539–44.

De Iuliis, E. and Ciancia, A. (eds) 1989 *Monte Sannace. Gli scavi dell'acropoli*. Galantina.

Dench, E. 1995 *From Barbarians to New Men*. Oxford.

Evans, E. C. 1939 *The Cults of the Sabine Territory*. New York.

Frederiksen, M. W. 1976 'Changes in patterns of settlement' in P. Zanker (ed.) *Hellenismus in MittelItalien*. Göttingen: 341–55.

Frederiksen, M. W. 1984 *Campania* (ed. N. Purcell). London.

Frézouls, E. 1983 'Le théâtre romain et la culture urbain' in *La città come fatta di cultura*. Como: 105–30.

Gabba, E. 1971 'Urbanizzazione e rinnovamenti urbanistici nell'Italia centro-meridionale del sec. I a.C.', *Studi Classici e Orientali* 20: 73–112.

Gaggiotti, M. *et al.* 1980 *Umbria-Marche, Guide archeologiche Laterza*. Bari.

Greco, E. 1980 *Magna Grecia, Guide archeologiche Laterza*. Bari.

Gros, P. 1994 'Les théâtres en Italie au Ier siècle de notre ère: situation et fonctions dans l'urbanisme impérial' in *L'Italie d'Auguste à Dioclétien*. Actes du Colloque internationale de l'École Française de Rome (CEFAR 94): 285–307.

Johnson, J. 1933 *Excavations at Minturnae* I *The Republican Magistri*. Philadelphia.

Jouffroy, H. 1986 *La Construction publique en Italie et dans l'Afrique romaine*. Strasbourg.

Keppie, L. F. 1983 *Colonisation and Veteran Settlement in Italy, 47–14BC*. London.

Laurence, R. M. 1994 *Roman Pompeii. Space and Society*. London.

Lomas, K. 1993 'The city in south-east Italy: ancient topography and the evolution of urban settlement, 600–300 BC', *Accordia Research Papers* 4: 63–78.

Lo Porto, F. G. 1971 'Topografia antica di Taranto', *Atti di 10° convegno di studi sulla Magna Grecia*: 343–83.

Owens, E. J. 1991 *The City in the Greek and Roman World*. London.

Pancrazzi, O. *et al.* 1979 *Cavallino I. scavi e ricerche 1964–7*. Galantina.

Patterson, J. R. 1988 *Sanniti, Liguri e Romani/Samnites, Ligurians and Romans*. Circello.

Patterson, J. R. 1991 'Settlement, city and elite in Samnium and Lycia' in J. Rich and A. Wallace-Hadrill (eds) *City and Country in the Ancient World*. London: 147–68.

Poccetti, P. 1979 *Nuove documenti Italici*. Pisa.

Poccetti, P. 1988 'Riflessi di strutture di fortificatizioni nell'epigrafica Italica tra il II e il I secolo a.C.' *Athenaeum* 66: 303–28.

Rawson, E. D. 1987 '*Discrimina Ordinum*: the *Lex Julia Theatralis*', *Papers of the British School at Rome* 55: 83–114.

Salmon, E. T. 1965 *Samnium and the Samnites*. Cambridge.

Small, A. S. 1991 *Gravina. An Iron Age and Republican Settlement in Apulia*. London.

Spivey, N. and Stoddart, S. 1990 *Etruscan Italy. An Archaeological Essay*. London.

Strazzulla, M. J. and De Marco, B. 1982. *Il santuario sannitico di Pietrabbondante*. Rome.

Sydenham, E. A. 1952 *The Coinage of the Roman Republic.* London.

Thomas, E. and Witschel, C. 1992 'Constructing reconstruction: claim and reality of Roman rebuilding inscriptions from the Latin west', *Papers of the British School in Rome* 60: 135–78.

Welch, K. 1994 'The Roman arena in late Republican Italy: a new interpretation', *Journal of Roman Archaeology* 7: 59–79.

Whittaker, C. R. 1994 'The politics of power: the cities of Italy' in *L'Italie d'Auguste à Dioclétien. Actes du Colloque internationale de l'École Française de Rome* (CEFAR 94): 127–43.

Zanker, P. 1988 *The Power of Images in the Age of Augustus.* Ann Arbor.

6

LANDSCAPE AND CULTURAL
IDENTITY IN ROMAN BRITAIN

David Petts

The aim of this chapter is to demonstrate how native and Roman elites in late
Iron Age and Roman Britain used the spatial organisation of both ritual and
urban landscapes to project and contest a series of specific social and cultural
identities. This interpretation of the Romano-British landscape utilises many of
the arguments developed by prehistoric archaeologists such as Richard Bradley,
Julian Thomas and John Barrett (Bradley 1993; Thomas 1991; Barrett 1994)
in order to reconstitute a landscape archaeology of Roman Britain that is laden
with meaning. By means of a case study of the landscape of Wessex and the
surrounding area, a locale which is traditionally associated with the ritual interpretation of the prehistoric landscape (Barrett 1994; Thomas 1991, 29–55), I aim
to show how the treatment of the area from the late Iron Age (*c.* 100 BC) to the
early post-Roman period (*c.* 450 AD) in Wessex both reflected and modulated the
way that Roman Britons situated themselves in relation to Roman imperialism,
and how this changed and developed in different periods according to specific
economic and social situations.

The control of the landscape has an obvious ideological impact, but the
control of access to certain areas and the importance of surveillance are equally
significant. The resources needed to physically change landscapes are large: the
group that can articulate the required resources is usually the dominant political
unit. This opens up the landscape as an arena for contesting power between elite
groups as they struggle for hegemony. This arena is not open to sub-groups and
is thus important for the construction of higher-level cultural identities rather
than for lower-level intra-group identities. In the Roman period there are only
a few potential hegemonic powers, namely local potentates and the representatives of the Roman Empire, and in the third and fourth centuries the Christian
Church. It is through the conflict of these powers that the landscape can be seen
to mould the cultural identity of the Roman Empire and its inhabitants.

It is through the processes of daily life that identities are formed, and it is
through the mundane generalities of day-to-day life that individuals are incul-
cated with the structures and strategies that form their society. All individuals

have a range of social persona relating to their roles within society. These roles can include positions in a kinship, religious groups or political affiliations. However, in all societies there is a tendency for certain identities to have greater importance, serving to tie together disparate elements within the group. Cultural identity can be defined as the means of centring individuals in relation to geographical and cosmological space, although within each society different elements may create different myths of being and cultural identity may often be contested. Cultural identity should not be separated from other forms of social identity. It is just one end of a sliding scale of perceptions. At the lower end are identities that serve to mark people out as different and serve to individualise the social actor; at the other end identities such as cultural identity serve to integrate the individual into a wider community.

Theoretical perspectives

Studies of Roman landscapes have shown a reluctance to engage with many of the new approaches to space that have been utilised in the study of the land-scapes of other periods in Britain (Tilley 1994). Instead traditional approaches to the Roman landscape have been characterised by a tendency to regard it purely as an agricultural resource (e.g. Vallat 1991; Shennan 1985, 1–2), and also, in many cases, attempts have been made to reconstruct the environmental and economic reality of the Roman countryside (e.g. Lambrick and Robinson 1979). In a recent overview of the subject, all the examples discussed were used to examine the economic and resource implications of the landscape (Fulford 1990): there were no substantive attempts to reveal its ritual and symbolic dimensions. A similar emphasis on the agrarian history of Roman landscapes can be found in the studies of field survey in the Mediterranean area (e.g. Barker and Lloyd 1991).

It is important to consider why Romano-British archaeology should have been so little touched by the conceptual advances that have been influencing other areas of archaeology. There are several reasons for this theoretical isolation. First there is a conceptual dividing line between Roman and Iron Age archaeology on one hand and earlier prehistory on the other (Hill 1989). It is widely accepted that earlier prehistoric landscapes are not constructed on developed economic principles and are instead influenced by non-economic factors (e.g. Barrett 1994; Harding 1990). It is easy to envision prehistoric landscapes being influenced by ritual factors, especially when the field archaeology is dominated by large-scale monuments such as Stonehenge and Silbury Hill. In contrast, in studies of the Roman landscape, monumentality is instead seen to have been predominantly confined to the urban arena, and the countryside is interpreted in terms of agricultural development. This settlement pattern of urban centres and an agriculturally productive countryside superficially appears to reflect modern concepts of a developed and 'rational' landscape. These *perceived* differences can be characterised as the difference that Chris Tilley has defined between

80

capitalist/Western and non-capitalist/non-Western space (Tilley 1994, 7–34). By this he means that 'Western' space could be defined as desanctified, rational and tamed whereas 'non-Western' space is symbolic and an-economic. Although as he points out (ibid., 21) these are ideal types they are useful as heuristic devices and appear to reflect the current polarised attitudes to the landscape.

The belief that the Roman landscape was essentially 'rational' has also arisen out of the methodological approaches used. Originally the study of Roman archaeology was site-based, dealing with each site as an individual unit (Fowler 1980, 1–21). In the post-war period there was an appreciation that these sites were not constructed in a void but instead operated within the context of the landscape as a whole. This change of emphasis led to the great rise of field survey in the study of Roman archaeology: a movement which had its roots in Italy in the work of the British School at Rome, led by John Ward-Perkins and his students (Barker and Lloyd 1981; Barker 1991). Such growth was additionally encouraged by the advent of the 'New Archaeology' (Trigger 1989), which led to the introduction of many new sampling and analytical techniques (e.g. Nance 1983; Plog 1976; Haselgrove *et al.* 1985). These surveys achieved two aims: first, they led to the discovery of many new sites, padding out the occupation record both chronologically and spatially (e.g. Barker and Lloyd 1991; Vallat 1991, 10–11; Hunn 1994, 7–13). Second, they allowed the economic aspect of the landscape to be more clearly defined. For example, manuring scatters could be traced, infield/outfield and crop rotation systems examined and attempts made to delineate estate boundaries (e.g. Gaffney and Tingle 1989, 224–38). All these studies were essentially map exercises, plotting points on a two-dimensional surface. The danger with this approach is that it may encourage 'cartographic' thinking, characterised by viewing the landscape from an all-encompassing, over-head, controlling perspective (Harvey 1989, 240–59). The map thus becomes a device for the 'homogenisation and reification of the rich diversity of spatial itineraries and spatial stories' (Harvey 1989, 252–3). In effect the wide number of possible perspectives available for looking at the landscape becomes threatened by a rational viewpoint with its roots in economic geography.

The approaches to landscape being developed by some modern prehistorians emphasise a move away from looking at abstract, objectified landscapes to meaningful subjective landscapes (Moreland 1990; Tilley 1994; Barrett 1994; Gosden 1994). Following Tilley it is possible to set up a number of dichotomies emphasising the difference between the two approaches. The traditional approach to prehistoric landscapes is essentially materialist and rational. It envisages space as an arena for social action where social systems are passively projected on to landscape with a lack of reflexivity. Space itself is seen as value-free and meaning-free. Most of all it fails to deal with landscape as an experienced phenomenon, a network in which socially informed individuals live their lives. The alternative 'human' space revels in the differences and variabilities within the landscape. Points on the landscape are not merely neutral areas existing in and for themselves, rather they are meaningful places gaining their importance in relation to other spaces, material conditions and the presence or absence of people. This is a reflexive relationship: place gains its meaning from people, whilst equally their persona as people changes according to their spatial context. The result of this relationship between places and people is that there is not a single, normative meaning to a landscape, but instead the landscape constitutes a manifold web of meaning couched within the day-to-day subjective existence of real people. Thus there are no fixed meanings within the landscape, and features within the landscape continue to have resonances well after the period of their construction. They are continually being reinterpreted. Whilst space is often capable of 'accommodating diverse meanings and practices' (Eade and Sallnow 1991, 15, quoted in Coleman and Elsner 1994, 73), certain hegemonic powers have the ability to manipulate spatial order to favour particular interpretations. This means that, although theoretically there is no limit to the production of meaning, the meaning of the landscape is ultimately constrained.

Recently there have been attempts to examine the symbolic importance of space in the Roman landscape. Alcock has examined the effect of Roman imperialism on the Greek landscape (1993, 1989). Her work particularly focuses on the way political, social and economic change affected the role of rural sanctuaries and monuments. This emphasis on the way in which monuments are reinterpreted is situated firmly in the tradition of landscape studies developed by the modern landscape prehistorians. Purcell has also examined the spatial dimension of imperialism (1990). His work on centuriation emphasises the role of imperialism in physically adding to a pre-existing landscape. His analysis of the way in which centuriation operated emphasises the way in which spatial practices can be used to incorporate a territory into a pre-existing Roman cosmological system. Both examples are rare demonstrations of the importance of geography in imperialism (Said 1993, 271–2). In examining Roman Britain using these approaches I want to explore the countryside in way that will uncover some of the ways in which landscape was experienced, for it is through the experience of such space that cultural identities may be externalised.

Roman Wessex: a case study

Context

By the late Iron Age (100 BC–AD 43) the hill forts traditionally associated with Iron Age Wessex had fallen out of use (Cunliffe 1984, 32–6). Whilst most settlements were small complexes of ditched enclosures such as those at Worthy Down and Tollard Royal (Cunliffe 1973; Wainwright 1968) there was also the growth of a new kind of settlement, the *oppida*. There were two main forms of *oppida*: enclosed *oppida*, which had a single defensive circuit surrounding the focal area of the site, as at Silchester (Fulford 1993), and the more dispersed territorial *oppida*, where a network of dykes and ditches defined a more polyfocal settlement area. Territorial *oppida* in Wessex include Bagendon, near Cirencester, and the

Gussage/Thickthorn Down complex in Dorset. These large sites may have acted as high order settlements and are frequently associated with imported pottery and early coin production (Cunliffe 1993, 223).

Following the Roman conquest some of these *oppida* developed into Roman towns (Fig. 6.1), such as at Silchester (Fulford 1993). Other *oppida* saw an end to occupation and were often replaced by a new Roman town close by. This occurred at Bagendon, where settlement ceased in the first century AD, to be replaced by a thriving town at Cirencester only a few miles away. Some of these towns had an administrative function and became the capital towns of the Roman *civitas*, territorial areas often based on earlier tribal territories. Cirencester became capital of the Dobunni, Silchester that of the Atrebates and Dorchester that of the Durotriges. Such towns were soon provided with the classic Roman civic complex of forum and basilica. There were also smaller towns such as Ilchester, Dorchester on Thames and Mildenhall (Burnham and Wacher 1990). These too may have had Iron Age antecedents, such as Dorchester on Thames, which is adjacent to a small *oppidum* at Dyke Hills.

Rural settlement was dominated by nucleated, village-type settlements such as Chalton (Cunliffe 1973). These were often related to extensive field systems which seem to have started to develop at the end of the Iron Age. Villas are known in Wessex but they are rarely found on the chalk uplands and tend to cluster round towns such as Bath and Ilchester. These villas remained small and there were few palatial sites, as known from the south-east, until the third century.

In the third and fourth centuries there was a great change in town life. There was a decrease in the construction of new public buildings, whilst at the same time rural villas became increasingly elaborate, often adorned with painted wall plaster and mosaics. Changes in the wider economy also led to a decrease in the amount of imported foreign goods, and local industries expanded to meet the demand (Millett 1990). Although Wessex remained prosperous throughout the fourth century there was an ever increasing threat from external raiding. In the final years of the fourth century and the first decades of the fifth a combination of British rebellions and trouble on the Continent meant there was a progressive withdrawal of troops and a corresponding reduction in the money supply. Increasingly taxation was commuted to agricultural renders and with the removal of the final troops in AD 410 the monetary economy rapidly ceased along with large-scale industrial production.

A new approach

Rather than approaching Wessex from the traditional perspectives I want to consider the landscape from the point of view of its inhabitants, drawing on the perspectives developed by Chris Tilley (1994). I want to show that people's perceptions of their place in society were influenced by their experience of the landscape. This approach emphasises the importance of a subjective understanding

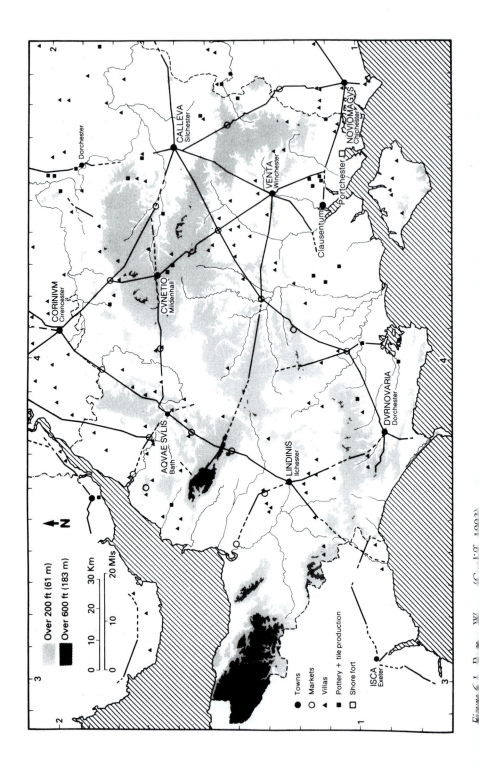

Figure 6.1 Dorset Wessex (Copestake 1992).

Over 200 ft (61 m)

Over 600 ft (183 m)

N

20 Mls

0   10   20   30 Km

0   10

●   Towns

○   Markets

▲   Villas

■   Pottery + tile production

□   Shore fort

CALLEVA
Silchester

Dorchester

VENTA
Winchester

NOVIOMAGVS
Chichester

Portchester

Clausentum

CORINVM
Cirencester

CVNETIO
Mildenhall

DVRNOVARIA
Dorchester

AQVAE SVLIS
Bath

LINDINIS
Ilchester

ISCA
Exeter

of Roman Wessex. Meaning is created only through individuals' engagement with their surroundings (Barrett 1994, 36). Thus meaning will always vary according to who is experiencing the landscape and in what context. The landscape is not reducible to one overarching meaning, it is inevitably contingent. By considering the reactions to the landscape of a range of individuals the impossibility of a totalising normative reading of the landscape will be shown.

Wessex has traditionally been one of the regions most intensively studied by prehistoric archaeologists and it contains many important examples of 'ritual landscapes' such as the areas around Stonehenge, Avebury and Cranborne Chase. It is also an area with extensive Roman occupation, and has a wide range of settlements, ranging from large towns such as Cirencester, Dorchester and Silchester to small villages and villas.

In the earlier prehistoric landscapes a person working on the land in Wessex would have been very conscious of the sheer importance of monuments in the landscape. They were continually elaborated and added to, and were respected by field systems (Fowler 1983, 190). The very act of moving through the landscape would have emphasised not only the importance of individual monuments, but also their connectedness through intervisibility. Sites were important not just in themselves, but in their relationship with others. Even the mundane practices of everyday agricultural activity would be spatially constrained by monuments. This would have emphasised the ritual significance of these basic activities, imbuing them with symbolic importance. The role of the individual in the landscape would be understandable only through the spatial movement associated with agricultural activities

In late Iron Age Wessex the farmer would have been less aware of the importance of these monuments. At Waylands Smithy on the Ridgeway in the north-west corner of the Berkshire Downs (Whittle 1991) a substantial Bronze Age long barrow survived fundamentally untouched through most of the Iron Age. With the development of field systems in the late pre-Roman Iron Age and early Roman period, the barrow was breached by lynchets (Whittle 1991, 65). A similar encroachment by field systems on to a barrow is also found at Norton Bavant in Wiltshire (Butterworth 1992, 6), where a Bronze Age round barrow was cut by early Roman ditches. The action of ploughing over and digging into these monuments each year would be a physical reminder of their symbolic redundancy. The physical movement of a farmer through the landscape would have been very different. New settlements did not respect the old landscape elements. The *oppidum* at Gussage Hill/Thickthorn Down (Barrett *et al.* 1991) overlies the Dorset Cursus: cutting rather than respecting a monument that had in earlier periods been a fundamental force in structuring the landscape. These new dyke structures would disrupt systems of connectedness between monuments. Whereas previously the farmer would see meaning in the entire landscape and agricultural activity, meaning would instead become focused in the *oppidum* and acts of exchange.

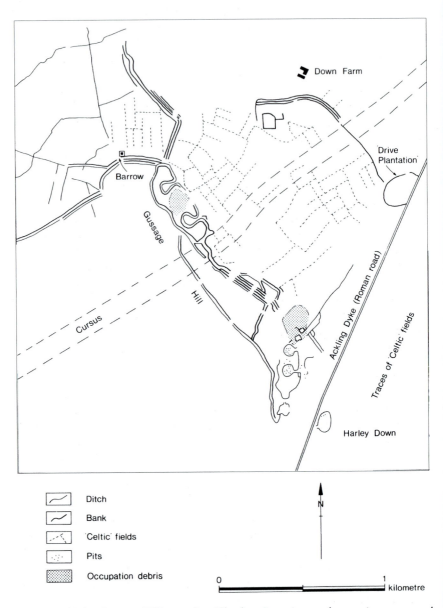

Figure 6.2 The Gussage Hill complex. The late Iron Age settlement is constructed across the line of the Neolithic Cursus (Barrett *et al.* 1991)

These transformations are recognisable in the development of the *oppida*, which may be seen at Bagendon (Gloucs.), Silchester (Hants.) and the Gussage Hill/Thickthorn Down Complex (Dorset, Fig. 6.2). *Oppida* became the focus of symbolic elaboration. The extensive dyke systems centred on these sites would have required a considerable investment of labour. The *oppida* also had an increasingly important ritual function, and became the location of temples and high-status burials. The farmer would see these sites as the main focus of community rituals. Rather than being spatially dispersed, the community would have become central, for gatherings and ritual activity were probably all focused on one location. Within the *oppida* there is evidence of a separation of different functions. In many ways an *oppidum* was a monumental landscape writ small. It was by movement through the *oppidum*, rather than the wider landscape as a whole, that Iron Age inhabitants of Wessex were able to centre themselves cosmologically, relating to areas of exchange rather than production.

The landscape of Roman Wessex would naturally vary according to who was experiencing it. A Roman official would have a very different perception of it from a native. A Roman official moving through Wessex would have been familiar with much of what he saw around him. The network of roads, towns and forts would all have acted as a reminder that the area was now part of the Empire, and also served to integrate native places of power with Roman ones. The main Roman route from Bath to London passed close by Silbury Hill and the Sanctuary, two important prehistoric sites (Malone 1989). The Roman road continued eastwards and crossed the Ridgeway (Fig. 6.3), an important trackway belonging to a transport network preceding that imposed on the landscape by the Romans. At this point there is a Bronze Age barrow. It can easily be seen how the simple placement of one Roman road can change the character of this section of the Wessex landscape. The landmarks which dominated the surrounding countryside were linked together by the road, which would also link them conceptually to Roman towns. The strong linearity of the Roman roads would also contrast strongly with the more sinuous contours of the Downland landscape, and may have suggested the subjection of 'nature' to the technological power of the Roman army. The primary Roman road in Dorset, Ackling Dyke, was also aligned on two important hill forts: Old Sarum and Bradbury Rings. The latter site seems to have acted as a major junction for several local Roman roads. Ackling Dyke with its distinctive banked construction was a major feature in the landscape of Cranborne Chase, and it has been suggested that it may have acted as an estate boundary. For a Roman traveller this annexation of native sites would have served to link them up with towns and forts, and would have added to the sense of an alien British landscape subjected and constrained by a familiar Roman one.

For the native, the view of the landscape would have been different. There would have been little long-distance travel for the majority of the population, and thus Roman roads would have been rarely used. Instead people would have continued using local routeways, not relying exclusively on the main Roman

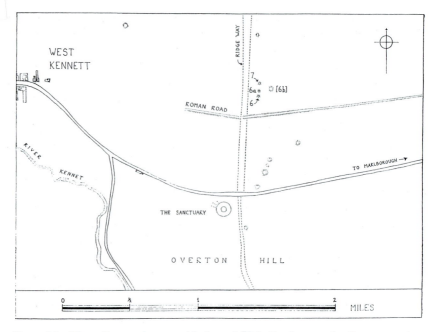

Figure 6.3 Three Roman barrows (6, 6a and 7) built close to the Roman road yet aligned with the prehistoric Ridgeway (*Wiltshire Archaeological Magazine*)

routes. It is possible that some relatively long-distance movement may also have used native tracks such as the Ridgeway. For the native, the main users of Roman roads would have been officials, traders and military units. Although journeys into the local town would have been rare, they would have been important. Local judicial functions, taxation and markets from which coinage could be gained to pay taxes would all be based in towns. To natives movement along Roman roads would have emphasised how roads linked the countryside with the coercive, economic and symbolic power of towns, and through towns with the Empire. This contrasts with the way in which the Roman viewed the landscape. For the Roman it was a landscape that emphasised familiarity and power; for the native it was ultimately a landscape of difference and powerlessness.

By the later Empire (*c.* AD 300–410) movement through the landscape of Wessex would have been very different. A traveller would notice that ritual life was evident throughout the countryside. Although there had always been temples on rural sites there was an increase in their number. These architecturally elaborate structures would be particularly noticeable, as they were often placed on prominent hilltop positions, or near earlier prehistoric sites, such as the Roman temple on Maiden Castle, an Iron Age hill fort.

For the residents of one of the many rural settlements in Wessex, prehistoric monuments in the landscape would have become once more important in their day-to-day life. Unlike the earlier period, monuments became important as 'places' once more. At the White Horse at Uffington there was the development of a late Roman burial ground in an earlier long barrow (Miles and Palmer 1995). Situated on the northern scarp edge of the Berkshire Downs, the White Horse would have dominated the view south of sites situated in the Vale of the White Horse, and would have acted as a conceptual dividing line between the Downs and the lowlands. It may well also have represented a divide between the two different forms of economic activity: a pastoral economy on the Downs contrasting with the lowland arable regime. Sites such as this would have been constantly confronted during the agricultural year. When ploughing, barrows would have been respected, and not incorporated into field systems. These barrows may well have served to define estate boundaries and their symbolic importance would have been enhanced, in some cases via the internment of the deceased within them at sites such as Codford St Mary (Fowler 1965) and Hetty Peglers Tump (Clifford 1966). For the viewer even the most mundane economic tasks would be increasingly carried out in a landscape imbued with ritual meaning.

The understanding of the landscape would vary according to the individual's social and cultural perspective. With a change in the function of towns, many previously civic functions would now occur in villas (Scott 1990). An official would have to travel through an increasingly non-imperial landscape. Access to villas themselves would be increasingly controlled, putting the villa owner at an advantage (Scott 1993). In the wider landscape, the official may simply not have been aware of the importance of many sites in the landscape. On a journey through the Avebury region, along the main Roman road, the landscape would seem superficially very similar to that of the early Empire. However, a knowledgeable local observer would appreciate that two of the barrows visible at the junction of the Ridgeway and the Roman road were not ancient but late second-century constructions (Smith and Simpson 1964). Although superficially similar to prehistoric barrows these Roman burials were of a distinctive construction with timber revetments. It is tempting to argue that the shape of the barrows may have mimicked the stepped and reveted shape of nearby Silbury Hill (Atkinson 1970, 314). Only someone with local knowledge would know that sites such as the West Kennet long barrow (Atkinson 1970, 314) and the Avebury stone circle (Smith 1965, 243) were sites of ritual deposition (Dark 1993, 135–9). The outsider would have seen a landscape similar to that of the early Romano-British period. The local travelling along the Ridgeway would see a landscape using traditional space, in the form of prehistoric barrows and the Romano-British barrows imitating them, the Sanctuary and Avebury. This created a juxtaposition that located power not in the context of Empire but in a reinvented native tradition.

Upon the withdrawal of Rome from active political intervention in the province of Britannia in the early fifth century there were yet more changes in the landscape. Importantly there was a dramatic decline in the extent of villa occupation. Life at such sites either ceased completely or continued in a greatly simplified manner. Movement through the landscape became increasingly controlled. A major change in the landscape at this time would have been the construction of large-scale ditch works which were either built anew or were refurbished prehistoric dykes: examples include Grims Ditch, Bedwyn Dyke, Bokerley Dyke and Combs Ditch as well as the great Wansdyke (Cunliffe 1993, 294–6). Wansdyke was a pair of major dykes crossing the Wessex heartland from the Savernake forest to Maes Knoll in Somerset, with a 15-mile gap in the centre (Myres 1964). These dykes seem to have developed at the same time as the elites started to reuse fortified hilltop enclosures such as Cadbury-Congresbury (Rahtz *et al.* 1992) and South Cadbury (Alcock 1995). The system of dykes and hill forts would have served to create a landscape in which movement was increasingly controlled and ordered. Although individuals would have been able to cross dykes easily, it would be difficult for large groups to move across them rapidly. Movement through dykes would be funnelled through certain easily controllable and observable points. Undoubtedly these developments were partly a reaction to the increasingly unsettled political climate and the level of warfare between the British and the Saxons. However, the hill forts, although equipped with ramparts and palisades, do not seem to have been constructed for military purposes, unlike similar examples in the north of Britain, and there is little evidence of violent destruction. They were probably a means of demonstrating the control which the elites wielded over both land and people. The collapse of the system of coinage would have caused tributes to be paid in agricultural produce and labour renders. These labour renders could have been used either for refortifying hill forts and dykes or for military service. The withdrawal of the Roman army left Britain without any external source of coercive power to mediate disputes between elites. For the first time since the Roman conquest, military action as a means of settling disputes was a viable option for the indigenous nobility. This would have changed the perception of land as a resource. Agriculturally productive land was now something that could be wrested from its owners by force. The construction of dykes and hill forts was not just a military strategy but would have acted as a very visible territorial marker to neighbouring groups. They would have required a large amount of labour to construct, and whatever the military purpose of these features they would serve as physical reminders of the ability of a polity to wield human resources on a large scale – human resources that could easily be turned to more direct military purposes. Moving through this landscape, the traveller would be constantly aware of the physical control over land and movement within it. Whereas the Roman landscape was designed to facilitate movement across country and over long distances and to tie distant areas together, both physically and conceptually, the sub-Roman landscape in Wessex was designed to impede long-distance travel and to emphasise the difference between neighbouring areas. The inhabitants were centred in a relationship not to Rome or even Britain but to local territorial power bases.

Conclusion

In the late Iron Age the native elites increasingly identified themselves with external sources of power, both symbolically and economically. They created a landscape that emphasised the importance of areas of exchange and played down the importance of agricultural production. The juxtaposition of temples and high-status burial sites with the *oppida* served to give foreign exchange an importance in society that went beyond the economic. It was only with the Roman invasion that the foreign links became specifically defined as 'Roman'. The emphasis on specifically Roman architectural traditions and the increased use of epigraphy would have served to place the native educated elite in a privileged position in a landscape where power was related to Rome. For the illiterate rural majority the importance of towns in creating a Romano-British identity would never have been as strong as it was for the urban aristocracy.

With the collapse of foreign trade and the increase of political instability that characterised the third and fourth centuries, as well as the decentring of the city of Rome as a focus of power, there was a change in the way the British perceived their overseas contacts. This was reflected in the way the landscape was utilised. There was a return to a landscape in which ideology was expressed in the context of local agricultural production. In the sub-Roman period, as power was increasingly devolved to the local level (Garwood 1989, 96–9) a landscape developed that emphasised control and coercion within small territorial areas.

The link between societies and the landscape they inhabit is crucial. Giddens (1981, 45–6) attaches a high level of importance to the concept of 'locale' in his analysis of social systems. It is only within spatial structures that social interaction can be played out (Barrett 1987). He suggests that a social system can be defined as a society if it shares a defined locale, legitimate prerogatives, shared institutions and inclusive identity (Firth 1996). The systems of power that operate in a society may control the use of and movement within a material environment, and it is these attempts by hegemonic powers to control the understanding of the landscape that constrains interpretation. While identity and self-perception may be in the last instance discursive they are limited by the control of the cultural locales within which they operate.

This chapter has shown that the Roman landscape can be understood in terms other than the strictly economic. It does not claim to replace the traditional approach but aims instead to move beyond it. If the nature of Roman imperialism is to be understood in a way that does not limit it to the simple flow of traded goods or the movement of armies it is important to consider what it meant to be a Roman, and live in a Roman way. Although the emphasis has been on the symbolic aspects of the landscape and not its economic role, the two positions should not be seen as in opposition to each other. The symbolic aspects of the landscape are not free-floating phenomena, but exist as specific ideological elements of the economic and political ebb and flow of the Empire. These spatial patterns are part of social conditions, not mere passive reflections, and instead the use of both urban and rural landscapes is a combination of the interplay of economic, political and social activity played out spatially. The economic is not privileged over the symbolic or vice versa, they play off against each other. The readings of the landscape offered above have been primarily those of the elites, both Roman and native. The mutability of the Romano-British landscape has been situated in attempts by both the Romans and the Romano-British to build up an ideological hegemony within a shifting political background. The changing use of the landscape can be seen as attempts by individuals and groups to affect the cultural identity of the population of Wessex for political ends. These are not the only possible readings. There were other groups within Romano-British society who may have understood the landscape in different ways: such as women, soldiers, town-dwellers and Christians. These are only some of the social personae that must be considered if a fuller under-standing of the Romano-British landscape is to be achieved.

Bibliography

Alcock, L. (1995) *Cadbury Castle, Somerset. The Early Medieval Archaeology*, Cardiff.
Alcock, S. E. (1989) 'Roman imperialism in the Greek landscape', *Journal of Roman Archaeology* 2: 5–34.
Alcock, S. E. (1993) *Graecia Capta. The Landscapes of Roman Greece*, Cambridge.
Atkinson, R. J. C. (1970) 'Silbury Hill, 1969–70', *Antiquity* 44: 313–14.
Barker, G. (1981) *Landscape and Society. Prehistoric Central Italy*, London.
Barker, G. (1991) 'Approaches to archaeological survey' in Barker and Lloyd (1991): 34–56.
Barker, G. and Lloyd, J. (eds) (1991) *Roman Landscapes. Archaeological Survey in the Mediterranean Region*, London.
Barrett, J. C. (1987) 'Fields of discourse: reconstructing a social archaeology', *Critique of Anthropology* 7: 5–16.
Barrett, J. C. (1994) *Fragments from Antiquity. An Archaeology of Social Life in Britain, 2900–1200 BC*, Oxford.
Barrett, J. C., Bradley, R. and Green, M. (1991) *Landscape, Monuments and Society. The Prehistory of Cranborne Chase*, Cambridge.
Blagg, T. and Millet, M. (1990) *The Early Roman Empire in the West*, Oxford.
Bradley, R (1993) *Altering the Earth*, Edinburgh.
Burnham, B. and Wacher, J. (1990) *The Small Towns of Roman Britain*, London.
Butterworth, C. A. (1992) 'Excavations at Norton Bavant Borrow Pit, Wilts, 1987', *Wiltshire Archaeological and Natural History Magazine* 85: 1–26.
Clifford, E. M. (1966) 'Hetty Peglers Tump', *Antiquity* 40: 129–32.
Coleman, S. and Elsner, J. (1994) 'The pilgrim's progress: art, architecture and ritual movement at Sinai', *World Archaeology* 26 (1): 73–89.
Cunliffe, B. (1973) 'Chalton, Hants: the evolution of a landscape', *Antiquaries Journal* 53: 173–90.
Cunliffe, B. (1984) 'Iron Age Wessex: continuity and change' in Cunliffe and Miles (1984): 12–45.
Cunliffe, B. (1993) *Wessex to AD 1000*, London.

Cunliffe, B. and Miles, D. (eds) (1984) *Aspects of the Iron Age in Central Southern Britain*, Oxford.

Dark, K. R. (1993) 'Roman-period activity at prehistoric ritual monuments in Britain and in the Armorican peninsula' in E. Scott (ed.) *Theoretical Roman Archaeology. First Roman Conference Proceedings*, Aldershot: 133–46.

Eade, J. and Sallnow, S. (1991) *Contesting the Sacred. The Anthropology of Christian Pilgrimage*, London.

Firth, A. (1996) 'Three facets of maritime archaeology: society, landscape and critique', paper circulated on Internet.

Fowler, P. J. (1965) 'A Roman barrow at Knobb's Crook, Woodlands, Dorset', *Antiquaries Journal* 45: 22–56.

Fowler, P. J. (1980) 'Traditions and objectives in British field archaeology, 1953–78', *Archaeological Journal* 137: 1–26.

Fowler, P. J. (1983) *The Farming of Prehistoric Britain*, Cambridge.

Fulford, M. (1990) 'The landscape of Roman Britain: a review', *Landscape History* 12: 25–32.

Fulford, M. (1993) 'Silchester: the early development of a civitas capital' in S. J. Greep (ed.) *Roman Towns. The Wheeler Inheritance*, CBA Research Report 93: 16–33.

Gaffney, V. and Tingle, M. (1989) *The Maddle Farm Project. An Integrated Survey of Prehistoric and Roman Landscapes on the Berkshire Downs*, Oxford: BAR 200.

Garwood, P. (1989) 'Social transformations and relations of power in Britain in the late fourth to sixth centuries AD', *Scottish Archaeological Review* 6: 90–10.

Giddens, A. (1981) *A Contemporary Critique of Historical Materialism* 1, *Power, Property and the State*, London.

Gosden, C. (1994) *Social Being and Time*, Oxford.

Harding, J. (1990) 'Using the unique as the typical: monuments and the ritual landscape' in P. Garwood, D. Jennings, R. Skeates and J. Toms (eds) *Sacred and Profane: Proceedings of a Conference on Archaeology, Ritual and Religion*, Oxford: 145–51.

Harvey, D. (1989) *The Condition of Postmodernity*, Oxford.

Haselgrove, C., Millet, M. and Smith, I. (1985) *Archaeology from the Plough Soil. Studies in the Collection and Interpretation of Field Survey Data*, Sheffield.

Hill, J. D. (1989) 'Rethinking the Iron Age', *Scottish Archaeological Review* 6: 16–24.

Hunn, J. R. (1994) *Reconstruction and Measurement of Landscape Change. A Study of Six Parishes in St Albans*, Oxford: BAR 236.

King, A. and Henig, M. (1981) *The Roman West in the Third Century*, Oxford: BAR 109.

Lambrick, G. and Robinson, M. (1979) *An Iron Age and Roman Riverside: Farmoor, Oxfordshire*, Oxford.

Malone, C. (1989) *The English Heritage Book of Avebury*, London.

Miles, D. and Palmer, S. (1995) 'White Horse Hill', *Current Archaeology* Vol. 12: 372–8.

Millett, M. (1990) *The Romanisation of Britain*, Cambridge.

Moreland, J. (1990) 'From the primeval to the paved: environment, perception and structural history', *Scottish Archaeological Review* 7: 14–22.

Myres, J. N. L. (1964) 'Wansdyke and the origins of Wessex' in H. R. Trevor-Roper (ed.) *Essays in History presented to Sir Keith Feiling*, London.

Nance, J. D. (1983) 'Regional sampling in archaeological survey: a statistical approach', *Advances in Archaeological Method and Theory* 6: 289–356.

Plog, S. (1976) 'Relative efficiencies of sampling techniques in archaeological survey' in K . V. Flannery (ed.) *The Early Mesoamerican Village*, New York: 136–55.

Purcell, N. (1990) 'The creation of provincial landscape: the Roman impact on Cisalpine Gaul' in Blagg and Millet (1990): 35–44.

Rahtz, P. *et al.* (1992) *Cadbury-Congresbury 1968–73. A Late/Post-Roman Hilltop Settlement in Somerset,* Oxford: BAR 223.

Said, E. (1993) *Culture and Imperialism,* London.

Scott, E. (1990) 'Romano-British villas and the social construction of space' in R. Samson (ed.) *The Social Archaeology of Houses,* Edinburgh.

Scott, S. (1993) 'A theoretical framework for the study of Romano-British villa mosaics' in M. Locock (ed.) *Meaningful Architecture. Social Interpretations of Buildings,* Aldershot.

Shennan, S. (1985) *Experiments in the Collection and Analysis of Archaeological Survey Data. The East Hampshire Survey,* Sheffield.

Smith, I. F. (1965) *Windmill Hill and Avebury. Excavations by Alexander Keiller,* Oxford.

Smith, I. F. and Simpson, D. D. A. (1964) 'Excavations of three Roman tombs and a prehistoric pit on Overton Down', *Wiltshire Archaeological Magazine* 59: 68–85.

Thomas, J. (1991) *Rethinking the Neolithic,* Cambridge.

Tilley, C. (1994) *The Phenomenology of Landscapes,* Oxford.

Trigger, B. (1989) *A History of Archaeological Thought,* Cambridge.

Vallat, J.-P. (1991) 'Survey archaeology and rural history: a difficult but productive relationship' in Barker and Lloyd (1991): 10–17.

Wainwright, G. (1968) 'The excavations of a Durotingian farmstead near Tollard Royal in Cranborne Chase, southern England', *Proceedings of the Prehistoric Society* 34: 102–47.

Whittle, A. (1991) 'Wayland's Smithy, Oxfordshire: excavations at the Neolithic tomb in 1962–3 by R. J. C. Atkinson and S. Piggot', *Proceedings of the Prehistoric Society* 57 (2): 61–102.

7

TERRITORY, ETHNONYMS AND GEOGRAPHY

The construction of identity in Roman Italy

Ray Laurence

The historian's conception of the process known as 'Romanisation' often depends on a bipolarity between the Romans and those conquered by them. In many ways, the Romans are represented as a nation state imposing their will upon subject peoples. However, as I will argue in this chapter, the concept of the nation state was not well developed in the Mediterranean, and in nearly all cases the ancient concept of 'Romans' as a people was highly negotiable and could be undercut by alternative forms of identity (Smith 1986, 6–21; cf. Gellner 1983). To understand these concepts, we need to have a clear understanding of how the ancients discovered and/or attributed ethnicities to others, and how these were represented by them.

It is in the work of the ancient geographers, in particular Strabo, Mela and Ptolemy, that we find discussion of and different approaches to the representation of ethnic groups in relationship to space and territory. The geographers had to make choices when describing the earth and its peoples in their accounts to distinguish the nature of the inhabited world (Barnes and Duncan 1992). In describing Italy, geographers provide us with a coherent body of knowledge about the representation of different peoples, which can be seen to have been driven by a concentration upon ethnicity as an organising feature.

However, first we need to set out a working definition of how ethnicity is formed. Ethnicity can be seen to be working upon certain variables in the ancient world; these are set out by Renfrew (1995, 130)

1   Shared territory or land.
2   Common descent.
3   A shared language.
4   A community of customs, or culture.
5   A community of beliefs, or religion.
6   A name, an ethnonym, to express group identity.

7   Self-awareness, self-identity.
8   A shared history, or myth of origin.

These variables need not all be present for ethnicity to be defined, but all contribute to the establishment of an ethnic identity for human groups that wish to set themselves apart from others. Direct evidence for the construction of ethnic identities in the Roman Empire is rare. What is far more common is evidence for the attribution of distinctiveness to regions and the peoples of those regions by outsiders. These accounts are investigated below to elucidate what were seen to be the organising features of ethnic identity in Italy. In no way are these accounts viewed as literal descriptions of a people's ethnicity or cultural identity as seen from the insider's perspective. Rather, what is analysed is the assertion through geographical description of difference in Italy – a region that during the first century BC became associated with a unified conception of Italy (*tota Italia*). This emphasis on difference is subsequently assessed in the light of the Augustan division of Italy into eleven regions associated with ethnonyms, which is contrasted with the use of ethnonyms in inscriptions by the local inhabitants.

The geographers' ethnicities

The general observations found in the modern literature on ethnicity and cultural identity are equally present in the writings of the classical geographers, who described physical features, named the places and cities of the human landscape and accounted for the variation of peoples, who were represented as a static entity in a set territory or place. However, the geographers did take account of discrepancies between the present situation of their time and the historical tradition (see below for discussion). Indeed, we should be clear about what the geographers were setting out to achieve through their activity of description before we go any further with the discussion of ethnicity. The Greek geographer Ptolemy (1. 1) provides a summary of the role of a geographer as compared with that of a chorographer:

> Geography is the imitative and representative description of the whole known part of the world, with everything which generally belongs to it. It differs from chorography in that the latter, considering the areas separate from one another, shows each of them with an indication of their harbours, their villages, and the smallest habitations, the derivations and detours of all the rivers, of the peoples and similar details. The actual aim of geography is solely to show the world in all its expanse, how it functions as much by its nature as by its position. It is concerned with general descriptions, like those of gulfs, large towns, peoples, great rivers, and everything which deserves to be shown as such. Chorography is concerned with the description of a part of the

whole, as one would show an ear or an eye. But geography embraces the totality of things as the image of a head depicts it [the human] in its entirety.

(Trans. Nicolet 1991, 119 n. 23)

Geography for the ancients represented the major features of the world without the minutiae and, from these descriptions, it should have been possible to draw a map of the world. The emphasis on map-making dictated a methodology that caused Strabo and others to describe the outline of coasts as a preliminary to any description of areas inland (Strabo 2. 5. 17; Janni 1984; on geographical methodology see Sordi 1988). This emphasis upon map-making, as Nicolet (1991, 95–122) has shown, can be taken as part of an imperial project to have the requisite knowledge to govern the empire (but see Leach 1988, 90–1 on alleged differences between Roman and Greek geography).

In contrast, the Augustan administrative system of eleven regions (Fig. 7.1) was not built around this geographical logic, with its emphasis on coastal description and map-making. Instead, as Nicolet (1991, 203) has observed, the arrangement of the regions was centred upon Rome, with the numbering running to the south from Rome through Latium and Campania (Region I), then across country to take in Apulia (Region II), then back to take in Region III. Following on from this, there is a jump to account for the peoples of the central Apennines and Picenum (Regions IV and V), then we have Umbria (Region VI) and Etruria (Region VII). At this point the system moves to the north of the Apennines to include Cispadana (Region VIII) and Liguria (Region IX). What is left over, the area north of the Po and south of the Alps, is split into two: the region of the Henetii (Region X) and Transpadana (Region XI).

1 Latium and Campania
2 Calabria and Apulia
3 Lucania and Bruttium
4 Samnium
5 Picenum
6 Umbria
7 Etruria
8 Aemilia
9 Liguria
10 Venetia and the Northern Adriatic Coast
11 Transpadine Gaul

Once the Augustan system of eleven regions had become established, some geographers combined the approach of describing the coastline with a view to map-making with reference to the Augustan regional division of Italy. Pliny, writing a little over half a century after the establishment of the eleven Augustan regions, describes first the coastline of Italy from its north-west to its north-east

Figure 7.1 The Italian regions established by Augustus (Nicolet 1991)

limit, setting the boundaries of the Augustan regions as he went and then adding, for the interior, a list of cities given alphabetically by Augustus. His need to describe the coastline causes him to reorder the regions: IX, VII, I, III, II, IV, V, VI, VIII, XI, X (Pliny, *NH* 3. 49–126).

However, the system of the Augustan regions could be disregarded by other geographers, who continued simply to describe the coast. Mela follows the coast, naming cities (places) and the four major inland cities: Rome, Capua, Bononia and Patavium. Similarly Strabo followed the coastline, but accounted for the ethnonyms as well as the cities and places of Italy in his account. The final extant version of Italy, Ptolemy's, set out a precise location of places via his concept of longitude and latitude, but he continued to group towns according to their territorial location and their ethnic name. Clearly, the Augustan division of Italy into regions did not eradicate alternative representations of Italy by geographers. It would seem that there was not one representation of space, but a number of versions representing the same territory and peoples.

Strabo in particular uses a concept of ethnicity, in his representation of Italy, which reveals the ancients' understanding of ethnicity. As a geographer Strabo was involved in the description of territory and had to face up to the task of creating a unified concept of Italy as a geographical unit out of a number of disunited parts. (See Coarelli 1988; Tozzi 1988; Prontera 1988 for detailed discussion; also notice the role of geography in creating a fiction of a whole or parts, see Duncan and Duncan 1992 or Barthes 1972, 81–4 on the Blue Guide.) At the same time, Strabo succeeded in emphasising the disunity of Italy through the detailed description of its parts, for instance Umbria.

His concern with meeting the requirement that a map might be drawn from his description of Italy causes him to emphasise the shape of Italy and its coastline. But, in a number of ways, he does more than this by describing the inland areas: he presents detailed information about the territory of various peoples in former times and in their present positions, and makes a link between territorial division and the ethnicity of the people living in that territory. Frequently he notes the loss of ethnic unity and cohesion in a region, which he accounts for. This account provides detailed information on how Strabo attributed an ethnic identity to other peoples and the geographical use of ethnonyms in the description of territory.

The relationship of an ethnos and a territory found in Strabo's account of Italy needs some detailed analysis. Traditionally, following Herodotus (8. 144), an ethnos could have been tightly defined: in the case of Greeks, a people sharing a common descent, a language, gods, sacred places, festivals, customs and ways of life, in spite of having no geographical unity of territory in space. Not surprisingly, Strabo accounts for the Greek involvement in Italy through colonisation, but resists any attempt to see contemporary Italy as a Greek world, unlike other writers, who attempted to draw comparisons to create a Greek past for Rome (e. g. Dion. Hal. *Ant.* 7. 72–3). Strabo is adamant that very few of these Greek cities had retained their Greek way of life, apart from Naples and Tarentum (Poccetti 1988; Lomas 1993, 34, 145, 162 on Tarentum and Naples) and, to a lesser extent, at Cumae (5. 4. 4). But, even at Naples, there was a major loss of what Strabo recognised as a Greek ethnicity: the population had been mixed with the Campani, and might have retained Greek institutions (the gymnasium, the ephebia, the phratriae) and the Greek names for things, yet Strabo was adamant that they were Romans (5. 4. 7). This loss of ethnicity and its replacement with a Roman identity have frequently been commented upon. However, seldom have they been placed in the context of a discussion of Strabo's account of a change in identity or ethnicity amongst the other peoples of Italy.

Strabo's geography of Italy, frequently, involves a discussion of the past, in which he relates the changes in population in the past (Poccetti 1988, 223–5). This often refers to the replacement of one people by another; for example in Campania (5. 4. 8) we can identify the Osci being driven out by the Tyrrheni, who were themselves removed by the Pelasgi, and the Pelasgi were to be conquered by the Samnites. Strabo accounts for such changes processually in terms of the ethnic replacement of one people by another in the past. Here he follows a fairly simple model of conquest and removal.

Strabo had a complex ideal of what constituted an ethnic identity in Italy and like Herodotus was concerned with common origins and descent when discussing either Greeks or Italian groups in Italy. This comes out in his discussion of the Sabini. He regards them as a very ancient people of Italy and indigenous to Italy, unlike so many other groups (5. 3. 1). He conceptualises their role as the original people of Italy from which many other peoples were descended in the manner of the descendants in the Greek colonies. Therefore, he relates that the Picentini (5. 4. 2) and Samnites were colonists sent away to other areas by the Sabini. The Samnites had their own descendants, the Leucani (6. 1. 2), from whom were descended the Brettii (6. 1. 4). Thus many of the peoples of Italy were represented as having a common origin similar to that of the Greeks.

For Strabo, a crucial element in the determination of ethnicity was language. Most of the languages of Italy do not receive a mention, but we can see that he links language with ethnic groups when he discusses Campania and in particular the Osci (5. 3. 6, 9). He finds it strange that the Osci had disappeared and had no presence in Italy, since the language still existed but was not associated with any particular ethnicity. Moreover, place names, so important for the telling of geography, referred back to an Oscan presence; for example, in naming Teanum Sidicinum he is forced to discuss the absence of the Sidicini (a people) and account for why the town is part of Campania. Similar problems occur with names such as the Ausonian Sea: the Ausones never lived near the sea, according to Strabo's investigation (5. 3. 6). Thus, elsewhere, language and place names could be seen to be coinciding with the ethnonym described in cases in which Strabo does not remark upon their lack of correspondence. It also demonstrates the importance of language in defining ethnicity for Strabo and the ancients, which we have already seen in his discussion of Naples. That city through the use of Greek institutions and language came close to being ethnically Greek, yet, upon closer examination, Strabo found that the city was ethnically Roman but was promoting its Greekness and its association with a Greek past.

As a geographer Strabo was describing different ethnic groups and accounting for their presence in relation to a defined territory. Ideally, for geographical tidiness, there should be a precise relation between territory and people, especially if it should be possible to draw a map afterwards from the description. Not surprisingly, problems occur. In discussing Umbria there was little concordance between where the Ombrici lived and the territory known as Umbria (5. 2. 10). The territory began at the Apennines and stretched to the Adriatic coast, with its ancient boundary with Cisalpine Gaul at either the river Aesis or the Rubicon in the past. However, now that Cisalpine Gaul was thought of as part of Italy, Umbria according to Strabo and others was seen to stretch as far as Ravenna, since the people living there were Ombrici. As we shall see later, this in no way corresponded to the administrative region known as Umbria.

Strabo takes another criterion in accounting for ethnicity and, in particular, its absence: dress and customs. He points out that the Leucani, Brettii and Samnites had lost those features that emphasised their ethnic distinctiveness: language, armour, dress and other attributes (6. 1. 2). To make matters worse, for Strabo, their settlements had either disappeared or were simply unremarkable. Such a situation creates unremarkable geography and little to account for or write about, although in discussing the Sabine settlements earlier Strabo lists them in spite of their lack of urbanity, owing to a need to account for the 'glory and power of Italy' (5. 4. 11), presumably in the past.

Equally, we can see a general erosion of neat boundaries in Italy and the formation of larger units of territory, alongside the loss of individual cohesion of ethnic groups. This is particularly apparent in Apulia, where the Peucetii were also known as Poedicli, and the Apuli (native name) could be called by the name Daunii, given to them by Greeks (6. 3. 1). These names and the division of Apulia according to different ethnic territories had collapsed:

> Since the terms Peucetii and Daunii are not at all used by the native inhabitants except in early times, and since the country as a whole is now called Apulia, necessarily the boundaries of these ethnics cannot be told to a nicety either and for this reason neither should I myself make positive assertions about them.
>
> (6. 3. 8)

Evidently, some ethnic boundaries had ceased to have any meaning for those living there and this could be recognised. However, it would appear that ethnic boundaries could have a rigidity once applied, as Nicolet (1991) recognises in the division of Italy into eleven parts by Augustus. Many of these boundaries corresponded to the traditional ethnonyms, with some break-up, with the Samnites being divided between regions 1, 2 and 4 (Nicolet 1991, 175–6). Interestingly, it was the Samnites who in Strabo's account had lost their ethnic distinctiveness and were not recognised as a separate region by Augustus, unlike the Umbrians, Etruscans or Ligurians. Not surprisingly, the division could not account for all possibilities and the heterogeneous nature of Italy. Those ethnic groups on the boundaries were likely to disappear from geography, just as the Osci on the boundary of Latium and Campania had disappeared from Strabo's geographical vision at some earlier date (5. 3. 6, 5. 4. 3).

Ptolemy's geographical account of Italy (3. 1), written in the second century
AD, confirms the persistence of the ethnonyms attributed to the peoples of Italy
by Strabo. Even with his use of longitude and latitude, Ptolemy first follows
the coastline of Italy, listing its towns, and then in the north lists the peoples
of the Alps, returning to his starting point in the north-west. Then he fills in
the interior, using a system of ethnonyms to group towns together. These are
subdivided to a greater extent than the divisions used by Strabo for the same
purpose. For example, Ptolemy's Umbria does not constitute such a large area,
since its northern sector is divided off under a separate ethnonym – the Senones.
There is a tendency to break the eleven large regions of the Augustan redivision
of Italy into smaller units, except in the cases of Liguria and Etruria, which
might be seen to have been thought to have a greater homogeneity compared
with other regions. Ptolemy makes every division possible, including that of
Apulia into Peucetii and Daunii, which Strabo had viewed as arbitrary, since the
inhabitants did not recognise such terms. Clearly, geography had created a map
which fixed the boundaries of territories to be associated with a stated ethnonym
and, as can be seen from Strabo's more extensive account, unified a history to
be associated with that ethnonym and territory. Ideally, the geographer should
have been capable of finding the appropriate customs and beliefs to associate
with the people inhabiting a particular part of the earth, but in Italy, owing to
personal knowledge, Strabo could find such attempts frustrated for the present
and needed to explain the inconsistencies with reference to the past (on Strabo's
knowledge of contemporary Italy see Coarelli 1988).

In no way should we view the statements of the geographers as a representation of reality or draw maps with ethnic boundaries based upon these sources
(Dench 1995, 1–3). The authors of the extant descriptions of Italy were using
information to create divisions of the world into regions. The problematic
nature of such divisions is clear. As any regional geographer will confirm, it is
relatively easy when mountains or rivers create a physical division in space. What
is more difficult is to find the boundaries when the physical geography provides
few clues (e.g. in Apulia) or too many features for the creation of simple division
(e.g. in the central Apennines, see Dench 1995, 1–3). Therefore, the subdivision
of space by ancient geographers does not directly represent the reality of ethnic
territories, but it does inform us of a view of the world that relied upon ethnicity
to define territorial divisions in space. As the geographers fixed these divisions
they were in effect creating a static notion of ethnicity for those regions – in
many cases they were aware of such arbitrariness but not capable of reconcep-
tualising an organising paradigm based on the concordance of territory and
ethnicity.

Understanding Romanness

So far we have largely dealt with the outsider's view of ethnicity and its mapping
on to other peoples. We need to examine the insider's point of view and switch to

a Roman source representing his ethnic group, Romans, in space and the relationship between that group and its territory. Velleius Paterculus (1. 14–15) in the first book of his *History of Rome* groups together various features of Roman history that he saw to cease to have meaning if inserted into his historical narrative. He creates lists of achievements, and one such list is the foundation of colonies and the extension of citizenship to others from 390 BC (the sack of Rome by the Gauls) down to 100 BC (the date of army reform and alteration of the nature of colonial foundations): 'It will perhaps not seem out of place, if, in this connection, we weave into our history the various extensions of citizenship and the growth of the Roman name through granting to others a share in its privileges' (1. 14. 1).

This view of the importance of citizenship would suggest that, for Velleius Paterculus, membership of a citizen body could constitute what it was to be Roman. It can be seen to be similar to the notions of French nationality that in the late eighteenth and nineteenth centuries was constituted above all through membership of the citizen body rather than being based upon language or ethnicity (Hobsbawm 1990, 88). The peoples to which Roman citizenship was extended included: the Aricians, the Campanians and a portion of the Samnites without suffrage, Fundi and Formiae, Acerra, the Sabines without suffrage, and finally suffrage was granted to the Sabines. The list stops at 100 BC and avoids the complication of the Social War, after which most of Italy gained Roman citizenship. The concept of citizenship overrides and distances Romanness from ethnicity, since citizenship is reported as being granted to peoples identified by their ethnonyms to distinguish them. Some of these ethnonyms accounted for peoples over a wide area and resident in a number of centres, for example the Sabines or the Campanians; others were of a more specific nature, for example the Fundani or Formiani referring to the peoples associated with the cities of Fundi or Formiae. This would seem to represent a universal approach by Rome towards others, whether a dispersed group of people or a very specific group of people centred around a city.

Clearly, there was a desire on the part of Rome to set up centres or cities amongst dispersed peoples. For example, in resettling the Picentes on the Gulf of Paestum, the Romans set up what Strabo calls a metropolis at Picentia as the centre of the newly established people in the area, who lived largely in villages (5. 4. 13). Strabo notes other metropoleis associated with other dispersed peoples in Italy: Mediolanum of the Insubres, Suessa of the Volsci (in the past), Corfinium of the Peligni, Teate of the Marrucini, Petelia of the Chones and Consentia of the Brettii (5. 1. 6, 5. 3. 4, 5. 3. 11, 5. 4. 2, 5. 4. 10, 6. 1. 3, 6. 1. 5; cf. Capua 5. 4. 10, and the rivalry for this title between Cnossus and Gortyna, 10. 4. 7). However, in most cases the word 'metropolis' tends to refer to what is termed '*civitas* capital' in discussing the urban pattern in Roman Britain: it was a central place for a large territory associated with a particular ethnonym.

To return to Velleius, he also lists the founding of colonies throughout Italy down to about 100 BC. The list can be seen as a complete naming of all

Roman colonies, because those founded after that date could easily be identified as colonies by their name, since the name included a reference to the general who had settled veterans in that place, for example Colonia *Cornelia* Veneria Pompeianorum (the town of Pompeii), founded by Lucius *Cornelius* Sulla. Thus Velleius is highlighting in effect the places that were not known or had simply been forgotten as colonies of the Roman people. The list effectively details all those who could be seen to be ethnically Roman or Latin – the differentiation of these as ethnonyms is less than easy in Velleius or other contemporary texts. (This is not to argue that there was not a legal distinction between these colonies originally.) However, what Velleius does provide us with is an account of a dispersed settlement pattern (of colonies) of those we might associate with the ethnonym 'Roman' in Italy and elsewhere in the Mediterranean. Parallel to Velleius' account of the colonies founded prior to 100 BC, there already existed a list of colonies drawn up by Augustus and enumerated alphabetically for each of the eleven regions of Italy. (Also notice how Livy pays particular attention to the founding of colonies in his *Summaries* and see also Plin. *NH 3*.) These lists of colonies marked the towns that had been associated with a Roman origin as distinct from the other towns of Italy. Significantly, colonies placed a particular emphasis upon the anniversary of their foundation and their continuity as settlements of citizens (Roman or Latin) established by Rome in the past and marked the day with a festival. Unlike the surrounding towns and territories, the colonies could point to a Romanness that others simply did not have (e.g. Cicero, *Pro Sestio* 131, on Brundisium and his arrival on the anniversary of the colony on 5 August; see also Puteoli, *CIL* 10. 1781; Interamna Nahars, *CIL* 11. 4170; see Harris 1977, 285 for discussion of these).

How other towns constructed their identity needs to be discussed. An example will suffice to illustrate the problem. Patavium in the region of the Henetii is seen by the geographers as exceptional. Mela picks it out as one of the four inland towns he mentions (the others are Rome, Bononia and Capua), and Strabo (5. 1. 7) views it as the best of cities, with 500 equites according to the AD 14 census. The town was the birthplace of Livy and so we have extra information about the construction of the town's identity (Liv. 10. 2). Moreover, as Harris (1977) stresses, the town had not been conquered by Rome but, instead, was firmly allied with Rome in wars against the Boii and the Symbri (Strabo 5. 1. 9). The town could celebrate the fact that it had never been conquered, and could recall the defeat of the Spartan general Cleonymus at the head of a Greek fleet in 302 BC. Livy points to the ancient beaks of ships fastened to the Temple of Juno and contests involving ships on the anniversary of the battle (Liv. 10. 2).

In terms of ethnicity, according to Strabo (5. 1. 4), there were two theories over the origins of Patavium: one stated that the people were part of the Celti of northern Italy, but the other suggested that the city had been founded by Antenor and the Eneti of Paphlagonia. The connection with Antenor was key if the identity of the town was to have a wider value, since it linked the Patavians with Rome through a common ancestral link back to Troy. Moreover the link with Antenor was actively marked by games, said to have been set up by him, every thirty years. Here we see a basically barbarian town appropriating the Trojan legend to be used symbolically to alter the city's ethnicity so that it may become closer to Rome, the major power in the region. (Compare Dench 1995, 61 ff. on similar actions by Greeks and peoples of southern Italy.) Equally, we should view this appropriation of Trojan mythology in the context of the increase in Roman influence in the region. This contact with Rome occurred in the early second century BC and was associated with the setting up of a local calendar beginning with year 1 (*CIL* 5. 2864, 2885, 2787, 2794, 2797, 3031, 2873, 3019, 2943; *ILS* 5650, 9420; *NSc* 1926, 352; see Harris 1977 for discussion). According to Harris (1977, 287), the calendar can be calibrated by cross-referencing the dates to locate year 1 as 173 BC. The significance of this year, in the context of Roman involvement in the region, may have been the alliance between Rome and the Henetii referred to by Strabo (5. 1. 4). No doubt, given the date, the setting up of a new calendar marked some involvement with Rome (Harris 1977, 287–8).

However, the town could distance itself from Rome culturally, for example to create a moral contrast between the chastity of women in Patavium compared with women in Rome (Plin. *Ep.* 1. 14. 6; Mart. *Ep.* 11. 16). As Dench (1995, 91) has shown in her study of the Sabines, this feature of morality simply contrasts anywhere in Italy with Rome, a city seen to have decayed or 'fallen' in the Roman imagination. Harris (1977) sees this feature as a symptom of others, alongside the previously discussed phenomenon, that represent attempts by the people of Patavium 'to preserve some independence from the dominant Roman culture'. This may be true, but he constructs the argument through a dichotomy of acceptance and resistance of Romanness which ignores the complexity and evolution of identity that could on one reading ally Patavium with Rome but on another could view the city and people as descended from the Celti.

Clearly, in Patavium identity could be refashioned in relation to Rome. The changing political situation associated with Rome's conflict with the Boii had altered and disrupted the traditional affinities between the Henetii of Patavium and the Boii. In consequence, we may say that the Patavians had redefined their identity to emphasise their link with Antenor of Troy and an origin myth that linked them with Rome. Equally, in the period following Rome's domination of the region, we might use an alternative explanation and state with Harris (1977) that the changing social context had disrupted the conventional ways of understanding. Both explanations can be used at different moments in time to stress the advantages of the negotiation of change in identity. More than anything, this illustrates how the nature of both identity and ethnicity was subject to negotiation through time (see Bentley 1989; Chapman *et al.* 1989, 11 on academic debate and the definition of ethnicity), rather than any truth about the use of fragmentary elements from antiquity that can be identified as being important for the construction of either identity or ethnicity in practice (see

Bentley 1989 on practice). What is clear is that outsiders, such as Strabo, could detect or attribute differences between the peoples of Italy, and that these differences were a valuable resource in terms of symbolic capital.

The Augustan regions: the state's geography

The emphasis on regional distinctiveness in the ancient geographers brings us back to the need for the division of Italy into larger units and, in particular, the division of Italy into the eleven Augustan regions. This system appears to have been quite different from the organisational methods of the ancient geographers already discussed. Nicolet has argued that the Augustan system of eleven administrative regions eroded local character in some cases, yet in others it can be seen to have been based upon existing regional entities (Nicolet 1991, 203, examples cited: Umbria Cic. *Mur.* 42; Picenum Sall. *Jug.* 30; Lucania Plin. *NH* 2. 147). However, Nicolet does not have the whole story. He tends to relate the regions to physical geography, which works in most cases – for example, Etruria was defined by its coastline, the Apennines and the Tiber. It is possible to view the order and arrangement of the regions in relation to a land-based geography, in which land transport rather than maritime transport was the organising feature. To explain, Region 1 includes two traditional groupings, Latium and Campania, which suggests that its organising feature was not this division but some other form of geographical organisation. In the context of the next region (Apulia), we can begin to see a geographical logic and a relationship between Regions 1 and 2; and this relationship can be seen to revolve around the long-distance transport routes (the Via Appia and Via Latina) across Italy in the direction of Brundisium. This unified geographical concept is accounted for by Strabo in his discussion of inland routes, but is fragmented because he emphasises a maritime organisation for his geography (5. 3. 6, 5. 3. 9, 5. 4. 11, 6. 3. 7; see Dench 1995, 180 on the absorbtion of these spatial concepts derived from Rome by Strabo). Moreover, in discussing the roads of southern Italy, he highlights the Via Appia and another route through Region 2 leading north from Brundisium to Beneventum, but then mentions a third road from Rhegium to the Via Appia (6. 3. 7). This third road coincided with the territory of the Brettii, Leucani and Samnitae, in other words Region 3. Therefore, in these three regions, we see an organisation based upon the geography of the major roads. From the point of view of cultural identity, Strabo stresses that in all cases these roads pass through the territories of more than one specifically identified ethnic group. In the case of Region 1 (Apulia), the road north went through the territories of the Peucetii and the Daunii, peoples whom Strabo had found impossible to separate, since they themselves did not recognise the division. Effectively, the organisation of the regions was defined by the extant road network, which had coincidentally been systematised during Augustus' lifetime (Suet. *Aug.* 37).

Elsewhere, the organisation of individual regions can be seen to have been based around land transport. Strabo's description of Umbria prioritises the Via

Flaminia (Pasquinucci 1988), from Ariminum to Ocriculum, as Umbria's defining feature. Towns are placed in relation to the road and Strabo can point to new towns being founded because of the road's presence (5. 2. 10). Certainly, in this case, Region 6 was traditionally associated with the ethnonym Ombrici, but as Strabo points out the presence of the Ombrici could be found as far north as Ravenna, yet the region did not extend that far and was confined to the area defined with reference to the Via Flaminia.

Looking at the overall division of Italy into Augustus' eleven regions, we begin to understand the principles based upon physical and human geography. Regions 1 to 3 have already been shown to have been based around the geography of land transport. Regions 4 and 5 can be seen to have followed from the previous division of Regions 1 to 3, as a simple northward progression to account for the central Apennines. Moving north from Rome, Regions 6 and 7 correspond to the northward route of the River Tiber, the boundary between the two regions. The four regions of recently enfranchised Cisalpine Gaul are dealt with by an east-to-west progression, first south of the River Po, Regions 8 and 9, and then to the north of the Po, Regions 10 and 11. This east-to-west progression broadly corresponds with the transport route – the River Po and the Via Aemilia.

This relation between the Augustan regions and the road system is confirmed by the source material, from the second century AD, referring to the administration of Italy and the offices of *iuridici, curatores viarum* and *praefecti alimentiorum*. A link is made in the titles and area of jurisdiction of these officials; for example a *iuridicus* could be appointed for a region known as the Flaminia and Umbria (*CIL* 2. 2634, 3. 6154, 6. 1509, 14. 3586; 11. 376 adds Picenum as well), which stresses the coincidence between the road structure and this ethnonym. To the north, Region 8 is simply referred to as the Aemilia (*CIL* 14. 3601, 3993) and an ethnonym is absent. However, to the south of Italy the emphasis on the roads as the division could be forgotten and a greater emphasis was placed on the ethnonyms associated with the regions, for example the *iuridicus* of Apulia and Calabria (*CIL* 9. 1572). In no example known to the author was the numerical identification of the regions utilised. In the north the regions are simply referred to, for example Transpadana (*CIL* 5. 1874, 4332, 4341, 11. 6338), which reflects maybe a suppression or loss of the ethnonyms attributed to the peoples of the region.

The presence or absence of ethnonyms in the epigraphic evidence for the organisation of Italy raises the question of what these ethnonyms referred to and why in some cases they survive whilst in others they are simply absent. We need to recognise that we are not dealing with a formal government structure when discussing the epigraphy that records ethnonyms associated with the office of *iuridicus*. In nearly all cases they were set up by a local population (e.g. the *ordo* of Ariminum sets up a statue and inscription to the *iuridicus* for the Flaminia, Umbria and Picenum: *CIL* 11. 376). We might argue that the ethnonyms could still have had meaning for the population from the fact that some regions were referred to simply by a number of ethnonyms, rather than the structures of land transport. However, this may be missing the point and underplays the power of geography to politically define territory and to name regions (see Pickles 1992). Once a territory has become associated with a set ethnonym, the ethnonym can remain in use for a considerable period of time. For example, Procopius (writing in about AD 500, *BG* 5. 15. 20–30) uses the same ethnonyms to describe Italy as Strabo 500 years earlier. Therefore, the naming of Italy by geographers fixed the populations of regions with an ethnicity that would continue to be associated with the individual regions. The populations of the individual regions need not have been directly identified with the ethnonym(s), which associated them with the region collectively. Indeed, identity could more easily be expressed through the structure of the local city, and it was only when the population came into contact with a central authority, the *iuridicus*, the curator of roads or the prefect of the *alimenta*, that there was contact with the notion of a wider collective region. This should not be seen as an argument that asserts that the ethnonym could not be used or appropriated in order to assert a collective identity, but I know of no cases where it was used for that purpose. (It is notable that Italian wines do not take ethnonyms, but prefer a specific name with reference to the point of maritime export Plin. *NH*, 14. 59–73; Varro, *RR* 1. 2. 6–8; for similar case of pottery see Plin. *NH* 35. 159–61). Perhaps we see in Italy, during the first two centuries AD, a shift from the ethnonym representing a people to the ethnonym representing a territorial division.

Imagining Italia

The eleven regions of Italy and their associated names (ethnonyms and others) were not a natural division of territory. For the regions to have coherence, they depended upon a mythology of descent that denied the basic heterogeneity of the Italian population to create a number of unified regions, which were associated with one or two ethnonyms. Such a view can be seen as a simple denial of history, which is summed up by the expression 'Once upon a time the land was assigned to specific peoples to cultivate, such as Etruria to the Tusci' (*Varro Men.*, frag. 17), or elaborated into a full geographical list of the peoples of Italy who were said to have been present at the battle of Cannae (Sil. Ital. 8. 356–617). The preservation and representation of ethnicity in history as part of a natural order are not unusual in the representation of identities – ethnic, national or local (Gellner 1983, 48–9; Hobsbawm 1990, 1–13; Reminick 1983, 8; Patterson 1975, 305–8; Jones and Graves-Brown 1995, 4–9).

Similarly, at a macro level, the population of Italy could construct itself as part of *tota Italia* or simply by citizenship as Roman. However, what is important, in the context of the use of ethnonyms by geographers, is the division of territory according to ethnonym and the association of a common mythology and history with that ethnonym, which could subsequently be unified under the relatively recent concept of *tota Italia* (Nicolet 1991, 194). This unification of the disparate elements should be seen as the creation of a new 'imagined community', Italy, with which all the disparate local histories and geographies could be unified (Hobsbawm 1990, 17, 48–9, on imagined communities). *Tota Italia* must be seen as an 'imagined community' and not as resistance to 'Romanisation' or the Italianisation of Rome. In fact *tota Italia* was part of the complex ideology that unified Rome and Italy politically. In many ways, the imagined community is not a description of the relationship, but a vehicle for achieving and stabilising that relationship politically. The static and unchanging association between ethnonyms and territory, found in the geographical writers, would have reinforced the stability of the political relationship between Rome and the population of Italy. Moreover, it might have hindered the renegotiation of ethnicity at a regional level and have caused the focus of any shift in identity to be concentrated at the level of the city and inter-city rivalry (see Chapter 5). In this light, we may view the concept of *tota Italia* and the use of ethnonyms in the definition of geography as a method of Romanisation that stressed the distinctness of the Italian peoples but united them politically with Rome at the centre. Such a viewpoint seems at first sight contradictory, but it may reflect the ideological and cultural complexity of the process known as Romanisation more realistically than a simplistic view based upon notions of domination and resistance and a duality between Roman and native culture.

Acknowledgements

This chapter was originally presented as part of a panel session on 'Outsiders in the Roman City' at the Classical Association annual conference (1996) in Nottingham. I would like to thank all present for their critical comments. The research was conducted whilst I was funded by the British Academy as part of its postdoctoral research fellowship scheme. Naturally I am indebted to the Academy for its support of my research. Any errors are of course my own creation.

Bibliography

Ardener, E. (1989) 'The construction of history: vestiges of creation' in E. Tonkin, M. McDonald and M. Chapman (eds) *History and Ethnicity*, London: 22–33.

Barnes, T. J. and Duncan, J. S. (1992) 'Introduction: writing worlds' in T. J. Barnes and J. S. Duncan (1992) *Writing Worlds. Discourse, Text and Metaphor in the Represen-tation of Landscape*, London: 1–17.

Barthes, R. (1972) *Mythologies*, London.

Bentley, G. C. (1989) 'Ethnicity and practice', *Comparative Studies in Sociology and History* 29: 24–55.

Bourdieu, P. (1977) *An Outline of a Theory of Practice*, London.

Coarelli, P. (1988) 'Strabone e il Lazio' in G. Maddoli (ed.) *Strabone e l'italia antica*, Perugia: 73–91.

Duncan, J. S. and Duncan, N. G. (1992) 'Ideology and bliss, Roland Barthes and the secret histories of landscape' in T. J. Barnes and J. S. Duncan (eds) *Writing Worlds. Discourse, Text and Metaphor in the Representation of Landscape*, London: 18–37.

Chapman, M., McDonald, M. and Tonkin, E. (1989) 'Introduction – history and social anthropology' in E. Tonkin, M. McDonald and M. Chapman (eds) *History and Ethnicity*, London: 1–21.

Dench, E. (1995) *From Barbarians to New Men. Greek, Roman and Modern Perceptions of the Central Apennines*, Oxford.

Friedman, J. (1994) *Cultural Identity and Global Process*, London.

Gellner, E. (1983) *Nations and Nationalism*, Oxford.

Harris, W. V. (1977) 'The era of Patavium', *ZPE* 27: 283–93.

Hobsbawm, E. J. (1990) *Nations and Nationalism since 1780. Programme, Myth, Reality*, Cambridge.

Janni, P. (1984) *La mappa e il periplo. Cartografia antica e spazio odologica*, Rome.

Janni, P. (1988) 'L'Italia di Strabone: descrizione e immagine' in G. Maddoli (ed.) *Strabone e l'Italia antica*, Perugia: 145–59.

Jones, S. and Graves-Brown, P. (1995) 'Introduction: archaeology and cultural identity in Europe' in P. Graves-Brown, S. Jones and C. Gamble (eds) *Cultural Identity and Archaeology. The Construction of European Communities*, London: 3–24.

Leach, E. W. (1988) *The Rhetoric of Space. Literary and Artistic Representations of Landscape in Republican and Augustan Rome*, Princeton.

Nicolet, C. (1991) *Space, Geography and Politics in the Early Roman Empire*, Ann Arbor.

Pasquinucci, M. (1988) 'Strabone e l'Italia centrale', in G. Maddoli (ed.) *Strabone e l'Italia antica*, Perugia: 45–59.

Patterson, O. (1975) 'Context and choice in ethnic allegiance: a theoretical framework and Caribbean case-study' in N. Glazer and D. R. Moynihan (eds) *Ethnicity: Theory and Experience*, Cambridge, Mass: 305–49.

Pickles, J. (1992) 'Texts, hermeneutics and propaganda maps' in T. J. Barnes and J. S. Duncan (eds) *Writing Worlds. Discourse, Text and Metaphor in the Representation of Landscape*, London: 193–230.

Poccetti, P. (1988) 'Prolegomeni ad una lettura dei dati etno-toponomastici dell'Italia Straboniana' in G. Maddoli (ed.) *Strabone e l'Italia antica*, Perugia: 221–63.

Prontera, F. (1988) 'L'Italia meridionale di Strabone' in G. Maddoli (ed.) *Strabone e l'Italia antica*, Perugia: 93–109.

Reminick, R. A. (1983) *Theory of Ethnicity. An Anthropologist's Perspective*, New York.

Renfrew, C. (1995) 'Prehistory and the identity of Europe, or, Don't let's be beastly to the Hungarians' in P. Graves-Brown, S. Jones and C. Gamble (eds) *Cultural Identity and Archaeology. The Construction of European Communities*, London: 125–37.

Roosens, E. E. (1989) *Creating Ethnicity. The Process of Ethnogenesis*, London.

Shennan, S. (1989) *Archaeological Approaches to Cultural Identity*, London.

Smith, A. D. (1986) *The Ethnic Origins of Nations*, Oxford.

Sordi, M. (1988) *Geografia e storiografia nel mondo classico*, Milan.

Thomsen, R. (1940) *The Italic Regions*, Copenhagen.

Tozzi, P. (1988) 'L'Italia settentrionale di Strabone', in G. Maddoli (ed.) *Strabone e l'italia antica*, Perugia: 23–43.

8

ROMANCING THE CELTS

A segmentary approach to acculturation

Alex Woolf

The term 'Romanisation' has become shorthand for what we, as archaeologists, perceive as the influence of Roman tastes and values on patterns of consumption and production in the non-Latin provinces of the Empire and in bordering territories. The identification of what processes in the past this actually reflects is rather less clear. A variety of possibilities exist and in all probability a combination of them has contributed to the production of the evidence. John Barrett, speaking in the session from which many chapters of this book were drawn, argued against the usefulness of the concept of Romanisation on the grounds, as I understood him, that aesthetics and values in Rome itself were fluid, dynamic and open to external influence and therefore could not provide a stable model for emulation (now published as Barrett 1997). What we have to ask ourselves is whether this perspective, in itself, is not ahistorical and whether it denies not simply agency but also motivation to individuals in specific historical conditions in the provinces. An attempt by a Briton or a Gaul to be more like the Romans he encountered cannot be discounted as a possibility merely on the grounds that the Romans themselves changed. Any given individual who encountered the Romans will have developed his or her own Platonic or Weberian ideal of what *romanitas* (to use another problematic word!) demanded, and the objective accuracy of these images is neither here nor there.

More interesting, perhaps, are the questions about the nature of the different aspects of Romanisation as it appears to us. Which features of Romano-British or Gallo-Roman culture resulted from deliberate attempts to 'become Roman', which represented utilitarian adoptions of superior technology and which resulted from an 'ethnically blind' processes of elite emulation, or redistributive consumption? The answers to such questions will be historically and regionally contingent and as such are likely to elude any broad theoretical analysis.

On glancing at a map of the Roman Empire, one of the first things one notices is that the *civitates*, the local administrative units, of northern Gaul and of Britain are, relatively speaking, so much larger territorially than those of Italy or the Mediterranean littoral. Whilst an average Italian city might have a territory comprising 100–200 square miles, it seems not to have been unusual for *civitates* in Britain and Gaul to be over 2,000 square miles in extent. In terms of sheer territory a British tribe such as the Iceni, with their capital at Venta (Caistor by Norwich), were on a par with the Latins or Etruscans, as peoples, rather than with any one of the score or so cities in Latium or Etruria. In terms of territorial extent it is the tribal divisions of Italy and the Greek world which seem to equate most naturally with the *civitates* of the north.

It is not within the scope of this chapter to discuss why it was that political unity should have been achieved at a tribal level in the north and at district level in the south, though doubtless the specific historical conditions of the Roman conquest may have had something to do with it. Instead I would like to discuss the implications for archaeological interpretation of the very different role of the urban centre and the curial elite in northern cities and then go on to discuss whether or not such process can be directly linked with the replacement of the Celtic languages by Romance.

Because of their small size the Mediterranean *civitates* were able to display and maintain a high degree of homogeneity. The civic centre was the local market for the whole territory. Town houses were no great distance from rural estates. Although curial membership was based upon property qualifications rather than any elective process the sheer 'locality' of each civic republic would have demanded a spread of residence mirroring, to some extent, our ideal of constituency representation, each citizen having as a local patron some *curialis*. Was anything like this possible in the north?

The policy followed by the Romans for establishing an administrative framework for their growing empire, in the western, barbarian, provinces at least, was to offer the various polities which they subdued, or allied themselves with, a republican constitution modelled more or less closely upon their own (see González 1986 for *Lex Irnitana*, the only western civic code extant). Thus the early Empire was technically a league of Rome and a vast number of allied states. From an imperial perspective the urban centres of these republics provided the contact points for tribute collection and for tendering additional contracts for the support of the superstructure: the army and the civil service.

Rome incorporated barbarian tribes as constituent *civitates* of her empire by enlisting the existing local elites to fulfil the role of local *senatores*, *curiales* or *decuriones*. This is well known, and twenty years ago Brunt (1975) emphasised the degree to which local leaders maintained traditional methods of articulating social relations. We have to ask ourselves what these methods were. How far might they have been accommodated within the imperial structure? And what evidence of such accommodation might we expect to find in the archaeological record?

In *The Romanization of Britain* (1990, 20), Martin Millett envisages, for the immediate pre-incorporation period, a 'division of society into a series of comparatively small-scale units, each with its own leader, and aristocratic elite. These clans came together to form larger groups assembled under a single leader at times of stress.' Such schema are common and not peculiar to Millett. It seems to me, however, that there are a number of problems with this model. In chief its failing seems to lie in its synchronism. We know from the archaeological record that different groups in the late pre-Roman Iron Age structured the deposition of archaeologically recoverable material in different ways (Hill 1989; Millett 1990; Cunliffe 1991). It can safely be assumed that such variation in depositional practice reflected, and helped to reinforce, communal differences which would have been manifested in many other material and behavioural traits than those which are recoverable today. Millett's model emphasises the pragmatic and situational nature of federations of local communities in a way which down-plays the tradition and history implied by the archaeological record and by ethnographic analogy. Even were we to accept that such federations were not wholly pragmatic we are still left with an essentially synchronic model of social and power relations. Each local community – let us use the word *plebs* – is essentially autonomous and sends its headman to join a committee which elects a leader in times of emergency. Such a model can easily be adapted to turn the committee into the *curia* of a Romanising *civitas*, providing an even spread of patron–client clusters throughout the territory.

At the heart of such analytical problems lies the unresolved question of the relationship between tribalism and territoriality. It is widely recognised that one of the major transformations in European society was the shift in power relations from a system articulated primarily through the control of people to one articulated primarily through the control of land. Indeed, the importance of this shift is so widely recognised that most scholars who have an interest in such matters locate it in the period of their own specialisation, whether that be the 'meso-/neo-' transition or the seventeenth century!

It seems likely that the key to the paradox lies in the fact that this phenomenon is not a single, locatable, transformation at all. The key to the articulation of power relations has always involved a series of complex reflexive relationship (a dialectic?) between considerations of land and of people. After all, the one is useless without the other. The various transformations that we can perceive in history and prehistory are, perhaps, part of a continuous process of readjustment and modification of the ways in which the interaction between land and people is organised and expressed.[1]

In an attempt to illustrate how north European tribal societies may have articulated considerations of land and people I wish to draw an extended analogy based on research into early historic Irish society. The map (Fig. 8.1), from Alfred Smyth's *Celtic Leinster* (1982, 148), may, I hope, help us explore *one way* in which late pre-Roman Iron Age societies *may* have dealt with this relationship between land and people. Leinster, roughly south-east Ireland, is named from the tribal grouping, the Laigin, who dominated it in the early medieval period (*c.* AD 500–1200). Its total area comprised about 3,500 square miles and is thus within the range acceptable for north-western *civitates* of the Roman Empire. It was divided up into between forty and fifty *plebes*, each with its own council and headman, much as in the model presented earlier. The headships of these *plebes*, however, were monopolised, *c.* 800, by only seventeen clans, and the great majority of them by only two clans: the Uí Dúnlainge (marked by dotted stippling), and the Uí Cheinnselaig (marked by vertical hatching). Over-kingship over the whole province was contested between the chiefs of these two dominant clans. The two ruling clans, together with a number of others (marked on the map by open squares) were classed as 'free' or as *prímsluinte*. It was the headmen of the *plebes* which they controlled who effectively formed the councils which chose the provincial king and debated 'foreign relations' and war. Those *plebes* which were controlled by 'unfree', or *forsluinte*, clans had little say in provincial policy decisions and were marked out by having to pay tribute, usually in livestock, to the chiefs of one or other of the dominant clans, who redistributed this wealth amongst their own clansmen. The exact status of the 'unfree' clans varied, with some of them (marked by crosses) being classed as 'non-Laigin', supposedly the remnants of some indigenous peoples (for further discussion of this see Charles Edwards 1993, 89–165). Within their own territories and amongst their own people the 'unfree' tribes operated with full autonomy, although the relatively restricted access to resources available to their chiefs almost certainly meant that ties of clientship amongst these peoples were less secure. The language used to articulate relations between *plebes* mirrored that used in establishing patron–client relations between individuals, with a distinction being drawn between relations of friendship (*cairde*) and relations of subjugation (*cáin*) (Stacey 1995, 99–111).

This type of complex relationship between tribalism and territoriality was not confined to Ireland, though the Irish sources are most amenable to its analysis, and can be seen in Scandinavia and in other parts of the Germanic and Celtic worlds. A particularly good example is found in Anglian Galloway. This region was a province of Northumbria for 200 years, from about 670 to 870. Place-name evidence makes it clear that dense Anglo-Saxon settlement was confined to three discrete areas covering a little under half the whole province, whilst contemporary documents treat the region as if it were totally English, masking the complexity of the situation on the ground (Brooke 1991). Here we see social hierarchies developed not simply along crypto-feudal lines, with kings, nobles and peasants divided into clear strata, but through a dynamic lineage-based system in which whole clans increase their corporate wealth at the expense of less successful lineage-based groups whilst maintaining internal social distinctions. Less successful clans may occupy, cumulatively, considerable portions of territory and yet, isolated from one another, both geographically and ideologically (through the suppression of shared ritual experience, for example), be virtually absent from any documentary record (cf. Evans Pritchard's description of political life amongst the Nuer, 1940, 139–248).[2]

The distribution of such clans in any given territory would have been constantly in flux. The search for land by clansmen and for material goods to redistribute as gifts by chiefs will have led to a variety of competitive strategies

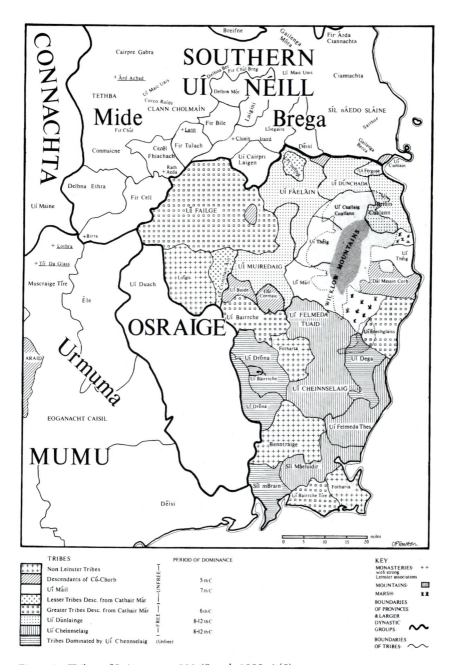

Figure 8.1 Tribes of Leinster, AD 800 (Smyth 1982, 148)

being utilised, from outright territorial and material aggrandisement, through war, feud and aggressive litigation to brokered marriage agreements and the monopolisation of external exchange mechanisms (cf. Durrenberger 1992). As individual groups began to dominate vast tracts of territory and multiply in membership so segmentation would take place and the competition would start again between the new subdivisions. In the south-western Irish province of Munster this can be seen very clearly by observing the group of lineages known as the Eóganachta. In the seventh century, when reliable records are first available, there were five distinct tribal areas controlled by septs of the Eóganachta covering between about a quarter and a third of the province. By the late tenth century well over half the province was in Eóganachta hands, but by this stage segmentation had taken place to such a degree that any meaningful corporate identity within the group had become so fragmented that, paradoxically, they lost the over-kingship of the province to another much smaller cluster of lineages, the Dál Cais. This kind of instability is inherent within the structure of segmentary societies and failure to recognise it has presented a great obstacle to our understanding of north European 'ethno-history'.

With the source material available to us today it would be impossible to prove beyond all doubt that such a model of a lineage-based segmentary society was applicable to the late pre-Roman Iron Age of Britain and Gaul. The widespread appearance of such social formations in medieval Celtic and Germanic societies which not only shared a wealth of cultural traditions with the late pre-Roman Iron Age populations but also had access to similar technological resources and exchange mechanisms must surely incline one to regard such analogues as at least as useful as the tendency of many European prehistorians to turn to sub-Saharan Africa for ethnographic models. It should be stressed here that this is not an application of synchronic 'Celticity', since similar models could as easily be applied to Germanic population groups and indeed may well be just visible in Tacitus' ethnography.[3] The fact that classical ethnographers stressed the role of clients as the social bread-and-butter of Gallic society has not, so far, been sufficiently appreciated by modern commentators, who do not seem to recognise the socio-economic implications of the distinction between clients and tenants and the role of redistribution in the competition for the former and of consumption in the control of the latter (e.g. Wightman 1978, but see Van Dam 1985, 7–56).

Archaeologically such a social formation proves problematic. A chief of a less successful clan or sept might command the loyalty of a number of households and yet have very restricted access to prestige goods or external sources of material wealth (much like the image of Rob Roy MacGregor as played by Liam Neeson in the Hollywood film epic) whilst relatively lowly members of a more successful clan might well possess commodities which, whilst not necessarily of great value in themselves, bespeak an air of sophistication befitting the connections of his own chief. In the course of field survey the house of the former may elude detection whilst that of the latter may be spotted by the rankest amateur. This site would be visible not on account of its importance in the Roman period but on account of its high degree of Romanisation according to modern archaeological perceptions. The settlement pattern characteristic or this sort of social formation in early medieval Europe appears to have been that of fairly uniform dwelling houses displaying status differences only in scale and located singly or in groups of less than half a dozen. It is also fairly typical that some level of craft production, including metalworking, is in evidence at every occupation site. This pattern would seem to fit fairly well with our understanding of late pre-Roman Iron Age settlement in Britain and northern Gaul, particularly if we accept, as I do, J. D. Hill's interpretation of the relationship between hill forts and unfortified settlements (1989, 22–4).

The application of such models to understanding the archaeology of the Roman Empire lies in the potential it has for explaining the uneven spread of Roman or Romanising features in both space and time. Had the Laigin, the Irish 'tribe' we looked at earlier, been incorporated as a *civitas*, or perhaps two, of the Roman Empire we might expect that the *curiales* would have been drawn from amongst the leading men of the two dominant lineages, the Uí Dúnlainge, the Uí Cheinnselaig and perhaps from the larger of the other 'free' clans, and it would be in their territories, penetrated by patronage chains originating at the centres of Roman power, that we might have expected the richest development of villas and the greatest evidence for the distribution of imported commodities (including slave or itinerant producers), and other aspects of the archaeological phenomena termed Romanisation. The 'unfree' tribes, however, as regions of high production and low consumption, would display a very different archaeological profile. Individual farms would concentrate on producing livestock and other produce which the headman of their own *plebs* would pass on to the civic *curia*, or, at least, to the *principales* who ran it.

During the *Principate* the civic *ordines* were responsible for organising the collection of imperial taxes, which they handed over to the procurator. Whilst official censuses were used to calculate the total sum required from each *civitas*, responsibility for collecting the sum lay with the curiales, and indeed later they were made personally responsible for any shortfalls; there seem to have been no checks to ensure that collection by them followed the census (Hopkins, 1980). In the early decades of incorporation it seems far more likely that tribal leaders would not have imposed extra burdens on their own followers but instead thrust the burden on to the shoulders of the less privileged clans.

A cursory examination of the archaeological record of the north-western provinces may suggest regions which entered the Empire as subject tribes within *civitates* bound to Rome as allies. The shadowy peoples of Lower Britain, such as the Setantii, Textoverdi and Carvetii, may not have been 'septs' or 'segments' of the Brigantes but actually non-Brigantian tribes originally tributary to their stronger neighbours until they were able to establish an independent connection with Rome. Such a model makes more sense of the massive size of Brigantian territory in the later first century. Indeed, it may be precisely because the regime of Cartismandua and Venutius benefited from their clientage to the Romans that the Brigantes were able to extend their own dominion so widely.

Less fortunate than these northern peoples, a number of which seem, eventually, to have achieved *civitas* status, may be the nameless inhabitants of the area on the left bank of the lower Trent, between Torksey and the Wharfe. Here a discrete region can be recognised through the distinct pattern and morphology of an extensive series of field systems, apparently established in the late pre-Roman Iron Age. Although these field systems seem to have remained in use at least into the early imperial period and quite possibly later, the final Iron Age phases and the Roman occupation are marked by the exceeding poverty of rural settlement sites (Chadwick and Cumberpatch 1995). The late pre-Roman Iron Age and Roman archaeology of northern Nottinghamshire, South and West Yorkshire and the eastern fringes of Derbyshire is concentrated on forts and fort-focused small towns and industrial sites . The rural districts were clearly areas of high production and low consumption apparently divided between the allied *civitates* of the Corieltauvi and the Brigantes. The fact that the northern part of this district re-emerged as the kingdom of Elmet in Late Antiquity may also signal a separate tribal identity. In Gaul the separatist tendencies of the Chateaudunois against the Carnutes in the same period are well known (*HF* VII. ii).

Of course, lineage-based clan competition of the kind that I have outlined above depends upon the ability of the clan leaders to provide constant opportunity for expansion. *Pax Romana* would reduce, though probably not eliminate, the opportunities for violent clan conflict, and the tendency to grant *civitas* status to further groups, as in the case of the Carvetii, would protect them from the aggrandising tendencies of their more powerful neighbours. This in itself, however, may contribute to further developments in the process of becoming Roman, although whether all of these could be archaeologically recognised as aspects of Romanisation is less clear.

In addition to the broader discussion of native interaction with perceived Roman values, which has certainly dominated the discipline in recent years, we must not forget the *coloniae*. Northern Gaul seems to have escaped colonisation, although Cologne, Orange and Vienne were established on its frontiers. In Britain *coloniae* were established at Colchester, Lincoln and Gloucester and later, perhaps, at London, as well as York. These last two centres are somewhat anomalous as *coloniae*, since they were not *de novo* foundations but grants of status to settlements which had grown up organically. More usually, however, *coloniae* were founded on appropriated land and populated with retiring veterans from the legions. The three 'normal' *coloniae* of Britain had previously been legionary fortresses and it seems likely that the colonists were largely veterans from the same legions that had provided the garrisons. At this early period (Colchester was founded in 49, Lincoln *c.* 90–6 and Gloucester *c.* 96–8; for dates see Millett 1990, 87) citizen legionaries, recruited, it must be remembered, some twenty years earlier, will almost certainly have been Italians, or natives of

Latin or Roman *coloniae* elsewhere in the provinces (Mann 1983, 23–5), and the normal language of discourse in these cities and on their associated farms is likely to have been Proto-Romance[4] from the start.

The *coloniae*, then, will have formed islands of *romanitas* and Romance in the Celtic countryside which, whether they acted, as Tacitus (*Annals* 12. 32) suggested, to set an example to their Celtic neighbours, might be expected to have manifested cultural variation from them. In addition to these formal *coloniae*, legionary veterans were settled individually in Britain (Mann 1983, 23–5), possibly in quite large numbers, since there were three legions permanently garrisoned on the island and plenty of land was available as a result of the prolonged military resistance offered by some tribes. We may have evidence for this in south-east Wales.

In this region the dominant late pre-Roman Iron Age tribe was the Silures. They put up staunch resistance to the Romans from the time of Caratacus and were not finally subdued before the governorship of Frontinus (*c.* 73–8). The Silures were eventually incorporated as a *civitas*, though we do not know exactly when, and an urban centre was established at Caerwent. By that time, however, there was already a legionary fortress at Caerleon, only eight miles away, established by Frontinus. From its foundation, up to about 280, this fortress was the principal base of Legio II Augusta. II Augusta had been the legion based at Gloucester before Gloucester became a *colonia* and it is quite likely that the majority of the colonists in that city were veterans from the unit. Likewise when II Augusta at Caerleon came to seek recruits the nearest substantial body of Roman citizens would have been the Glevenses (the men of Gloucester). The fierce resistance put up by the Silures will almost certainly have ensured that large swathes of their territory fell into the hands of the military or the imperial fisc, and this land will have provided opportunities for future settlements of II Augusta veterans. Indeed, the only explicit evidence we have of settled II Augusta veterans comes from Caerleon itself. Further evidence of this wide-scale colonial settlement in Siluria can be inferred from Late Antique evidence. Unlike their western neighbours the Demetae, whose name survived into the Middle Ages, despite an apparent Irish conquest, as Dyfed, the Silures have no post-Roman existence. Their territory, however, is distinguished in the paltry records which remain by its very Roman character (Davies 1978) and was known by the name Glywysing. Glywysing appears to mean 'men of Glywy', and Glywy is an acceptable Welsh form of the name Glevum: Gloucester. The possibility that, as land-holding *incolae*, the descendants of II Augusta veterans of Italian descent maintained a corporate interest as a powerful faction within the old Silurian Republic, and contributed to the establishment of Gwent's peculiarly Roman character in late antiquity, should not be discounted.

Throughout this chapter I have tried to emphasise the fact that 'Romanisation' is an archaeological phenomenon the exact anthropological or historical meaning of which is unclear. Earlier I also briefly drew a distinction between 'Romanisation' and 'Romancing' and I would now like to clarify exactly what I intended by that distinction. One of the most enduring legacies of the imperial expansion of Rome was the spread of the Latin and Proto-Romance languages. Today Romance languages dominate Portugal, Spain, France, Italy, Romania and Moldova and play a major role in Switzerland, Belgium, Luxembourg, Yugoslavija (*sic*), Bulgaria, Greece and the Ukraine, as well as in various modern post-colonial nations. For much of the Middle Ages the range of Romance dialects within Europe and the Mediterranean basin was wider still. Such an effective diffusion of language, in most cases completely replacing the native languages encountered by the Romans, is almost unparalleled in the pre-modern history of expansions in which no programme of ethnic exclusion was practised.[5] Indeed, in most cases where we have sufficient historical documentation to analyse language history in post-conquest situations it is the language of the conquerors which disappears, leaving only a handful of lexical loans and phonological features in the later stages of the indigenous language (cf. Norman French in England).

As with the Hellenisation of western Asia, and the modern colonial and nationalist ventures of European states, the Romancing of the west probably owes much to the importance of literacy and formal education in the classical tradition. Roman educational ideals, however, unlike post-Enlightenment trends in a similar direction, were not universally inclusive. Although military service and slavery exposed some members of the lower orders to Latinity and vernacular Romance the extent of language replacement in the later Empire requires an explanation which goes beyond the trite appeal to 'elite emulation', which usually fails to consider the problems that would be encountered by would-be emulators in gaining adequate access to elite models to explain such masterful reproduction of form (though not dealing in detail with the spread of Romance both Renfrew 1987 and Hodges 1989 cite the 'elite emulation' model as a catch-all explanation of language change). Clearly, more complex social processes must have been in play, and not necessarily the same processes which were involved in the transmission of material culture traits. This is why it is important to draw the distinction between the Romanisation of the archaeological record and the Romancing of ethnolinguistic identities. Once more I wish to appeal to medieval Ireland to present a model for such processes.

The examination of lineage dynamics made possible by the nature of the Irish sources suggests a possible avenue for speculation in this area. Mac Fir Bhisigh's law, formulated by the Irish scholar Duabhaltach Mac Fir Bhisigh in the seventeenth century, provides a key to understanding the workings of such patrilineal clan societies. It states:

> It is customary for great lords that, when their families and kindreds multiply, their clients and their followers are oppressed, injured and wasted.
>
> (trans. Charles Edwards 1993)

What Mac Fir Bhisigh is trying to encapsulate in this statement is the situation which arises when territories for expansion are not available to clan leaders. In order to maintain their position as redistributors of wealth Irish chiefs habitually responded to territorial restriction by tightening their definition of kinship and promoting close kin, or the more useful of their clients, at the expense of the more distant or less useful members of the tribe. Thus even when the extent of the territory under the control of a chief or head man remains constant the internal demography can be manipulated to benefit the central segments of the tribe.

Donnchadh Ó Corráin (1972, 44–5) has pointed out, to illustrate this process, that in the mid-ninth century the portion of the Dál Cais clan occupying, and controlling, East Clare consisted of fifty land-holding households. Two hundred and fifty years later, at the beginning of the twelfth century, upwards of 200 of the households of this region were Dál Cais. There is no evidence of population growth; what had happened was that the Dál Cais had, piecemeal, ousted a considerable proportion of the non-Dál Cais population. The same pattern occurs time after time, ultimately resulting in the expanding clan becoming too large to function effectively and falling prey to internal segmentation in which the whole pattern begins again. The constant need for segments to find new names to distinguish one from the other leads to great difficulties in following the trajectories of tribal history, particularly in contexts less well documented than medieval Ireland. In Roman Iron Age Germany the Suevi seem to have been undergoing this process, with whole segments of the tribe, such as the Alamanni, developing independent corporate identities and major tribal status themselves (cf. Gluckman 1965, 136 ff.).

As Goody (1976) has shown, and Hopkins (1983, 31–119) confirmed, it is natural that some lines should prosper and some fail. Level playing fields, however, rarely exist in complex societies and, in the *civitates* of the *Principate*, one can be sure that the patrilineages of the *curiales* were more likely to flourish than those of less well connected individuals. Where few opportunities existed for placing kinsmen on new estates, or in civil or military service, Mac Fir Bhisigh's law will have led to the gradual disappearance of the least well connected lines and their replacement in the countryside by 'gentlefolk in distress': the poor relations of the great and the good.

This factor of lineage replacement is almost certainly of crucial importance when discussing the long-term Romancing, though not necessarily Romanising, of the west. Whilst the latter process is largely dependent upon continued access to centres of production and distribution, the former is carried out not primarily through adult education but through what linguists term 'normal transmission' (i.e. learning from the example of childhood carers). Emphasis on normal transmission rather than formal education would also explain the Proto-Romance, rather than classical Latin, origin of the later vernaculars. The full acculturation into Roman or Romanian *mentalités* occurred at the level of the *curiales* who routinely interacted with imperial officials, who performed imperial service and whose children were educated in the public grammar schools (e.g. Kaster 1988), and owned trans-marine slaves. These children will have grown up to become Romans, bilingual, at least, in Latin.

The workings of Mac Fir Bhisigh's law will have ensured that not all those who experienced the benefits of public and private education of this sort found places on civic *curiae* themselves. Many will have succumbed to the downward cycle of social mobility which typifies lineage-based society (Barth 1959). Yet we can be sure that the use of the Romance language, and those aspects of *romanitas* which cost little in economic terms to retain,[6] would have been maintained on account of the privileged status, and practical advantages in legal cases, with which they were associated. Along with the descendants of veterans these 'gentlefolk in distress' will have made a great contribution to the Romancing, if not necessarily the Romanising, of the countryside. In short this model requires only a relatively small percentage of the population to shift from being preferential Celtic-speakers to preferential Romance-speakers, but for that portion of the population to have a far greater long-term reproductive capacity than the rest of their compatriots.

This is not, of course, to say that all fifth-century peasants were the descendants of first-century aristocrats, only that many of them must have facilitated the propagation and development of Romance culture in many areas. The relationship between these processes and the Romanising tendencies observable in the material record is far from clear and may be non-existent or at best tangential. The question of whether linguistic or material expression is the true key to cultural identity is a chimera. Both are equally valid mechanisms for expressing varying ranges of ideas, and, though long periods of processual inertia or geographical isolation can lead to the illusion of some direct link between them in some contexts, it is hard to establish on theoretical or methodological grounds.

The dynamic social processes which I have outlined above are likely to have been endemic within the *civitates* of the *Principate* when tribal authorities maintained some real autonomy, but it is less clear that they would have been perpetuated under the *Dominate*. The registration of land and the expansion of the cash economy radically changed the relation between lordship over people and lordship over land (see Garnsey and Saller 1987, *inter alia*). Elites became ever more integrated into Empire-wide patronal networks, and, with the decline of the *civitates*, fewer depended upon the support of their fellow tribesmen (Jones 1964). The apparent depopulation of the late antique landscape, borne witness to by our difficulty in identifying fourth and fifth-century rural settlement, may well be the result of the poverty of peasant dwellings rather than their absence (Woolf forthcoming).

Late Roman society was a fully stratified one in which the social worlds of *humiliores* and *honestiores* barely intersected. Fourth-century peasants lived in a far more parochial and stable world than their first or second-century ancestors, albeit one with narrower horizons. In stratified societies trends in social mobility are more likely to be upward than downward, since successful aristocracies survive by adopting an expansivist hegemony which recruits from below. The crucial factor in the failure of much of Britain to successfully Romanise, or Romance, may well have been the timing. It is, perhaps, not so important that Britain was under the Roman yoke for 350 rather than the 500 years Gaul enjoyed as that the lost 150 years were late Republican and early Imperial years when downward social mobility and material acculturation will have been far more typical than in the later period.

Notes

1 Indeed, such a series of reflexes might well be postulated as the archetypal example of structuration theory in action (Giddens 1984, 281 ff.).

2 This Galwegian model may well be worth considering as an explanation of the conflict between Caesar's description of the Belgae as being partly of Germanic origin and our inability to distinguish any non-Celtic elements amongst the names of their leaders and *oppida*.

3 And perhaps for Slavonic-speaking Europe as well; the present writer is not qualified to comment. It does occur to one, however, that the Solonic and Cleisthenic reforms of the Athenian constitution could be seen as attempts to wipe out similar tendencies in Archaic Greek society.

4 Using the comparative method of linguistic reconstruction on the modern Romance languages, it can be shown that the vernacular language which spread through the Empire was not identical to literary Latin but resulted from the convergence of Latin and other related Italian languages, with considerable interference from Gallic, etc.; this language is termed Proto-Romance (Wright 1991).

5 For a more detailed discussion of comparative examples of ethno-linguistic and language replacement see Woolf (1997).

6 It may be possible to see the spread of the 'aisled house' as a material expression of *romanitas* that required little in the way of privileged access to external sources of supply (cf. Millett 1990, 201).

Bibliography

Barrett, J. C., 1997, 'Romanization: a critical comment', in D. J. Mattingley (ed.) *Dialogues in Roman Imperialism* (*JRA* Suppl. 23), Portsmouth: 51–64.

Barth, F., 1959, *Political Leadership amongst the Swat Pathans*, London.

Brooke, D., 1991, 'The Northumbrian settlement in Galloway and Carrick: an historical assessment', *Proceedings of the Society of Antiquaries*, Scotland, 121: 295–327.

Brunt, P. A., 1975, 'Did imperial Rome disarm her subjects?' *Phoenix* 29: 260–70.

Chadwick, A. and Cumberpatch, C., 1995, 'Further work on the Iron Age and Romano-British landscape at Edenthorpe', *Archaeology in South Yorkshire, 1994–1995*, South Yorkshire Archaeology Service.

Charles Edwards, T. M., 1993, *Early Irish and Welsh Kinship*, Oxford.

Cunliffe, B., 1991, *Iron Age Communities in Britain*, London.

Davies, W., 1978, *An Early Welsh Microcosm*, London.

Durrenberger, E. P., 1992, *The Dynamics of Medieval Iceland. Political Economy and Literature*, Iowa.

Evans-Pritchard, E. E., 1940, *The Nuer. A Description of the Modes of Livelihood and Political Institutions of a Nilotic People*, Oxford.

Garnsey, P. and Saller, R., 1987, *The Roman Empire. Economy, Society and Culture*, London.

Giddens, A., 1984, *The Constitution of Society*, Cambridge.

Gluckman, M., 1965, *Politics, Law and Ritual in Tribal Society*, Oxford.

González, J., 1986, 'Lex Irnitana', *Journal of Roman Studies* 76: 147–243.

Goody, J., 1976, *Production and Reproduction*, Cambridge.

Hill, J. D., 1989, 'Rethinking the Iron Age', *Scottish Archaeological Review* 6: 16–24.

Hodges, R., 1989, *The Anglo-Saxon Achievement*, London.

Hopkins, K., 1980, 'Taxes and trade in the Roman Empire, 200 BC–AD 400', *Journal of Roman Studies* 70: 101–25.

Hopkins, K., 1983, *Death and Renewal*, Cambridge.

Jeffrey, L. H., 1976, *Archaic Greece. The City States c. 700–500 BC*, London.

Jones, A. H. M., 1964, *The Later Roman Empire, AD 284–602. A Social, Economic and Administrative Survey*, Oxford.

Kaster, R. A., 1988, *Guardians of the Language. The Grammarian and Society in Late Antiquity*, California.

Mann, J. C., 1983, *Legionary Recruitment and Veteran Settlement during the Principate*, London.

Millett, M., 1990, *The Romanization of Britain*, Cambridge.

Ó Corráin, D., 1972, *Ireland before the Normans*, Dublin.

Renfrew, A. C., 1987, *Archaeology and Language. The Puzzle of Indo-European Origins*, London.

Smyth, A. P., 1982, *Celtic Leinster*, Dublin.

Stacey, R. C., 1995, *The Road to Judgment. From Custom to Court in Medieval Ireland and Wales*, Philadelphia.

Van Dam, R., 1985, *Leadership and Community in Late Antique Gaul*, California.

Wightman, E., 1978, 'Peasants and potentates: an investigation of social status and land structure in Roman Gaul', *American Journal of Ancient History* 3: 97–128.

Woolf, A., 1997, '*Ethnic Replacement in post-Roman Britain*', unpublished Sheffield Ph. D. thesis.

Woolf, A., forthcoming, 'Adventus, Patrocinium and the urban landscape in late Roman Britain', in R. Samson (ed.) *Proceedings of the Third Theoretical Roman Archaeology Conference*.

Wright, R., 1991, *Latin and the Romance Languages in the Early Middle Ages*, London.

9

A SPIRIT OF IMPROVEMENT?

Marble and the culture of Roman Britain

Raphael M. J. Isserlin

The spirit of improvement had passed the Alps, and been felt in the woods of Britain, which were gradually cleared away to open a free space for convenient and elegant habitations. York was the seat of government; London was already enriched by commerce; and Bath was celebrated for the salutary effects of its medicinal waters.

(E. Gibbon, *Decline and Fall of the Roman Empire*, chapter II)

Foreign stone, native soil: whose culture, whose identity?

Rarely can the verdict of one of the Roman Empire's most eloquent scholars, and the archaeology of his native province, have been quite so at variance. Gibbon was wrong on the nature of the Romano-British countryside, and in the towns he mentions (not to mention many more he did not) decades of research would have given him pause for thought (and pithy comment). It was not always thus. In 1776 volume I of his *Decline and Fall* was published; twenty-one years later, Samuel Lysons published Woodchester villa with its mosaics and Roman marble statues. Vindication of Gibbon's views seemed certain – though we now know Lysons's discovery to have been quite exceptional. But in one respect Gibbon was right: his brilliant thumbnail sketches of imperial building policy underline the significance of marble as a cultural indicator. It is something which classical archaeologists, architectural historians and students of building materials (notably the late John Ward-Perkins) have not been slow to grasp (e.g. Dodge and Ward-Perkins 1992). Yet investigators of the past of Gibbon's *own* country have too frequently ignored it. Twenty-five years ago Williams remarked that imported stones should not be forgotten (1971, 180). Little appears to have changed. Recent works on Romano-British provincial architecture mention marble either fleetingly or not at all (de la Bedoyère 1991; Holbrook and Haynes 1996). This rarity (more precisely, *apparent* rarity) after several centuries of investigation has something to tell us too – and not only about scholarly traditions. Absence and presence are important bearers of meaning in any contextual analysis. The incidence of a 'classical' stone in a 'barbarian' world

125

surely merits such a treatment if we are to understand how, why (and on what occasions) nature's deficiencies in not providing the material in the province were rectified. In particular we would do well to adopt two exemplars: the use of marble as exterior decoration; and its employment in interior decoration (for an earlier attempt at the latter, e.g. Liversidge 1969). We may say that these correspond to the external display of values as communicated to the man (or woman) in the street, whether by the state or by individuals – and those with which they actually felt 'at home'.

Imperial culture, provincial canvas

It was Augustus' proud boast that he had 'left a city of marble which he had received built of sun-dried brick' (Suet. *Div. Aug.* 28. 3). Could the same thing ever be said of Britain, invaded a generation or so after his death? With a tradition of timber building in the south of the province, and none whatever of brick-making before AD 43, the introduction of decorative stone from abroad – and the quarrying of stones with similar potential (such as Purbeck or Raunds marbles) within it – represented not an advance but a quantum leap.

Because there was no gap to bridge, but rather a vast chasm, the introduction of these materials spoke, in every way, of a new culture and a New Order. It was, however, not a solely Roman one. Marbles had been worked in Egypt and Greece long before Rome's rise to power: in exploiting their stones, she showed herself heir to their achievements. In transporting them to Britain, she demonstrated herself to be doing more than showing-off shiny stone (impressive though that was). She was giving the myth of *imperium sine fine* tangible substance. It was this identity that was being handed down to her newest province, by the all-conquering emperor. Minimalists today may argue that the quantity of marble used to decorate a few fora, some gateways, temples and a few opulent town houses was never very large, and this is certainly true: but then the amount of stone used for building in the province was never very large, either, viewed against the amount of wood used for most domestic buildings. But both rural and urban structures can be useful means to a single end: projecting the image of *Romanitas* to a provincial audience.

Urban culture: a battleground of images?

If the parade was the traditional means of demonstrating the triumph, the best way of immortalising the deed was the arch. Claudius may have attempted to equal Augustus' feat, but, though proof is elusive, the possibilities are intriguing. The western gateway (or 'Balkerne Gate') at Colchester would have been one of the first things to greet the visitor to the *colonia* arriving from a fledgling London. It has been redated to AD 49(/55) – 60/1 (Period 2: Crummy 1992, 16–17). It was originally free-standing and is best envisaged as an arch (a similar one was incorporated into the walls of Rome). There is no real archaeological basis for the date of AD 49 (any more than the year of conquest, AD 43) for the Colchester example: but its Roman counterpart has recently been demonstrated to be linked with Claudius – and its completion was subjected to some delay (Barrett 1991). Delay of a few years might be even more expected in a more remote province – but its inception might easily be attributed to Claudius. We may note that the marble from nearby contexts probably came from it and the nearby temple and shrine (of which more shortly).

Such dualism would be logical: province and homeland linked by the same monumental form, dictated by the victorious emperor first in Britain, then back home, and designed to reinforce the Italianate (Roman?) identity of the *coloni*. A rather later Romano-British example of decoration to this form of monument, incidentally, is implied by Carrara marble from the vicinity of the (Antonine) archway at the *municipium* of Verulamium (Wheeler and Wheeler 1936) – while the brick core of the archway by the theatre of the same settlement would have required facing in something (Kenyon 1934, 238)!

Such an official message of welcome – to the province, not to a cult precinct or a city – would have been written even larger at Richborough, where the victorious army had landed. A *quadrifrons* arch was erected to greet the new-comer to the province on the site of the old supply base: it was perhaps 25 m high. It too was clad in a white marble veneer, some of which came from Carrara. (Travertine from Etruria was apparently also used (Strong 1968, 47) – so far, unique to the province.) The marble sheets had assembly marks incised into their reverse (*RIB* 58–65; the highest surviving number is DLXX […], i.e. 570: *RIB* 65). This numbering must imply pre-assembly and the marking-out of specific items in a masons' yard in Britain – or even on the quarry floor, back in Italy. A drawn design of such a high order would also have embraced the inscription of the monument, of which few fragments survive (*RIB* 45–57). The building of this particular item may have started in AD 84, under Domitian, and here too work proceeded at a leisurely pace for twelve to fourteen years (Cunliffe 1968; Strong 1968, 72–3). At Dover, too, the *pharos* could have been clad in marble, but proof-positive is lacking. But recent (unpublished) work at Caesarea Maritima in Palestine shows that the *pharos* there was apparently coated with a mixture of powdered marble and cement. Were marble to have been used in monuments in Dover or Boulogne their visibility (and, especially at night, inter-visibility) could have been vastly increased by that stone's reflective power.

In theory – and in practice?

It is, however, to Colchester that we return. One particular example shows that a gap between study of the architecture of the classical world and its application in Britain has developed in Romano-British studies through insufficient research into building materials and techniques. The temple of Claudius played a significant part in the history of Roman Britain during the first century AD. That is peculiarly fitting – for it was a large building. We can best appreciate quite how large it was if we indulge in a prodigious feat of mental levitation. If we lifted up Colchester Castle (itself no mean example of Norman engineering) we would see that its foundations encased and overlay a platform built of Ragstone rubble, septaria and Kentish Rag (Wheeler and Laver 1919, 145–6; Hull 1958, 166), and that other portions, most notably the processional front steps, were levelled off in brick (Drury 1984). This last was intended as a suitable backing for a stone veneer: and for buildings in other provinces such as Italy, or elsewhere, the technique usually meant the use of marble. The significance of this is rarely (if ever) commented upon in Britain. The Roman temple stood on this vaulted podium, now shorn of marble facing and all its pier bases (Fig. 9.1), but the form of classical temples atop podia is familiar enough from, for example, the Maison Carrée at Nîmes in Gallia Narbonnensis (as Wheeler noted nearly eighty years ago: Wheeler 1920). But what of the superstructure? It may be suggested that here too marble was employed, but where and to what end?

Vitruvius' ratio of width : height has been applied to suggest a height for the temple (this width approximating to that of the podium). At 3.5 m, this podium is 0.5 m taller than that of the temple of Venus at Baalbek, Syria; at 9.0 m its columns would have been the same height as those of the Maison Carrée; its entablature and pediment 5.0 m high. Its probable overall height (17.5 m [59.1 *pedes*; 60 would have been desirable]) was effectively double the height of a traditional 'Pimperne-type' roundhouse (8.0 m: MacDonald 1986, 136–9; Reynolds 1979, 100). The area of podium (24 m × 31.5 m [81.08 × 106.4 *pedes*]) should be compared with Lyons (41 m × 32 m: Fishwick 1995, 13). Clearly, the Romans wished to impress. Roman architects did not just use height and space to make a statement (the *insula* precinct which it occupied measured some 4.5 *actus*) but also the display of marble.

Robbing (and piecemeal excavation) makes it difficult to prove precisely where (or when) marble was used: the material rarely survives in structural contexts. It is thus difficult to assign it to a particular emperor's building project. A Flavian rebuilding of the Claudian structure is generally accepted (= Periods IIIA, IIIB, *c.* AD 62–100: Drury 1984, 25 ff.), after clearance of Boudiccan destruction debris and subsequent lustration: nor are Hadrianic or Antonine endowments impossible. Whether or not the emperor Claudius was worshipped during his lifetime, as an 'imperial' project, the builders of the *insula* XXII temple precinct would have had access to official marble quarries. One example should be noted when we attempt to visualise Colchester, both as a building and as an object of donations. At Smyrna (Izmir) in Turkey Hadrian immortalised his donation to a temple of goods and cash by an inscription which specifies the marbles of which columns were made: ' . . . 72 of Synnadan marble, 20 of Numidian and 7 of porphyrite for the anointing room . . . ' (*IGR* IV. 1431). The porphyrite was almost certainly the Purple Porphyry which came from

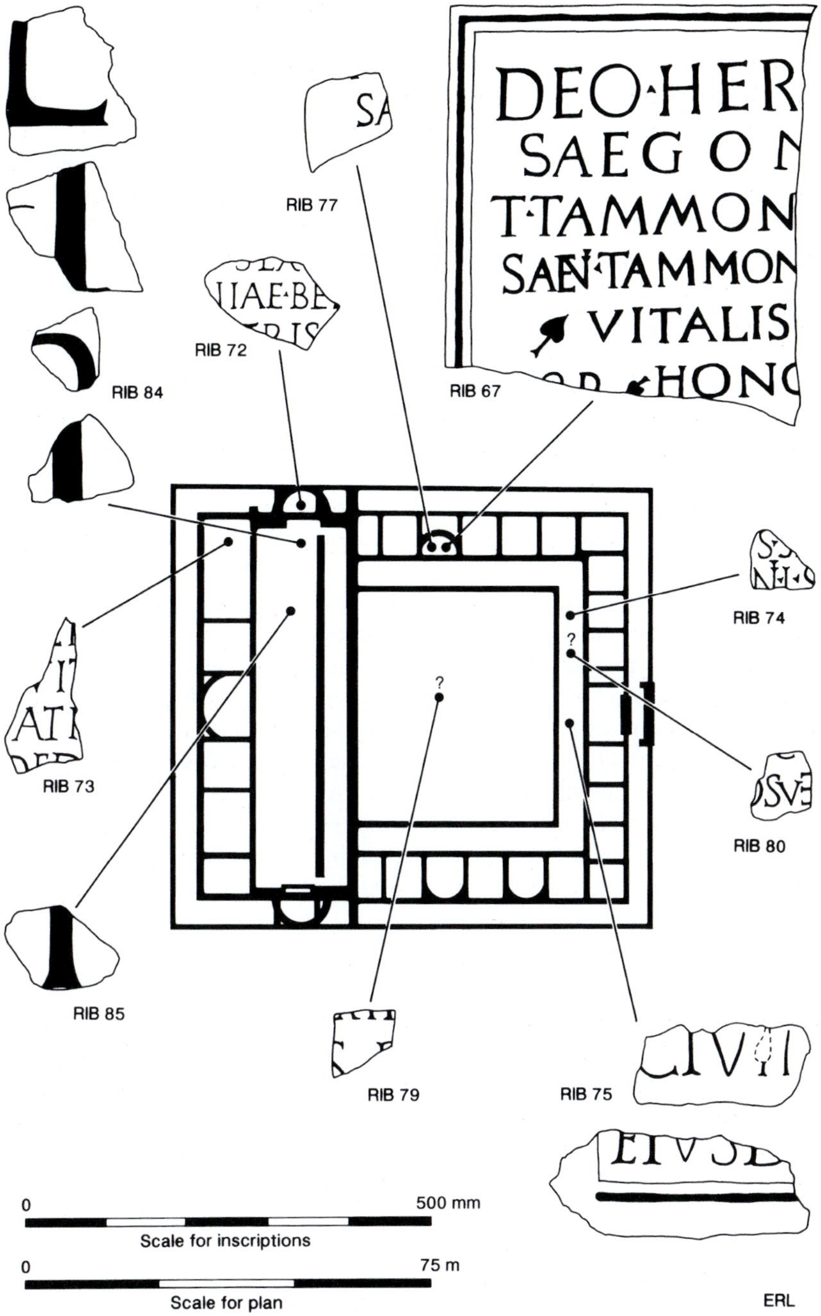
DEO·HER
SAEGON
T·TAMMON
SAEN·TAMMON
VITALIS
HONO
RIB 67
SA
RIB 77
IIAE·BE
RIB 72
RIB 84
RIB 74
ATI
RIB 73
SVE
RIB 80
RIB 85
RIB 79
LIVII
RIB 75
EIVS
0
500 mm
Scale for inscriptions
0
75 m
Scale for plan
ERL

Figure 9.1 Forum of Silchester (masonry, second-century phase) and distribution of inscribed Purbeck marble decorative elements, by room or open area. Find spots approximate (Boon 1974; *RIB* I)

the Djebel Dokhan, in the Eastern Desert of Egypt. All the stone types that the inscription mentions occur at the precinct of the imperial temple at Colchester (Synnadican being another name for Docimian marble; and Numidian for *Giallo Antico*). Rescue excavation around the entrance and enclosure wall produced portions of *Giallo Antico* (from Numidia), *Pavonazetto* (from Phrygia), *Africano* (from the Turkish Aegean), *Rosso Antico* (from the Peloponnese) and Green (Spartan) Porphyry (Hull 1955, 48–9). This gave the entranceway and southern arcade a monumental aspect. The distribution of this and other material is shown in Fig. 9.1. *Cipollino*, Purbeck and Carrara-type marbles have been found at others, together with alabaster (Hull 1958, 174, 188–9; Lewis 1966, 62). These may not necessarily derive from the primary phase. They could be from structural components (such as veneers, columns) or statues donated at any period in the lifetime of the temple (as at Narbonne: *CIL* XIII. 6038; Fishwick 1991, 540). Surrounded by colonnades built of yellow, green, red and purple stone, the *ara provinciae* and the temple exterior would have stood out in their monochrome austerity. Hadrianic involvement at Colchester and Smyrna may be indicated.

One other analogy should be noted. At the shrine of Augustus in Lyons, the columns used for the Hadrianic reconstruction of the altar were of Syenite Granite from Egypt (Fishwick 1987, 105; a pink-red stone with white, grey and black inclusions) and white marble was also employed at that site. Presumably at Colchester, too, the altar was clad in marble. Concrete bases of the statuary known from texts (Tacitus, *Ann.* XIV. 32) have been recovered by excavation (Hull 1963, 176) but afford no real clue as to the nature of the material used. Though it is probable that the plinth would have been of marble, and flanked the altar, the suggestion has to be treated with caution (Fishwick 1995, 24–5).

Finds of brick piers (and stucco) stylistically relate to the inner arcade and engaged piers of the Period IIIA (Flavian) rebuilding of the temple (Drury 1984, 42). The columns of the outer arcade (and especially the facade) would have been of more weatherproof material (and surely amongst the first items to be robbed). It may well be that they were of marble (as at the temple of Augustus at Emerida in Lusitania (Keay 1988, 123). A case against the *universal* employment of the medium is easily assembled, for limestone was certainly used in visible contexts – of a large inscription, only the fragmentary letter A (in Caen stone; and with traces of red paint) comes from a frieze around the temple court-yard, not the main building; the frieze has been calculated at 0.6 m/2 *pedes* (Drury 1984, 39). So not all decorative structural elements were of marble in one of the prestige projects of the province. We may recall that at Aquae Sulis the local Bath Stone was used for the facade and piers of the temple in prefer-ence to marble (of which only small amounts have been found: Cunliffe and Davenport 1985, 132) and at Nîmes, too, local stone was used. The use of solid marble blocks (cf. Pliny, *NH* 36. 50) is unlikely.

The distribution in the rest of town

Purbeck and Africano marbles, together with Pavonazetto were recovered in mid-first-century contexts, in an area where (for a time) the *ara provinciae* probably lay, adjacent to the former fortress-annexe (Crummy 1984, 29). These items too probably derive from construction levels, and (we may surmise) indicate a grand Claudian intent (Fig. 9.3). Purple and Green Porphyry (not all necessarily first-century at that) has also been retrieved from *insula* XXIX, close to the temple (Hull 1958, 96). Whether or not this indicates a monumental quarter (some commentators have doubted it), other monumental buildings are known from documentary references – a senate house (*curia*) and a theatre (*theatrum*) (Tacitus, *Ann.* XIV. 32) – and decoration involving marble would surely have been intended for them too (a screen-wall veneered in Purbeck marble lay south of the theatre in *insula* XIII: Crummy 1992, 385). At other more recently excavated *domestic* sites in Colchester, the overall range of marbles is similar to those found in public buildings, though in lesser quantities, and, in some cases, reused from them (Crummy 1981, 29). Their distribution (not just public buildings) is notable in the southern part of the town, as is the intensity of excavation (Table 9.1).

Table 9.1 Distribution of marbles in Colchester tenement *insulae*

Site	Marble type	Authority
Insula II	Unspecified	Hull (1958, 79)
Insula IX	Porpyhry, Purbeck	Hull (1958, 96)
Insula XXI	Unspecified	Hull (1958, 160)
Insula XXVIII	Unspecified	Hull (1958, 197)
Insula XXIX	White and yellow; Green Porphyry	Hull (1958, 202–3)
Insula XXXIII	White	Hull (1958, 209)
Insula XXXV	Purbeck or other	Crummy (1984, 29)
Insula XXXVI	Purbeck or other	Crummy (1984, 29)
Northern ditch	Purbeck	Crummy (1992, 370)
Extra-mural 'villa'	Purbeck or other	Crummy (1984, 29)

Sources Various.

Other temples

While the temple of Claudius is the key to understanding Camulodunum, as it was intended to be the focal point of the *colonia* – indeed of the whole province – donations to lesser shrines should not be neglected (*RIB* II). For example, marble occurred elsewhere in pre-Boudiccan Colchester at the extra-mural site of Sheepen, where in Period IV fragments of Purbeck marble and other 'imported marbles' were found, some in a pit (Hawkes and Hull 1947, 349). Unique not just to the *colonia* but to the province, on an altar of Purbeck arble, is the statement specifying the stone of which it was made: '*aram opere maronio d(e) s(uo) d(edit)*' (*RIB* 193). The Purbeck marble statue of an eagle from a Neronian pit near the forum at Exeter (Bidwell 1979, 132) is suggestive of many more items now lost. However slight the evidence, rural temples should not be forgotten: a marble relief is known from Uley, Gloucs. (Henig 1995, 96) and another temple at Maiden Castle produced marble (Wheeler 1943). Temple sites are inherently more likely to produce statues of deities. The London *mithraeum* assemblage (as well as cult impedimenta, statues of Mithras, Minerva, Serapis, Bacchus and Mercury) may be as exceptional as the underground (?*favissa*) conditions which ensured its survival (Toynbee 1986). Nor is such statuary the only example in the medium from the capital, marble statuary having been retrieved from the Walbrook many years before (Haverfield 1906). The watery context of a marble statuette dredged up from the Thames is thus not exceptional for this particular medium (Cuming 1857); a marble head of ?Trajan, dredged up from Bosham, Sussex, may originally derive from a temple (?) at Chichester (Henig 1984, 73).

Quite how far down the monumental scale the use of marble may extend is unclear. At Silchester (not the greatest of provincial towns) Egyptian porphyry excavated at *insula* XXXIIB. 3 (a ?priest's house) may have originally come from the temple in the adjacent *insula* XXX (where Purbeck marble is known: Boon 1974, 155–6). But, though neither settlement nor structure is large, according to current theory, imperial generosity (or private initiative) is indicated. More debatable is the evidence for Purbeck marble (but not necessarily anything better) decorating a temple in Silchester *insula* XXXV (*RIB* 69, 70, 71; Boon 1973, 113 for an alternative reading of *RIB* 70). Both individual and corporate donations are attested; and statues are known from the foundations of the temple – but not of marble.

Occasionally, other interesting patterns can be identified. Adjacent to the 'triumphal arch' at Verulamium lay the 'triangular temple' of *insula* VII, using Carrara-type and Purbeck marble: associated debris suggests that both monuments were parts of an integrated scheme (Wheeler and Wheeler 1936) – using black and white decoration. A shrine near the Balkerne Gate at Colchester (see earlier for the portal) also used Purbeck marble – fragments have been found in the fortress ditch near by (Crummy 1984, 123). Here too such dualism of arch and shrine, and at least a two-tone colour scheme, is conceivable (indeed, it has been suggested that other colours were used too: Crummy 1984, 29). These fragments may have come from statues (cf. Frere 1983, 77 on another thoroughly robbed arch at Verulamium).

The ideal sequence, moving from outside to inside the town can be articulated as:

Liminal	Point of transition	Intramural
external temple →	city gate →	internal temple
(± shrine)	(free-standing arch?)	

That a colourful appearance was thought desirable in a city gateway through the judicious use of marble veneer finds surprising artistic confirmation in a recently excavated first-century mosaic from Fishbourne, Sussex. It depicts a town wall with gateways through the use of red, grey and black *tesserae* (Cunliffe and Rudkin 1994, 37). Such an image was clearly familiar enough (to a certain clientele) for it to be used in a domestic or palatial context. The considered choice of colour would reinforce the presence of arches as armatures in the street plan (MacDonald 1986): first at entry to the city, and then to its most important part, the forum, they would have been useful directional indicators in a not totally literate society. Conversely the use of colours such as black (Purbeck marble) and purple, or purple-and-white (Pavonazetto; Africano) at, if not actually on, the *ara provinciae* is significant for its bold innovation; and not even evident at the Carrara marble *ara pacis* in Rome (such a colour scheme would, incidentally, be quite in keeping with a possible Flavian date of rebuilding). The same stone types may have been used in a colonnade or south wing of the structure.

Civic values: the fora

So far we have dealt with external space. Decorating the heart of the 'classic' Roman city, the forum may have been rather different: our evidence is least badly known from within the basilica, its prime structure. Again, the occurrence of this material is best understood in relation to colour schemes. The nature of the transition to the forum which gateways formed was remarked upon earlier.

The second-century forum at Silchester is especially notable for its profligate use of Purbeck marble: quantities of this have been recovered, including a series of a dozen or so inscribed fragments. Most of them can be located to the west, north and east ranges; it is presumably an accident of survival that no material is recorded from the south (where a copper-alloy eagle survives; its Purbeck marble cousin from Exeter will be recalled), but this nevertheless affords a unique insight into the place of marble in decorative schemes for Hadrianic/ Antonine civic architecture in the province. Portions of tutelary deity, of appropriately superhuman scale, recovered from the *aedes* that were the focal point of the basilica (executed in Portland stone: Boon 1973) remind us that not every city could aspire to its gods being of imported stone.

The Purbeck marble material represents a series of inscribed statements about funding and dedications, almost certainly in the form of plaques rather than continuous friezes (*RIB* 67, 72, 73, 74, 75, 79, 80, 82, 85). The disposition of these, as far as can be established, is displayed in Fig. 9.2. These would probably have been set off by a frieze or dado at the top of the wall of the basilica, or displayed at suitable locations along the ambulatory – presumably, in Purbeck marble. Two items from the basilica, however, took the form of large inscriptions, possibly for larger-than-life statues (*RIB* 84, 85),

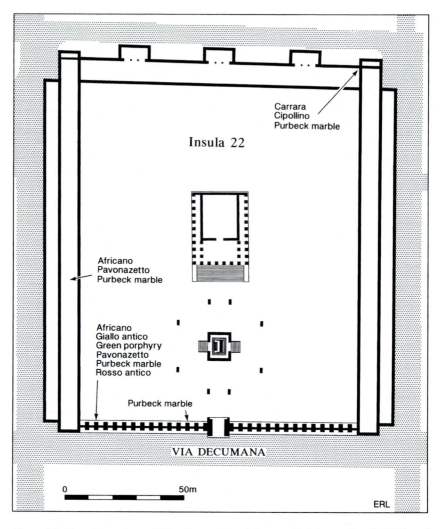

Figure 9.2 Temple precinct of Claudius at Camulodunum/Colchester (*insula* XXII) and distribution of marble decorative elements; superstructures of altar and temple reconstructed (Crummy 1980; Hebditch 1971; Hull 1958; Cotton 1958; Drury 1984)

and survive particularly badly. Conceivably they may relate to the tutelary deity mentioned earlier. Not all need be contemporary in origin (indeed, *RIB* 67 may have been reused: Boon 1973, 112–13 and n. 47). But many of them may have been on display at the same time, reflecting the cumulative pattern of donation and urban culture which the forum was supposed to embody.

But did it? In addition to these black or grey elements, the western range, or basilica, used white Italian marble for the dado for the focal point or *aedes* in its centre, and it has been suggested that the green and white Pyrenean marble found in *insulae* I and II (to the north and west of the forum and basilica respectively) also came from the building (Boon 1974, 115). If so (and assuming that these stones do not belong to the private structures that are known to have existed in these *insulae*) we may assume that a wider, more colourful scheme existed beyond mere black-and-white. While this may be so, it is possible to get an alternative overall impression based on the material of known provenance. This is, as the choice of material for the statue in the *aedes* suggests, one of poverty but also studied conservatism: coloured plaster (red, blue and green in the *aedes* of the basilica; red, yellow, white, green and yellow in the northern apse: Boon 1974, 115–16): no quantities of marble veneer here! Red paint was used to highlight letters on the Purbeck marble slab from the inner ambulatory (*RIB* 75), so in semi-exterior positions the use of another colour is attested. This example, incidentally, serves to remind us that high-lighting by the use of paint is a neglected element in colour schemes involving marble: a slightly more familiar example from the ancient world is the traces of painting the eyes of marble statues. Particularly notable for our purposes is the dedication slab to Hercules Saegon[...] by Titus Tammonius Vitalis, son of Saenius Tammonius (*RIB* 67), found in the north range: clearly this individual had access to the marble that the province produced. But not necessarily more if the presence of painting as an alternative to marble is recalled.

Though information from the monumental entrance to the forum is missing, it may be supplied by other sites. An inscription slab from the forum at Verulamium *insula* XII was in Purbeck marble: the same element as at Silchester. Recovered as unstratified fragments, it is, internal evidence suggests, Agricolan (Frere 1983, 69–72). Recent reassessment suggests two panels were actually recovered, one from either side of an archway (Keppie 1991, 144 n. 27) – though the white marbles from city gateways are not present in an assemblage recovered under salvage conditions, the same arrangements of elements seems highly likely. The ?capitolium or imperial cult temple used Purbeck and white marbles (Lewis 1966, 67; Frere 1983, figs 22–4). In Canterbury, Roman build-ing debris from a public building (the ??western portion of the basilica) included cornice- and wall-veneer fragments of *Giallo Antico, Pavonazetto, Porfido Verde Antico, Verde Antico, Porfido Rosso Antico,* Carrara-type marble and other stones (Frere *et al.* 1987, 95–8, 250). The red, white, green and purple colour scheme is reminiscent of the material from the Silchester forum – and may imply access to greater resources than were commanded by that community, where painted plaster sufficed.

A simple colour scheme (employing black and white marbles) is reinforced by material from the *colonia* of Glevum (Gloucester), where the same elements may have been intended for display in the forum: portions of white marble (so far

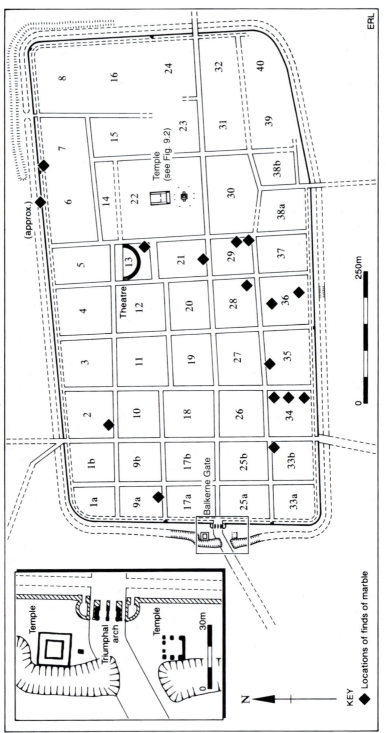

Figure 9.3 Colonia of Camulodunum/Colchester and distribution of marble (including Purbeck marble), by *insula* (presence/absence only; compare Table 9.2) (Crummy 1984; Crummy 1992; Hull 1958)

unidentified) have been found, together with Purbeck marble in construction levels (Hurst 1972, 55). Though the forum structure to which they relate was originally thought to be Flavian (Period III), an early second-century or Hadrianic date is now thought more likely. (I am grateful to Dr Henry Hurst for this information; Hurst, in progress.) Nevertheless, such a stark colour scheme has respectable Flavian antecedents, which it would echo. For Purbeck and white marbles were employed in the ?*capitolium* or imperial cult temple (Verulamium 3) at the head of the forum (Lewis 1966, 67).

Of the marble building material from the second-century forum in London, the largest such structure north of the Alps, little has been published – because little survives (like the temple of Claudius at Colchester that inverse law of archaeological survival, that the more spectacular the structure, the more badly it was robbed, applies). The apse of the eastern antechamber (which is where statues would have stood – the less publicly visible portions of the structure) had, at one earlier stage in its life, been covered with white marble plaques; the walls had been plastered to receive them. Portions of panelling with double margins have been recovered, but not *in situ* (Milne 1992, 137 and pl. 33). As with sites elsewhere, there is a contrast, for no marble is known from the more 'public' areas, where the colour scheme was more austere, employing just red, pink and white paint. The colour scheme in the eastern antechamber was at its most sophisticated in a later remodelling. Murals in many shades and colours were created (white, yellow, orange, pink, red, green, blue, purple and brown) and scrollwork involving leaves and branches (Milne 1992, 102 and fig. 37). This was a traditional design – which could be traced back to the *Ara Pacis* in Rome (Castriota 1995 for details). This was very much a display of Roman values. Again, two interpretations are possible: either that this cheaper medium clearly supplanted any demand for marble, for none is known from this phase, implying that the trend was not just 'one-way'; or that it also complemented *robbed* marble and may give a hint of the splendours of 'missing' material. For a red granite column base (?*Granito Rosso* from Syene) unearthed decades earlier in Cornhill probably relates to the forum (Thomas 1926) – but this is in every way an exception (it will be recalled that it was used in Lyons). Broadly, the material from this site bears out our notions of decoration in the *fora* elsewhere in the province – and, conceivably, the building was even more luxuriously tricked out. The trend in Roman conservatism is evident: harking back to solid, traditional values.

Any study of the public buildings of a town should include bath houses too: and these should exhibit, one may suppose, the same range of responses and sensitivities as temples and *fora* but reports on building materials (marble in particular) are rare. The Huggin Hill bath house has yielded several portions of Purbeck marble inscription (Hassall and Tomlin 1992, 308).

Official (and military) use

This survey treats of the employment of marble primarily in relation to the civilian population in Britain, but any study should extend to the garrisons and officials stationed there also. Though our evidence is pitifully small, it does not mean to say the employment of marble was virtually non-existent here either. A clear (and until recently unique) indication of involvement in the military field is *RIB* 330, an inscription carved on a slab of statuary Tuscan (?Luna/Carrara) marble from Caerleon – with the lettering picked out in red paint (as with *RIB* 75 in the Silchester forum, elements of a red-and-white colour scheme). It dates to AD 99/100. The discovery of fragments of another inscription on white marble up to 24 mm thick at Southwark, south of the Thames, reminds us that in this sector of society, too, unexpected but pertinent discoveries are to be made (Hassall and Tomlin 1985, 317–22, Nos 1 and 2). Dating from AD 212–17, and listing legionaries by cohort, it may refer to soldiers selected to serve as, or guarding, members of the governor's staff: and the significance of the governor (and the army) in obtaining marble is stressed below. From elsewhere in Southwark come fragments of a platter or basin in Carrara and Thasos marble, in pre-Flavian and later structures, at a site considered to be a *mansio* (Cowan 1992, 115) – rare *in situ* finds. Clearly this was for 'personal' and official use, proclaiming the identity of the state, and the high living standards to be expected of it, to anyone making use of official facilities, in both the exterior (inscription) and interior (vessels). Material from another *mansio* (Chelmsford, Essex), though superficially promising, is frustratingly enigmatic. The excavator's archives preserve a wide variety of materials (Purbeck, Pentelic, Proconnesian and Carrara-type marbles; Pavonazetto and *Marmor Africano*; *Granito del Foro*; *Marmor Greco Scritto* from Bona/Ippona in Africa). Potentially this is a vast haul. Alas, very little of it is stratified. Far from being associated with the *mansio*, the material may have been collected during service in the Mediterranean during World War II (Drury 1988, 77–90 and microfiche 1A)! Nevertheless, many of these types are known from elsewhere in the province, so their presence in the building, while incapable of being proved, would not be surprising either.

Ordering the stone, transport and extraction

We have seen that considerable care was taken in the way marble was used. Once plans for a building had been drawn up and quantities of raw material estimated, the marble could be ordered. Inasmuch as marble quarries were often in state hands (Dodge and Ward-Perkins 1992, ch. 2), permission to use the material had to be obtained via the imperial court (Evans 1994, 145). This could take a while: a handily placed *patronus* or influential official might 'ease the path' of an application. The benefits obtained from the emperor Hadrian for Smyrna (Izmir) were achieved through the agency of the rhetorician Antonius Polemo

(*IGR* IV. 1431; Millar 1992, 184, 421). The role of such intermediaries in the process of smoothing the path of British applications to use material is likely. Two *patroni*, both of Italian origin, are epigraphically attested as having some sort of connection with Britain: M. Vettius M. f. An. Valens, from Rimini (*CIL* XI. 383; active in the late 120s–130s AD: Birley 1981, 215), and [C.] Iulius Asper, from Tusculum (*CIL* XIV, 2508; active in the early third century AD: Birley 1981, 433–4). Presumably Vettius could have had something to do with the procurement of marble for, say, the temple of Colchester under Hadrian (if we can identify this process archaeologically; perhaps we may have seen a large part of the material evidence already). For according to the well known statement that 'in almost all the cities he both built something and gave games': *SHA Hadrian*, 19. 2) we can reasonably expect some sort of Hadrianic donation to the prime temple of the province, even a remodelling. Numidian marble was rarely used in the province where it was quarried, and it has been suggested that this was because the locals were denied access, but it was employed in Italy relatively often (Fant 1993, 155). Perhaps Colchester was one of the rare occasions when it was employed in Britain too (its apparent absence from London has been noted: Pritchard 1986, 188). In particular, the association of one individual member of the imperial staff with Britain *and* with marble are beyond doubt: M. Aurelius lib. Marcio. He was a freedman procurator of Britain (*ILS* 1477; Birley 1981, 304–5). Before he came to the province he was in charge of the marble quarries, and he returned to Rome to deal with aspects of the capital's theatres. He probably arrived in Britain some time after AD 161 (a date as late as AD 211 may even be possible). If the earlier date is correct, we might try to connect his presence with activity at an 'appropriate' site type which has yielded marble, if of the 'right' date. The theatre–temple complex at Verulamium springs to mind: major alterations to the theatre in Period III are artefactually dated to AD 150/170 (Kenyon 1934). M. Aurelius lib. Marcio's arrival may fall mid-way in this date range: was he in some way involved in the project? The excavated remains of the theatre archway (for example) were only a brick core: precisely the medium on to which marble was fastened (Kenyon 1934, 238). Again, the theatre–temple complex at Canterbury must also have had a sponsor. The site has yielded Carrara-type marble, red and green porphyry, *Verde Antico*, *Pavonazzetto* and pink (?Numidian) marble (Blagg 1995, 1299) – as well as decorative stone from Purbeck, from Sussex and Egyptian onyx. Together these wall veneers and pieces of *opus sectile* flooring make a statement of social connections and urban ambition as eloquent as the text of any inscription.

A speedy imperial assent also depended upon exactly where the emperor was at the time. If we take a third-century example – a request to use Egyptian porphyry on some British monument, when the emperor Severus was already based in York – it might take relatively little time (paradoxically, excavation of the *principia* has not produced any marble, but the structure was very heavily robbed: Phillips and Heywood 1995). After commissioning came requisition: the order then had to be transmitted to the quarries in Egypt and we have approximate details of timings for this 'leg' of the journey. For in AD 211 the emperor Severus died in York, and the writer of a dated papyrus from Oxyrynchus in Egypt mentions that the news had just reached him, 256 days later (*P. Oxy.* 56; Duncan-Jones 1990, 15–16 and tables 9, 10). But there was still some distance to go to the quarries in the Eastern Desert, so some more time could be added. Moreover, once an order for stone was received at the quarry, there is no guarantee that it was acted upon straight away.

Much work was prefabricated as rough-outs, and then finished on site. Classical literature leaves us virtually ignorant of quarry production rates: the (?fourth/fifth-century) *Passio Sanctorum Quattuor Coronatum* suggests that it was possible (albeit with Divine help) for a gang of five workers (subsequently martyred) to cut (finish?) a column of porphyry in twenty-six days at one quarry, maybe Mons Claudianus in Egypt (Peacock 1995). Modern observations rely on humdrum experimental work carried out in connection with the two quarries whose products reached Britain (albeit in small measure). Their results are illuminating. Saw-marks on the faces of the quarries of Numidian marble have been observed. The rate of extraction for a slab, cut with a suspended saw shared by two men, was 0.25 m^2 a day. Of the volume of material extracted from the quarry face from which a block or column might be shaped, over 50 per cent was waste chipping (Röder 1988, 95). At Thasos experimental work on a block of marble used modern iron tools. A block (measuring $1.0 \times 0.5 \times 0.25$ m^3, only two faces already exposed) was separated from the quarry face. To extract this 0.125 cubic metre (or approximately 357 kg) of material took a pair of workers 22.5 hours. Concentrated work was impossible for more than five minutes at a time, it was reported, and every two hours or so the chisel had to be changed (Korzelji 1988, 35–9). With softer ancient iron, this would have kept a small army of smiths busy resharpening tools.

The term 'army' is particularly appropriate, for it was the Roman army which oversaw the work. It has been reckoned from documentary and epigraphic evidence that the eleven main marble quarries operating in the second century AD throughout the empire consumed the efforts of 27,000 workers, of whom perhaps 5,000 were skilled: virtually all were convicts. The workers operated in groups of fifty, divided into teams of ten, each with an overseer. The annual cost to the imperial treasury, at subsistence rates, was 3,712,500 sestertii (Fant 1988, 153 and nn. 33, 35). But the number of staff involved throughout the Empire was the equivalent of four to five legions: as many troops, perhaps, as were involved in the invasion of Britain in AD 43. It was with this system that the province was linked architecturally, and judicially.

Moreover, though shipped from the quarry, material did not always arrive. Two second-century cargoes, both comprising stone of the sort used in Britain, illustrate this – though we do not know if it was their ultimate destination; it could well have been. Both come from wrecks at the bottom of the Mediterranean. Some 200–30 tonnes of marble column drum, slab and architrave were destined for a *capitolium*, allegedly that of Narbo (Narbonne). The pieces had been quarried at Luna before the ship was lost *en route* off St Tropez (Parker 1992, 376). Two vessels of such capacity might carry the 400 tonnes of Carrara stone facing required for the monument at Richborough (as computed by Blagg 1990a, 40), and probably the contractors to erect it – a mason's mallet was found in the Torre Sgarata wreck, which was carrying marble from Thasos. This vessel also contained sarcophagi, blocks and veneers (Parker 1992, 429). The longer the journey the greater the risk: other such vessels doubtless await discovery in the Bay of Biscay and the English Channel. Portions of column and amphorae found (as this chapter was being written!) in the Solent (Mary Rose Trust, unpublished) are potentially of the highest significance in this regard, as the site is not so far from Fishbourne or Chichester. As none of the material in these wrecks was ever salvaged, the only thing to do was to start again with further requisitions and quarrying . . . The unfinished condition of the Continental material implies that it would have been shipped as semi-finished blanks and fine detail completed on site, to avoid damage. Such rationalist assessment of the process has not always applied to material shipped to this country, incidentally. The Carrara marble and Bulgarian limestone used for the ornate carved architectural detail of a Hindu temple at Neasden, London, completed in 1995, was shipped to India for completion before being transported to England for erection – because labour costs were lower (C. de Rouffignac, pers. comm.).

The numbers of workers were certainly very great, but insignificant compared with those of the Empire as a whole. In considering the relationship between marble and cultural identity on the one hand, and slave labour and production on the other, the underlying principle of utilitarianism expounded by Jeremy Bentham ('the greatest happiness of the greatest number') is directly relevant. It too led to quarries staffed by prison labour creating material for public works. In Roman times the number of workers involved and their welfare were irrelevant: it was the demonstration of power (here control and production) to a rather large audience: the means to a didactic end. The conditions under which the pieces had been obtained formed as handy a cautionary tale as any Roman matron (or not-so-nanny state) might require for her errant offspring. To illustrate the relationship between *vis*, *potestas* and *imperium* to the naive *Brittunculi*, marble could scarcely have been bettered. The results were not, however, always what might have been desired: the embodiment of this philosophy that Colchester was intended to be (and some attempt has been made in this chapter to reconstruct the appearance of the *arx aeternae dominationis* from excavated material) was a failure; the building was left in ruins before being completed.

Marble for eternity

Marble was a mark of opulence, certainly, and its use was confined to Romans in the first instance, but its adoption should also signify identification with Roman values by provincials. This reflects the place of the individual in the scheme of things: in relation to other individuals, and to the state. But what of the after-life, with its opportunity to reflect a splendid (or traditional) image? Documentary evidence in the form of a will provides a fascinating insight into the process of the selection of materials. The chieftain of the Senones in Gaul specified the design (and even the marble source) of his mausoleum: it was to use Luna marble (*CIL* III. 5708; second-century). This suggests a certain sensitivity to the new medium amongst the upper stratum of provincials, and perhaps access to pattern books, too, with alternative marbles or native stones being rejected during discussions with an architect.

Such connoisseurship should not be confined to Gaul: counterparts across the English Channel should exist. Nevertheless, such parallels as do appear in the archaeological record of (south-eastern) Roman Britain are rare. An inscription in marble would complete the process of immortalisation: a portion of one from the mausoleum at Stanwick villa, Northants., mentions a 'son of Titus' (Hassall and Tomlin 1992, 312). Few, if any, examples have been reported from the *civitas* capitals or the northern military zone (though note *RIB* 463: Chester – Purbeck marble). The expense of marble sarcophagi was colossal, even excluding workmanship. A single sarcophagus and lid consumed enough marble to cover 3,000 m^2 of wall or floor surface with a 1 cm thick veneer (Dodge and Ward-Perkins 1992, 42). London, the provincial capital, produces but two sarcophagi, third and third/fourth-century (Toynbee 1964, 211–12; marble type unspecified). Nevertheless, one or two examples of commemorative plaques are known from funerary monuments of Londinium: a slab of blue-grey marble was set up to Luceius Pompeius Licetus Da [.] This particular individual came from Arretium (Hassall and Tomlin 1989, 326). It would be a suitable memorial to an Italian far from home. A much more fragmentary example from a cemetery associated with a timber mausoleum is also known ([…]TUS[…|…]C[…]: Hassall and Tomlin 1992, 308) – but enough to indicate sex and cultural affinity. Not all were so treated. The tombstone of the procurator J. Alpinus Classicianus was of British limestone, not marble (*RIB* 12). This puts Neronian gratitude for helping save the province in perspective! The rarity of sarcophagi may be significant as any social mortuary theory suggesting 'richness' predicated merely on the presence of portable grave goods (e.g. Philpott 1991). Marble grave goods are rare, incidentally: a statue of Bacchus with a panther from Spoonley Wood (Gloucs) (BM 1922, 28 and pl. II) is (so far) unique in its British funerary context. An early/mid-third-century sarcophagus at Welwyn, Herts., is of Pentelic or Parian marble (Rook *et al.* 1984, 150, 159) – and suggests an opulent villa near by.

The *atelier* which the excavators of the Welwyn sarcophagus suggest was based at or near the site is perhaps unlikely, given the probably non-urban nature of the settlement. Much more likely is that some masons finished off the item on-site, it having been shipped out from the quarries as a semi-finished blank, in which the detail was less prone to damage during shipment. Such workers are likely to have been based elsewhere, and to have travelled to the site just for the particular project: British (or possibly Gaulish) hands may have finished the piece at Bradwell, Bucks. (Toynbee, quoted in Green 1974, 382). An unassuming villa – with mausoleum – is known at nearby Bancroft (Williams and Zeepvat 1994). Conversely the excavated portions of the building complex at Fishbourne, West Sussex, have yielded various marbles (of which more shortly). Whether or not this was the palace of Cogidubnus (and not all accept this: Black 1987, 14; Cunliffe 1991), the tomb which represented the occupant's final home (be it of client king or some other exalted personage) is scarcely likely to have been any less splendid than his earthly residence. It remains, however, to be found. Taken together however, the elements from various sites (statue, sarcophagus and mausoleum) suggest the main elements were in place of funerary gardens – occasionally. The evidence – precisely because so highly limited – may appropriately reflect the resting-places of a small (rural?) elite, and their affinities, or origins too. As in death, so in life.

The imitation of Roman values: rural culture

Although attention has been paid to the urban aspects of marble, there is good evidence from modern excavation of a few rural sites, usually thought of as villas, which should not be overlooked either. The prime example of a rural site employing marble yet known in Roman Britain is Fishbourne, West Sussex. (Cunliffe 1971). Seen from the point of view of the province as a whole, it is an outstandingly early assemblage (Dodge and Ward-Perkins 1992, 15, 31) and is therefore described separately from those listed in Table 9.1, though it far excels any site listed there in range, if not in content. Nor is the dating unchallenged (Black 1987), so that the extent to which it can be related to the 'client king' Cogidubnus is uncertain. It has been suggested that he did not live long enough to see commissioned work come to fruition (a possibility, incidentally, which reappears in another guise with reference to the Balkerne Gate archway at Colchester, if it was inspired by Claudius). But, on the basis of the excavators' published dating, Purbeck marble, Pouillenay marble from the Côte d'Or in France and Carrara marble occur in Neronian construction levels (Cunliffe 1971, 16; cf. Cunliffe 1991).

The presence of the French brown-pink breccia (i.e. an element other than monochrome) and the significance of the access to stone types which at this stage occur only in official monuments in the province becomes more marked during the Flavian period. These two latter stones were supplanted and others now became the norm, either lavished on wall veneers or used in *opus sectile* floors. For materials now included white marble (from Erdek in Turkey), *Marmor*

Docimenicum (from Phrygia in Turkey), *Semesanto* (from Skyros in Greece), *Porfido Verde Antico* (from Laconia in Greece), *Breccia Violetto* (from Tuscany), *Venata Crocicchio* (from Versalia in Italy), *Brèche Romaine Jaune Foncé* (from the Haute Garonne in France), and either *Campan Vert* (from the Haute Pyrenees) or *Vert d'Estour* (from the Pyrenees) (Cunliffe 1971, 16–17). The choice of these stones for their colours can only really be understood in the context of the decorative scheme as a whole (which it is not proposed to go into in detail). But in addition to black and white, stones mottled with pink and veined with purple; brown; deep green; grey-veined; light brown; and green and white were now used. This is classic Continental taste. Paler echoes of these schemes may be found in other, less spectacular, rural sites (Table 9.2). Some unidentified stones could be of considerable interest in our understanding of patterns of supply; most are decorative architectural elements from sites recorded as 'villas'. At Piddington, in addition to the stones in Table 9.2, two unidentified marbles have been noted (one white-and-grey-veined, the other magenta-and-white; R. Friendship-Taylor, pers. comm.). Likewise exotic stones of unknown type have been reported at Abbotts Ann, Hants. ; Ashtead, Surrey; Fingringhoe, Essex; and Folkestone, Kent (Clarke 1982, table 1).

Table 9.2 Marble building components in rural establishments

Civitas	*Site*	*Stone*
Regni	Angmering, Sussex	Italian, unspecified
		Peloponnesian;
	Buriton, Hampshire	(?Green Porphyry *or* Cipollino)
		Italian siltstone
Trinovantes	Rivenhall, Essex	Purbeck marble
		Red Porphyry
		Cipollino
	Coggeshall, Essex	St Beat, Pyrenees
Catuvellauni	Boxmoor, Hertfordshire	Carrara
Silures	Ely, Glamorganshire	Italian, unspecified
		Peloponnesian
		(?Green Porphyry *or* Cipollino)
Dobunni	Woodchester, Gloucestershire	Proconnesian
		Campan rose
		Campan vert
		Purbeck marble
Corieltauvi	Piddington, Northamptonshire	Green Porphyry
		Carrara-type marble
		Red Porphyry
		Tournai limestone
Brigantes	Barnburgh, South Yorkshire	Green Porphyry
Parisi	Rudston, East Yorkshire	Green Porphyry

Sources Buckland (1988, 269); Clarke (1982, table 1, adapted); Friendship-Taylor and Friendship-Taylor 1989, 5; Isserlin 1995, 99; Rodwell and Rodwell 1993, 1–2).

Private display and interior decoration

Apart from the high status of the owner, recipient or donor, one factor that makes an item prestigious is the expense involved in its creation. Jewellery is a good illustration of this (Clarke 1985 for a broad philosophy; Johns 1996 for British examples). The rarity of raw materials also determines this; or, in the case of marble, its inaccessibility. Another (here particularly relevant) is the amount of labour required in its creation. To be sure, neither material nor labour was in short supply in the Roman Empire: slaves and criminals were employed in the extraction of marble (*damnatio ad metallas*) – and in its administration too. Finally the rules of a culture (in Roman times, sumptuary laws) govern the employment of marble (Isager 1991) in specific sectors of society.

Earlier studies of 'Romano-British marbles' concentrated on furniture or statuary collected during the Grand Tour to grace the British stately home (Michaelis 1882). Such all-too-portable antiquities effectively exclude themselves from this study; nevertheless, reassessment of the provenance of selected examples may be in order, if it can be shown that they were excavated in Britain. Rare stratified examples remind us that in one sector of society, the *coloniae*, high-quality furniture was used. (Hassall and Rhodes 1974, 71, 79 for a Purbeck marble *candelabrum* from Gloucester; Walker and Matthews 1986 for a marble table leg from Colchester.) More bafflingly, a small octagonal plaque of *Pavonazetto* inlay, from post-Roman accumulation in the area of the eastern defences of Gloucester, may be a portion of furniture, possibly a table (Hurst 1986, 45 No. 58). In a *civitas* capital, Canterbury, it has been suggested, pieces of veneer from furniture may be distinguished by their fineness (4–7 mm thick): pink (?Numidian) marble; *Porfido Verde Antico*; *Semesanto* (Blagg 1995, 1298).

Such an exercise is beyond the scope of the present study, though it is always possible that more 'classical' material than we realise (and now in museums or private collections) may have been finished in Roman Britain, or come from Romano-British sites. For instance, the white marble head from Blackheath, two miles south of Camulodunum (Hinks 1935) would be well suited to a suburban, extramural villa. But too often, the identification of provincial *ateliers* is basically a matter of stylistic judgement and art-historical assessment of unstratified material (as Henig concurs: 1995). The (?Greek, ??Pentelic) marble busts at Lullingstone are examples of stratified material, albeit in a 'funerary' context: the house shrine (Toynbee 1987, 53). At Barburgh and Rudston portions of marble may have derived from statues (Buckland 1988, 269). So too may the pieces of Parian and Pentelic marbles (Rook 1986, 163). A cockerel of Carrara marble from Bradwell villa, Bucks., was part of a larger piece and probably accompanied Mercury (Green 1974). Purbeck marble occurs in a first-century context at the hilltop site of Old Sarum, Wilts.: Beavis 1971, 185) and also at the small town of Hibaldstow, Lincs. (Finch-Smith unpublished, quoted in Buckland 1988, 21). Woodchester produced pieces of statues (of Cupid and Psyche, and Luna), building veneer or furniture of Pentelic, Carrara and other unidentified marbles (Lysons 1797, pls XXXVI–XXXX; Clarke 1982) in a style that has not been equalled since (not least, in publication).

Excluded, too, are mosaics, the petrology of their components too rarely studied. Potentially these may conceal a considerable amount of information. If it is assumed that many *tesserae* were shaped from the offcuts which a mosaicist would have obtained from a masons' yard, that many structures no longer survive beyond a few courses high, with all marble decoration robbed, need be no hindrance to our understanding of the supply of marble to a settlement. Thus (Dr D. S. Neal informs me) while not a few London mosaics include *tesserae* of marble (and in this regard we should recall the *tesserae* of Mediterranean material from a first-century London mosaic: Sanderson, in Milne and Wardle 1993, 56), the same may not hold good of other settlements such as Colchester or Verulamium. Site-specific statements made on such a basis may be a different matter, however, since an urban stockpile might be some way distant from a particular structure. Unless mosaics with marble *tesserae* belong to a particularly large and imposing building project, with its own mason's lodge on (or very close to) a site, caution is advisable.

Possibly some of these *villae* or *domus* were not just the homes of the rich but imperial properties. In both town and country, quite modest houses might use painted wall plaster and mortar floors (Blagg 1990b, 207) but perhaps only two or three dwellings in each of the eighteen *civitates* from Brigantia southwards might use marble: perhaps fifty to sixty in all. Perhaps 2,500 possible *villa* sites are known, 1,500 of which are probable (Scott 1993, vii). If there was an average of thirty-three prominent families per *civitas* (assuming an even distribution of population throughout all the *civitates* of the province – an improbable state of affairs), perhaps one in ten had access to marble. Though notably absent from the Roman military north, like so many aspects of *Romanitas*, marble does occur in small quantities across the Irish Sea, in graves; these examples may, however, have been chips taken by medieval pilgrims as souvenirs of trips to Rome (Lynn 1984). Whether or not this outlying material is of Roman date, the picture from these rural sites in mainland Britain is not in conflict with the notion that marble was a 'prestige' commodity, subject on the one hand to the rules and regulations of Rome (restriction of supply; sumptuary laws) and, on the other, to the codes of a Barbarian society, where exotic goods were the purlieu of a privileged elite (Hedeager 1992, 8–90, 173–7).

Some of our evidence implies access to networks of manufacture and distribution, as well as demand. But what if the demand were there yet the access to the materials was not? Images had to be projected even though the sumptuary laws might forbid the use of marble. The imitation of marble by painting was a means of fulfilling demand while making ends meet, more familiar from domestic contexts in Italy: frescoes from the 'First Style' of Pompeii onwards (if not before) show how marble columns and other decorative features were imitated. This is very much the counterpart of the much-maligned *luxuria* which Scaurus exhibited in a domestic context, in erecting 38 ft tall marble pillars for his own mansion in Rome (Pliny *NH*, 36). From the final days of the Roman Republic onwards, possession of marble represented a level of wealth and its display embodied connections with power to which few individuals could attain (Fant 1993, 146–7) – a situation which was not to change. In consequence, it is hardly surprising to find that at tenements in Colchester, Verulamium and Cirencester, from the Flavian to the Antonine periods, people resorted to employing murals imitating black, white, pale blue, yellow, green, and red marble (Ling 1985, 22, 26). In some sectors of first-cenury London 'society' marble was in demand and available: *Rosso Antico* is known from Flavian contexts in Britain (Sanderson, in Milne and Wardle 1993, 57) at a time when other buildings near by could only aspire to mud-brick (an efficient but hardly glamorous material). This imitative trend continued into the third and fourth centuries at Leicester (Ling 1985, 31). But there were occasions when mixed media were used: one mid-second-century Verulamium tenement (*insula* XIV) used a Purbeck marble rail – and wall paintings too (Frere 1985, 79). Quite what circumstances require the use of marble in what are frequently cob or timber-framed buildings is rarely discussed. What would be possible in Pompeii (with weighty marble veneers affixed to timber framing and panels infilled with brick noggin) is rather less so in Britain (for veneers attached to panels of wattle-and-daub). Thresholds of Purbeck marble are, however, known (and lintels too??); domestic *lararia* remain also possibilities. Painted plaster applied to a brick or stone core is a technique known at Verulamium *insula* XIV (Frere 1971, 59 ff.), so veneering is also technically feasible. The rhetoric of display takes on a different note: the context is private (dwelling of mortal, not god, or emperor) and the *locus* is almost certainly inside, not outside: here colour (as opposed to monochrome) is used to project an image and this is matched quite well by developments in wall painting and in mosaics.

Conclusion: a prestige commodity

Little, surely, could be more illogical than to extract calcium carbonate by the tonne from one part of the surface of the planet (whether Italy, the Aegean or Egypt) and to shift it to another. Southern Britain scarcely lacks limestone or chalk. But in a world of that most renewable of energy sources, muscle-power, the Romans had no need of twentieth-century logic. The importance that Roman people put upon the marbled form this metamorphosed rock offset the 'worthlessness' of those who quarried it. Throughout this chapter the emphasis has been upon Britain as an *importer* of marbles, against the back-ground of a province largely self-sufficient in stone. (Marble would never have formed a major part of the building material used in the province.) Geology could scarcely dictate otherwise. Indeed, the presence of marble in pre-Flavian

London (Pritchard 1986, 185; Perring 1991, 11), Chichester (*RIB* 91, 92) and Colchester (Crummy 1984, 29) suggests a desire on the part of the new masters to exploit local stone – a viable alternative to importing the material – as early as possible. This process of assertion (and reassertion) of their cultural identity could only be beneficial. Potentially the province may have been a (small-scale) *exporter*. Cross-Channel trade in pottery is not unknown and Marquise limestone was apparently transported from the Pas-de-Calais for use at Richborough (Worsaam and Tatton- Brown 1990, 57). Black (Tournai?) limestone was also shipped to the province (Piddington). When the singularly opportune coastal location of the quarries at the Isle of Purbeck in Dorset is considered, we may ask if any Purbeck marble found its way to northern Gaul. Examination of museum collections (necessary to understand Gallo-Belgic attitudes to marble) could prove rewarding.

The introduction of marble to the province epitomises a crisis of cultural *identity*. Whose crisis? In antiquity, it took several forms: choice, access to the material, and how to get it from A to B. There were, too, the difficulties of conformity to a code of *urbanitas* which this embodied, in petrified form; and of the choice of how to display, and how to pay for, a very costly material. Under the circumstances, the reactions of the Britons to the temple of Claudius are entirely logical – if extreme. The trend, from the case studies here given, of what we may consider Roman 'conservative' taste, is also an act of intrusion In the first instance, use and display were for a select few – in select contexts. How far it spread is debatable, and understanding the success or failure of the Roman intent depends upon the resolution of a second crisis: crudely, did Britannia *have* any marbles to 'lose'? *Our* crisis is one of *identification* and *publication* – a crisis caused by not grasping the limited but important significance of its incidence; and in failing to understand the potential of what structural material was robbed in late or post-Roman times.

For we still do not know, within the tight little world of provincial urbanism and its architecture, what the 'norm' was. Codifying the recurring presence of stratified (and then unstratified), architectural elements enables us to understand the rhetoric of display at a provincial level. In this, context (of settlement type, of building and of date) is crucial to an understanding of social significance. It is moving between the structural to the social by means of material of known provenance that is the act of interpretation, in the country as in the towns.

For example, *Giallo Antico* is apparently absent in London (Pritchard 1986, 188). But, as we have seen, it has been observed in Colchester at the temple of Claudius, the theatre temple-precinct at Canterbury, and it also occurs (albeit in a post-medieval context) at York (Buckland 1988, 188). Is this evidence of the peculiarities of supply, of fashion, of patronage – or the vicissitudes of robbing? Again at one group of Lincoln sites, including one at Flaxengate, many of the marble types otherwise familiar in Roman contexts (*Cipollino, Pavonazzetto, Rosso Antico, Verde Antico*) occur in *post-Roman* contexts: Peacock and Williams 1992).

At another, Lincoln, Flaxengate, site by now familiar kinds (*Rosso Antico, Verde Antico*; Carrara-types; and *Pavonazetto*) are present from stratified *Roman* assemblages, suggesting that post-Roman robbing was widespread in the town. But a totally different picture emerges in that Italian marble – material from near Piedmont, from near Verona and from Valsesia – is also apparent (Dunham and Butler in Coppack 1972, 83–4). If these latter identifications are correct, then not only the colonial but the provincial *corpus* has to be widened, for these stones have not otherwise been reported from Roman Britain (to the best of this author's knowledge). A not dissimilar message comes from a consideration of the material from the Canterbury theatre–temple complex: only 27 per cent of recorded fragments came from contexts of Roman date (Blagg 1995, 1298 – and these few kilos are all that survive of the tons of material used to decorate the building).

Nor do we always really know what marble *meant*. Its place in the scheme of things may not have been what it seems to us today. Great strides have taken place in identifying marble types, but the application of red paint to inscription panels of Caen stone (Colchester), Carrara marble (Caerleon), Purbeck marble (Silchester) and another (of unclassified marble) in Southwark should indicate caution. Are we dealing with stones that were imported because they were 'exotic' – or because they were a particularly good background? The definition of these elements depends on identifying marble types: in the past, macroscopic comparison with specimens of known provenance, but now also possible through scientific means. Even relatively recent finds may be fruitfully re-examined, such as the Walbrook mithraeum assemblage. Recent work suggests that as well as Carrara-type marble (which was originally suspected), *Pavonazetto* and Proconnesian marble were also present (Matthews *et al.*, in Shepherd forthcoming). It is this definition of the subject matter which is, nevertheless, the primary requirement if we are to understand supply, demand and command 'economics' in a third-world context. Recent work will undoubtedly require revision of earlier identifications of archaeological material, but many may still stand: and a preliminary *ballon d'essai*, synthesising the more accessible published work is in order – if only to reassert the importance of the subject in a province where it has too easily been overlooked.

Envoi

Roman culture went so far, in conquering 'hearts and minds' – in some ways, very far – but no further. Two illustrations suffice, one literal, the other metaphorical. That Rome *could* have got as far as the isle of Iona, but never did, is from the Roman architect's point of view an opportunity missed. It produced marble and serpentine which would certainly have been to the Roman taste. As decorative stone it was valued by medieval builders (exported as far as Johannesburg in 1894: Viner 1992, 5–8). Iona's remoteness need have been no more off-putting than the Eastern Desert of Egypt. Imperial whim in the first century AD, and military necessity in the second, however, decided otherwise: *imperium sine fine dedi*? The Welwyn sarcophagus (above, p. 142) lay within a mausoleum surrounded by a ditch: clearly *Romanitas*, of which this was a symbol, had worked. Marble was but a part of the total cultural package, and symbols are capable of subversion, especially when translated far away from their original cultural environment. A series of skeletons was deposited at the base of the ditch in orderly fashion (Rook *et al.* 1984) – satellite burials. In a pre-Roman context such things might be interpreted as 'ritual killings': but in a *Roman* one the implications are profound indeed (Isserlin 1997). In such cases, context, as Tiberius realised, is all: 'Marble monuments, if the verdict of posterity is unfriendly, are mere neglected sepulchres' (Tacitus, *Ann.* IV. 38).

Acknowledgements

I thank Dr R. Laurence for admirable restraint in the face of a late and unwieldy text. My thanks also go to: Dr H. Hurst for information relating to Gloucester; J. Shepherd for information relating to Walbrook; Professor D. P. S. Peacock and Messrs E. W. Black, C. R. Wallace and Ms R. Tyrell for helpful comment; my examiners, Mr B. R. Hartley and Professor M. Fulford, for reading my thesis on which this is based; Mr E. Lyons for illustration. None is to be held responsible for the content.

Bibliography

Barrett, A. A. 1991: 'Claudius' British victory arch in Rome', *Britannia* 22: 1–19.

Beavis, J. 1971: 'Some aspects of the use of Purbeck marble in Roman Britain', *Proceedings of the Dorset Natural History and Archaeological Society* 92: 181–204.

Bidwell, P. T. 1979: *The Legionary Bath-house and Basilica and Forum at Exeter*, Exeter Archaeological Report 1 (Exeter).

Birley, A. 1981: *The Fasti of Roman Britain* (Oxford).

Black, E. W. 1987: *The Roman Villas of South-eastern England*, British Archaeological Reports (British Series) 171 (Oxford).

Black, E. W. 1987: 'The Period 1C bath-building at Fishbourne and the problem of the "Proto-palace"', *Journal of Roman Archaeology* 6 (1993): 233–9.

Blagg, T. F. C. 1995: 'The Roman marble and stone inlay' in K. Blockley, M. Blockley, P. Blockley, S. S. Frere and S. Stow (eds) *Excavations in the Marlowe Car Park and Surrounding Areas*, Archaeology of Canterbury V (Maidstone), 1298–1303.

Blagg, T. F. C. 1990a: 'Building stone in Roman Britain', in Parsons (1990), 33–50.

Blagg, T. F. C. 1990b: 'First-century Roman houses in Gaul and Britain' in T. F. C. Blagg and M. Millett, (eds), *The Early Roman Empire in the West* (Oxford), 194–209.

Boon, G. C. 1973: 'Serapis and Tutela: a Silchester coincidence', *Britannia* 4: 107–14.

Boon, G. C. 1974: *Silchester. A Mirror of British Archaeology* (Newton Abbot).

British Museum. 1922: *Guide to the Antiquities of Roman Britain in the British Museum* (London).

Buckland, P. C. 1988: 'The stones of York: building materials in Roman Yorkshire' in J. Price and P. R. Wilson (eds) *Recent Research in Roman Yorkshire. Studies in Honour of Mary Kitson Clark (Mrs Derwas Chitty)*, British Archaeological Reports (British Series) 193 (Oxford), 237–87.

Castriota, D. 1995: *The Ara Pacis Augustae and the Imagery of Abundance in later Greek and early Roman Imperial Art* (Princeton, N. J.).

Clarke, G. 1982: 'The Roman villa at Woodchester', *Britannia* 13: 197–228.

Clarke, G. 1985: *Symbols of Excellence* (Cambridge).

Coppack, G. 1972: 'The excavation of a Roman and medieval site at Flaxengate, Lincoln', *Lincolnshire History and Archaeology* 8: 73–114.

Cotton, M. A. 1958: 'The excavations of 1950' in R. M. Hull (ed.) *Roman Colchester*, Research Reports of the Society for the Antiquaries of London 20 (Oxford): 180–9.

Cowan, C. 1992: 'A possible mansio in Roman Southwark: excavations at 15–23 Southwark Street, 1980–86', *Transactions of the London and Middlesex Archaeological Society* 43 (1992): 3–193.

Crummy, P. 1980: 'The temples of Roman Colchester' in W. J. Rodwell (ed.) *Temples, Churches and Religion in Roman Britain* (BAR 77) (Oxford): 243–84.

Crummy, P. 1984: *Excavations at Lion Walk, Balkerne Lane, and Middleborough, Colchester, Essex*, Colchester Archaeological Report 3 (Colchester).

Crummy, P. 1992: *Excavations at Culver Street, the Gilberd School, and other sites 1971–85*, Colchester Archaeological Report 6.

Cuming, H. S. 1857: 'Head of a Roman statuette of marble found in the Thames', *Journal of the British Archaeological Association* 13: 317–19.

Cunliffe, B. W. 1968: *Fifth Report on the Excavations of the Roman Fort at Richborough, Kent*, Reports of the Research Committee of the Society of Antiquaries of London 23 (London).

Cunliffe, B. W. 1971: *Excavations at Fishbourne 1961–1969*, Reports of the Research Committee of the Society of Antiquaries of London 26 (2 vols) (London).

Cunliffe, B. W. 1991: 'Fishbourne revisited: the site in its context', *Journal of Roman Archaeology* 4: 160–9.

Cunliffe, B. W. and Davenport, P. 1985: *The Temple of Sulis Minerva at Bath*, Oxford University Committee for Archaeology (Oxford).

Cunliffe, B. W. and Rudkin, D. J. 1994: *Fishbourne Roman Palace. A Guide to the Site*, 3rd edn, Sussex Archaeological Society (Chichester).

de la Bedoyère, G. 1991: *The Buildings of Roman Britain* (London).

Dodge, H. and Ward-Perkins, B. (eds) 1992: *Marble in Antiquity. Collected Papers of J. B. Ward-Perkins*, Archaeological Monographs of the British School at Rome 6.

Drury, P. J. 1984: 'The Temple of Claudius at Colchester reconsidered', *Britannia* 15: 7–50.

Drury, P. J. 1988: *The Mansio and other Sites in the South-eastern Sector of Caesaromagus*, Chelmsford Archaeological Trust Report 3. 1, Council for British Archaeology Research Report 66 (London).

Duncan Jones, R. 1990: *Structure and Scale in the Roman Economy* (Cambridge).

Evans, E. 1994: 'Military architects and building design in Roman Britain', *Britannia* 25: 143–64.

Fant, J. C. 1988: 'The Roman emperors in the marble business: capitalists, middlemen or philanthropists?' in N. Herz and M. Waelkens (eds) *Classical Marble: Geochemistry, Technology, Trade* (NATO ASI Series, Series E: Applied Sciences 153) (Dordrecht): 147–58.

Fant, J. C. 1993: 'Ideology, gift and trade: a distribution model for the Roman imperial marbles' in W. V. Harris (ed.) *The Inscribed Economy: Production and Distribution in the Roman Empire in the Light of Instrumentum Domesticum* (*Journal of Roman Archaeology* Supplementary Series 6) (Ann Arbor): 145–70.

Fishwick. 1987: *The Imperial Cult in the Latin West. Studies in the Ruler Cult of the Western Provinces of the Roman Empire* I, 1 (London, New York, Copenhagen and Cologne).

Fishwick. 1991: *The Imperial Cult in the Latin West. Studies in the Ruler Cult of the Western Provinces of the Roman Empire* II, 1 (London, New York, Copenhagen and Cologne).

Fishwick. 1995: 'The Temple of Divus Claudius at Camulodunum', *Britannia* 26: 11–27.

Frere, S. S. 1983: *Britannia. History of Roman Britain*, 3rd edn (London).

Frere, S. S., Bennett, P., Rady, J. and Stow, S. 1987: Canterbury Excavations: Intra- and Extra-Mural Sites, 1949–55 and 1980–84, *The Archaeology of Canterbury* VIII (Maidstone).

Friendship-Taylor, R. M. and Friendship-Taylor, D. E. 1989: *Iron Age and Roman Piddington: An Interim Report* (Hackleton).

Green, M. 1974: 'A marble cockerel from the Bradwell Roman villa', *Britannia* 5: 381–3.

Hassall, M. and Rhodes, J. 1974: 'Excavations at New Market Hall, Gloucester 1966–7', *Transactions of the Bristol and Gloucestershire Archaeological Society* 93: 15–100.

Hassall, M. W. C. and Tomlin, R. S. O. 1989: 'Roman Britain in 1988' II, 'Inscriptions', *Britannia* 20: 326–45.

Hassall, M. W. C. and Tomlin, R. S. O. 1992: 'Roman Britain in 1991', II, 'Inscriptions', *Britannia* 23: 308–32.

Hassall, M. W. C. and Tomlin, R. S. O. 1995: 'Roman Britain in 1994' II, 'Inscriptions', *Britannia* 26: 371–90.

Haverfield, F. J. 1906: 'On two marble sculptures and a Mithraic relief of the Roman period found', *Archaeologia* 60: 43–8.

Hawkes, C. F. C. and Hull, R. 1947: *Camulodunum. First Report on the Excavations at Colchester, 1930–9*, Reports of the Research Committee of the Society of Antiquaries of London 14.

Hedbitch, M. 1971: 'Excavations on the south side of the temple precinct at Colchester 1964', *Transactions of the Essex Archaeological Society* 3: 115–30.

Hedeager, L. 1992: *Iron-Age Societies. From Tribe to State in Northern Europe, 500 BC to AD 700* (Oxford).

Henig, M. 1984: *Religion in Roman Britain* (London).

Henig, M. 1995: *The Art of Roman Britain* (London).

Hinks, R. P. 1935: 'A Roman portrait-head from Essex', *British Museum Quarterly* 9: 139.

Holbrook, P. and Haynes, I. (eds) 1996: *Architecture in Roman Britain*, Council for British Archaeology Research Reports 94 (York).

Hull, R. M. 1955: 'The South wing of the Roman forum at Colchester: recent discoveries', *Transactions of the Essex Archaeological Society* (new series) 25: 24–61.

Hull, R. M. 1958: *Roman Colchester*, Research Reports of the Society of Antiquaries of London 20 (Oxford).

Hull, R. M. 1963: 'Roman Gazetteer' in I. A. Richmond (ed.) *A History of the County of Essex* III, Victoria County History, 35–203 (London).

Hurst, H. R. 1972: 'Excavations at Gloucester, 1968–71: first interim report', *Antiquaries Journal* 52: 24–69.

Hurst, H. R. 1986: *Gloucester: The Roman and Later Defences. Excavations on the E. Defences and a Reassessment of the Defensive Sequence*, Gloucester Archaeological Reports 2 (Gloucester).

Isager, S. 1991: *Pliny on Art and Society* (London).

Isserlin, R. M. J. 1995: '"Roman Coggeshall II": Excavations at "The Lawns"', *Essex Archaeology and History* 26: 82–104.

Isserlin, R. M. J. 1997: 'Thinking the unthinkable: human sacrifice in Roman Britain?' in K. Meadows (ed.) *TRAC '96. Proceedings of the Sixth Theoretical Roman Archaeology Conference*, Sheffield 1996 (Oxford).

Johns, C. M. 1996: *Jewellery in Roman Britain* (London).

Keay, S. 1988: *Roman Spain, Exploring the Roman World* (London).

Kenyon, K. M. 1934: 'The Roman theatre at Verulamium', *Archaeologia* 84: 213–61.

Korzelji, T. 1988: 'Extraction of blocks in antiquity: special methods of analysis' in N. Herz and M. Waelkens (eds) *Classical Marble: Geochemistry, Technology, Trade* (NATO ASI Series, Series E: Applied Sciences 153) (Dordrecht): 31–40.

Lewis, M. J. L. 1966: *Temples in Roman Britain* (London).

Ling, R. 1985: *Romano-British Wall Painting*, Shire Archaeology 42 (Aylesbury).

Liversidge, J. 1969: 'Furniture and interior decoration' in A. L. F. Rivet (ed.) *The Villa in Roman Britain* (London): 127–72.

Lynn, C. J. 1984: 'Some fragments of exotic porphyry found in Ireland', *Journal of Irish Archaeology* 2: 19–32.

Lysons, S. 1797: *An Account of the Roman Antiquities discovered at Woodchester in the County of Gloucester* (London).

MacDonald, W. M. 1986: *The Architecture of the Roman Empire* II, *An Urban Appraisal* (Yale).

Michaelis, A. 1882: *Ancient Marbles in Britain* (Cambridge).

Millar, F. 1982: 'Emperors, frontiers and foreign relations', *Britannia* 13: 1–24.

Milne, G. 1992: *From Roman Basilica to Medieval Market. Archaeology in Action in the City of London* (London).

Milne, G. and Wardle, A. 1993: 'Early Roman development at Leadenhall Court, London, and related research', *Transactions of the London and Middlesex Archaeological Society* 44: 23–169.

Neal, D. S. 1976: 'Three Roman buildings in the Bulbourne valley', *Hertfordshire Archaeology* 4: 1–135.

Page, W. 1920: *A History of the County of Hertford. Celtic and Romano-British Remains*, Victoria History of the Counties of England, 119–172.

Parker, A. J. 1992: *Ancient Shipwrecks of the Mediterranean and the Roman Provinces* (BAR Int. Ser. 580) (Oxford).

Parsons, D. (ed.) 1990: *Stone Quarrying and Building in England, AD 43–1525* (Chichester).

Peacock, D. P. S. 1995: 'The *Passio Sanctorum Quattuor Coronatum:* a petrological approach', *Antiquity* 69: 362–8.

Peacock, D. P. S. and Williams, D. F. 1992: *Imported Roman Marble from Lincoln,* Ancient Monuments Laboratory Report 36/92 (London).

Perring, D. 1991: *Roman London* (London).

Phillips, D. and Heywood, B. 1995: *Excavations at York Minster* 1, *From Roman Fortress to Norman Cathedral,* ed. M. O. H. Carver (Swindon).

Philpott, R. 1991: *Burial Practices in Roman Britain: A Survey of Grave Treatment and Furnishing, AD 43–410* (BAR 219) (Oxford).

Pritchard, F. 1986: 'Ornamental stonework from Roman London', *Britannia* 17: 169–89.

Reynolds, P. 1979: *Iron Age Farm. The Butser Experiment* (London).

Richardson, B. and Tyers, P. 1984: 'North Gaulish pottery in Britain', *Britannia* 15: 133–41.

Röder, G. 1988: 'Numidian marble and some of its specialities', in N. Herz and M. Waelkens (eds) *Classical Marble: Geochemistry, Technology, Trade* (NATO ASI Series, Series E: Applied Sciences 153) (Dordrecht): 91–6.

Rodwell, W. J. and Rodwell, K. 1993: *Rivenhall: Investigations of a Villa Church and Village (Vol. 2)* (Council for British Archaeology Research Report 80) (London).

Rook, A. 1986: 'The Roman villa site at Dicket Mead, Lockleys, Welwyn', *Hertfordshire Archaeology* 9: 79–175.

Rook, A. J., Walker, S. and Denston, C. B. 1984: 'A Roman mausoleum and associated marble sarcophagus and burials from Welwyn, Hertfordshire', *Britannia* XV: 143–62.

Scott, E. 1993: *A Gazetteer of Roman Villas in Britain* (Leicester Archaeological Monographs 1) (Leicester).

Shepherd, J. forthcoming: *The Temple of Mithras, London. Excavations by W. F. Grimes and A. Williams at the Walbrook* (London).

Strong, D. 1968: 'The monument' in Cunliffe (1968): 40–73.

Thomas, H. H. 1926: 'Base of granite preserved in the Guildhall, London', *Transactions of the London and Middlesex Archaeological Society,* new series 5: 337–9.

Toynbee, J. M. C. 1964: *Roman Art in Britain* (Oxford).

Toynbee, J. M. C. 1986: *The Roman Art Treasures from the Temple of Mithras,* London and Middlesex Archaeological Society, Special Paper 7.

Toynbee, J. M. C. 1987: 'The Lullingstone Busts' in G. W. Meates *The Lullingstone Villa (Vol. 2: The Wall Paintings and Finds)* (Maidstone).

Viner, D., 1992: *The Iona Marble Quarry,* 2nd edn (Iona).

Walker, S. and Matthews, K. 1986: 'A fragmentary marble table-leg from Colchester', *Antiquaries Journal* LXVI: 369–71.

Wheeler, R. E. M. 1920: 'The Vaults under Colchester Castle: a further note', *Journal of Roman Studies* 10: 87–9.

Wheeler, R. E. M. 1943: *Maiden Castle, Dorset,* Reports of the Research Committee of the Society of Antiquaries of London 12.

Wheeler, R. E. M. and Laver, P. G. 1919: 'Roman Colchester', *Journal of Roman Studies* 9: 136–69.

Wheeler, R. E. M. and Wheeler, T. V. 1936: *Verulamium, a Belgic and two Roman Cities,* Reports of the Research Committee of the Society of Antiquaries of London 11 (London).

Williams, J. F. 1971: 'Roman building materials in south-east England', *Britannia* 2: 166–95.

Williams, R. J. and Zeepvat, R. J. 1994: *Bancroft Roman Villa* (Milton Keynes).

Worsaam, B. C. and Tatton-Brown, T. W. T. 1990: 'The stone of the Reculver columns and the Reculver cross' in Parsons (1990): 51–69.

10

MATERIAL CULTURE AND ROMAN IDENTITY

The spatial layout of Pompeian houses and the
problem of ethnicity

Mark Grahame

In this chapter I wish to ask whether there was such a thing as a Roman cultural identity? At first sight, the answer to this question may seem obvious. After all, for generations scholars have spoken about various aspects of 'Roman civilisation' and this discourse has been predicated on the belief that there are certain essential features of Roman culture that define it as 'Roman', as opposed to anything else. These features can be objectively described and are taken collectively to constitute a specific cultural identity. By recognising what characterises this identity we are able to state with certainty that 'this is "Roman"', while 'that is not'.

This objective definition of Roman culture is usually taken to reflect a self-conscious awareness by those who lived in the Roman world of their innate 'Romanness'. Consequently, Roman material culture – both literary and archaeological – demonstrates that the 'Romans' did think of themselves as having been 'Roman' and because they did so the material culture that they produced automatically reflects this shared sentiment. The circularity of this argument should be obvious and stems from the (often implicit) assumption that since all human beings have an identity – a set of ideas about who they are and with whom they belong – a collective, 'cultural' identity is inevitably part of being human. The issue of cultural identity in the Roman Empire has consequently been one of *description*: clarifying the content of a Roman identity. In this chapter, however, I wish, first, to problematise the issue of cultural identity, by reviewing the theoretical developments in anthropology and archaeology, in order to show that *in theory* the emergence of a cultural identity is not inevitable, but is predicated on the existence of certain social and historical circumstances, which are far from universal. Second, I wish to turn to examine the case of the Roman house in the Campanian region of Italy, during the first century AD, as a demonstration of the 'problem' of establishing whether a self-conscious identity did exist or not.

Choosing the heartland of 'classical' Italy is obviously important in attempting to locate a Roman cultural identity, as it is here where we might feel that the establishment of a common sense of 'Romanness' would be at its most developed. Indeed, it has been argued that, by the reign of Augustus, Italy was experiencing a high degree of cultural unification and so Campania cannot be dismissed as a provincial 'backwater' separate from the trends in Rome itself (Wallace-Hadrill 1994, 15). This conclusion is useful since it makes available to us the uniquely preserved archaeological material from Pompeii, because the suggestion cannot be reasonably made that Pompeii reflects local, Campanian, developments and not global, Roman, ones.

However, an objection to this conclusion might be that the population of Pompeii was originally made up of different ethnic groups, with the Romans not arriving until the 80s BC; quite late in the development of the town. Therefore, how representative of 'Roman culture' can Pompeii be? Wallace-Hadrill (ibid., 184–5) provides us with an answer by arguing that 'Romanness' in Italy was the outcome of a long process. Pompeii was drawn into the orbit of Roman political, military and cultural influence during the second century BC. Although, language, standard measurements and the legal status of citizenship were still non-Roman, in many other respects, most notably in the sphere of material culture, Pompeii was becoming 'Romanised'. This process intensified during the first century BC with Pompeii's conquest and conversion to a Roman colony. The local elites drew increasingly on the material culture of the dominant elite in Rome as a means of enhancing their own social standing. This process of self-assimilation blurred the distinction between 'Italian' and 'Roman' to the point where to be Italian meant to be Roman. From this point of view Pompeii does represent a Roman and not a Campanian cultural identity, at least as far as 'Romanness' was defined during the first century AD.

However, although this addresses the methodological point of the utility of the Pompeian evidence, there is a more telling answer to the above objection. The assumption that Pompeii was originally made up of different ethnic groups returns us to the proposition that a cultural identity is inevitably part of the human condition. By turning to the theoretical literature on the subject I now wish to show that this is not the case.

Culture, ethnicity and identity

Let us begin with the concept of 'culture' itself. The idea of 'culture' has its roots in the Western experience of colonialism. Confronted by societies apparently so different from those in Europe, the emergent discipline of anthropology posited that each human society was governed by its own set of norms, values and ideas that guided behaviour within it. Cultures were consequently objective, homogeneous entities defined as different one from another by the unique system of rules determining conduct within them. Although each culture was different this did not make them equal. Nineteenth-century practice was to arrange different cultures in a hierarchy of presumed technological and social complexity from 'savagery' to 'civilisation' (e.g. Tylor 1865). This conception of culture was imported into archaeology and was used mainly by prehistorians to explain the changes they observed through time in the patterning of material objects. Constantly recurring assemblages of different types of artefacts were regarded as the physical manifestation of particular social groups (e.g. Childe 1956). In other words, an *archaeological culture*, defined by material culture patterning, was equated directly with a *society*.

The concept of the archaeological culture has been found to be unsatisfactory on a number of counts (Shennan 1989, 5–14), but perhaps the most damning has been the recognition by anthropologists that 'society' and 'culture' are not one and the same thing. Leach (1954), drawing on his research among the Kachins of northern Burma, showed that members of a social group need not share the same set of cultural traits. It was clear that individual social perceptions of with whom they identified did not correspond neatly to anthropological perceptions of homogeneous groups. Thus 'ethnicity' emerged as a key problem with the debate ensuing as to whether the analytical units for ethnic groups should be based on the observer's criteria or on indigenous distinctions (Bentley 1987, 24). As Bentley has pointed out, by the late 1960s the latter position had prevailed. Obviously enough, ethnicity must refer to the self-conscious identification that individuals have with a particular social group and not to arbitrary distributions of material defined by an external observer.

The rejection of the idea that anything useful about ethnicity can be inferred from objectively observable distributions of cultural traits has generated uncertainty amongst archaeologists as to whether it is possible to recognise ethnic groups from archaeological material. To complicate matters further it has become increasingly clear that ethnicity is not a universal feature of human societies, but is contingent upon certain conditions prevailing. So, we cannot even be sure that ethnicity is being expressed in any given distribution of material objects, however homogeneous they may appear to be. As Shennan has observed, ethnic identity appears to be created only when other forms of identity are being destroyed and this is a process usually associated with the origins of the state (1989, 16–17). Consequently, the idea that ethnic groups (i.e. non-state 'peoples') were precursors of the state has to be treated with some suspicion. As Fried (1967) showed, 'tribes' as real entities were an artefact of colonialism. Prior to colonial intervention there had been a fluctuating pattern of groups that were 'fixed' by the imposition of an administrative structure external to them.

However, even if we accept that ethnicity is caused by the intervention of an outside agency, there is still uncertainty as to why ethnicity actually arises in the first place. A debate has ensued as to whether ethnicity originates from a desire for a sense of 'rootedness' and 'belonging' in a world that is constantly changing, or whether it is the pursuit of common interests that generates an ethnic sentiment (Bentley 1987, 25). The contrast between the *primordialist* and *instrumentalist* theories of ethnicity means that archaeologists are uncertain not only about whether they can recognise ethnic groups from patterning in archae-ological material, but also about whether that same evidence shows that the appropriate social processes that lead to the formation of the presumed ethnic identity were in operation.

Culture, then, has ceased to be an objective reality, but is now conceptualised as being part of the subjective process by which individuals come to recognise themselves as belonging to one group as opposed to another. Belonging to a group is, of course, only one aspect of identity and if we are to unravel the problem of cultural identity then it would be useful to distinguish between the various aspects of identity. First, we might recognise a *social identity*, which includes such relationships as family ties, personal networks of friends and other associates, peer group membership, class allegiance, social status, and the like. Second, we might identify a *political identity*, which would include such aspects as citizenship, membership of a body politic, party affiliation and nationality. A specifically *cultural identity*, in other words *ethnicity*, requires the self-conscious recognition by a group of individuals of commonalities that emerge through their conformity to similar ways of acting and being. These are likely to be expressed through the possession of similar cultural traits, such as language, styles of dress, personal adornment, material objects and particular ways of behaving. Of course, the problem with this definition of ethnicity is that *all* aspects of identity will be expressed through such cultural traits, so without ethnographic data to tell us whether the individuals sharing common cultural traits do actually recognise themselves as belonging to a distinct group, it seems that we cannot automatically infer the presence of an ethnic identity. Such is the problem of recognising ethnicity through material culture that there would seem to be no other option than to suggest that it simply cannot be done. However, as Shennan has recently pointed out, to do so would be unsatisfactory, even if tempting, as the concern for the presence or absence of a cultural identity at different times and places is certainly a valid and interesting one (1989, 14).

The question consequently becomes methodological: how can we recognise a cultural identity through patterning in archaeological material, when that material may also be expressing other aspects of identity? We obviously need a theoretical discourse to guide our investigations, and to provide this I wish to draw on Bentley's (1987) discussion on how ethnicity arises in practice (also discussed in Shennan 1989, 14–17). According to Bentley, the difficulty with both the primordialist and the instrumentalist views of ethnicity is that they seek objective explanations for the subjective experience of ethnic sentiment. Instead he argues that ethnic identity formation must be seen as a process playing a role in social reproduction as a whole. Second, ethnic identity must be seen as being in a tension with personal (social and political) identity. As an ethnic identity emerges it requires individuals to conform to common ways of doing and being. Individual interests are consequently submerged into those of the group. Finally, Bentley makes the vital point that an ethnic identity cuts across class boundaries. The most useful example of this is contemporary Afro-

American society. Studies have shown that 'black Americans characteristically perceive and symbolise their experiences differently from white Americans and in a manner not attributable to class differences alone' (Kochman 1981, cited in Bentley 1987, 33).

Despite the obvious complexity of ethnicity it has long been recognised that material objects play a significant role in communicating information about aspects of identity. Badges of office, national flags, the Crown jewels and Mercedes-Benz cars all have something to say about the individuals who possess and use them. However, we need an analytical framework that helps us decide which of any array of material objects used by individuals are indicative of an ethnic identity. To do this I wish to introduce into the discussion the concept of 'style'.

Stylistic variation in material culture

It has been rightly claimed that the issue of 'style' lies at the heart of all archaeological interpretation, whether overtly discussed or not (Conkey and Hastorf 1990, 1). This, of course, raises the inevitable question 'What is style?'. The answer that now seems to be almost universally accepted by archaeologists is that style is a particular 'way of doing' (Wiessner 1990). The importance of this definition is that it means that 'style' does not reside in the form of any material object, but rather in the behaviour that produces it. Style becomes linked with ethnicity because individuals are all enculturated into social and physical worlds not of their making. Through interaction with this world individuals come to understand how to function as social beings. A great deal of this knowledge never achieves the level of spoken discourse, but it is implicated in the way individuals behave, which includes, of course, the objects they make and use.

Sackett has consequently argued in a series of a papers (1982, 1985, 1990) that material culture inevitably carries information about ethnic identity, since it is produced in ethnically bounded contexts. Style, then, is generally *passive*, that is, there is not a deliberate intention to signify anything: particular ways of doing are simply the product of patterns of enculturation. Following from this Sackett has developed what he terms the 'isochrestic' model of style. 'Isochrestic' is a neologism, 'from the Greek which translates as "equivalent in use" and which connotes that there is more than one way to skin a cat' (1990, 33). According to Sackett, when confronted by a task there are, theoretically, a number of possible ways of carrying it out. The choice of one option as opposed to any other depends purely on one's upbringing. It follows that isochrestic variation in material culture is diagnostic of ethnicity (ibid.).

However, a passive view of style is not entirely satisfactory because it is not too difficult to think of material culture objects that are used actively by individuals in order to assert identity. A national flag is a useful example, symbolising as it does nationality and nationhood. Style can therefore be *active* in that individuals make or do something in a particular way in order to communicate something about themselves and their relation to others.

Wiessner (1983, 1984, 1985, 1989, 1990) has engaged in a debate with Sackett over precisely this point. She argues that active style has two aspects, which she terms *assertive* and *emblemic*. Assertive style is variation in material culture that is 'personally based and which carries information supporting individual identity' (1983, 258). Wiessner goes on to make the case that assertive style has no distinct referent. An earring, for instance, does not necessarily signify anything, but it does communicate something about the individual who wears it. It is assertive style, Wiessner argues, that has the potential to diffuse through enculturation and 'acculturation' since it is communicated through interpersonal contact. Emblemic style, on the other hand, is formal variation in material culture 'that has a distinct referent and transmits a clear message to a defined target population about conscious affiliation or identity' (Wiessner 1983, 257).

Underlying, and supporting, this distinction between assertive and emblemic style Wiessner sees the social-psychological process of 'identification via comparison'.

> Through comparing themselves with similar others, people evaluate their characteristics and abilities against those of others surrounding them . . . and develop a self-image which they try to present positively to others.
>
> (1989, 57)

Using this framework, Wiessner is able to integrate Sackett's view with hers. Isochrestic variation effectively provides the passive background, the 'palette' of choices, from which individuals are able to choose certain aspects, which are then made active, in order to assert personal identity or to communicate social group membership.

However, there is a problem with Wiessner's model of style and this can be seen in that Wiessner makes the point that the referent for emblemic style will normally be a social group. However, as we have seen, 'social groups' do not correlate with 'ethnic groups'. There could be a conscious attempt to identify with others of the same social class and so the material objects used to signify class allegiances would also in these circumstances be 'emblemic'. However, as we have seen, ethnicity has to transcend such social boundaries.

Wiessner neglects this problem, most probably because the societies with which she is concerned tend not to exhibit class divisions. Nevertheless, this does not render the distinction between emblemic and assertive style useless, it merely means that emblemic style can be seen to have two dimensions, which I intend to call, following Macdonald (1990), *status* and *etiquette*. 'Status' obviously refers to variation in material culture that is emblemic of a position in a social hierarchy. Individuals not only communicate their position but also their identification with those who share a similar status. 'Etiquette', on the other hand, is emblemic of variation in material culture that is designed to promote ethnic affiliations. We can summarise the relationship between these various aspects of style in diagrammatic form as in Fig. 10.1.

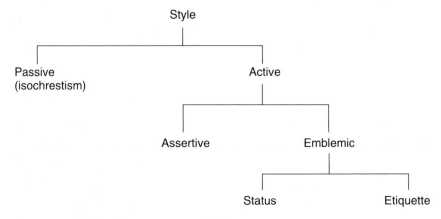

Figure 10.1 Relation between aspects of style

As Shennan (1990, 19) argues, the benefit of Wiessner's distinction between assertive and emblemic style is that it can be usefully related to Bentley's ideas on the formation of ethnic group identity, and the subdivision of emblemic style into status and etiquette above does not affect this. The two link because ethnicity is, after all, a process of comparing oneself with others, in the way Wiessner suggests. This unity consequently provides us with an analytical framework within which to attempt to locate cultural identity from distributions of material remains.

Identity and Pompeian houses

Establishing an analytical framework is one thing, applying it to archaeological material is another. To do so we obviously require a body of evidence with which to work. It has already been argued that Pompeii provides us with such a body of evidence, but, of course, the quantity and quality of the material at Pompeii are overwhelming and we obviously need to be selective. The most accessible aspect of Pompeii for analysis is undoubtedly the physical fabric of the city. This is fortunate, since ethnographic studies have shown repeatedly that there is one cultural artefact which is central to the definition of identity in many cultures, namely the house. As Parker Pearson and Richards (1994) have shown, the way people build their houses, orient them in space and decorate them encodes cultural meanings that express aspects of identity. A common way of building and decorating houses will consequently be indicative of a shared set of values, which, in turn, will indicate a cultural identity.

Indeed, Knights (1994) has recently interpreted the Roman house in precisely this way. He sees the house as expressing the relationship of the Romans with the cosmos. The house was more than just a place to live, it embodied features that linked the world of the mundane with the cosmological world of the spirits. The disposition of rooms within the house served as a constant reminder to the Romans of where they 'belonged', literally, according to Knights, enabling them to locate themselves in the wider scheme of things. This relationship to a shared cosmological framework, embodied and expressed in the very fabric of the house, defined and helped perpetuate a common sense of cultural identity.

In terms of the above framework house layout may be seen to be emblemic of etiquette. This, of course, would be true only if it could be demonstrated that the Roman house possessed a relatively standard spatial layout and, indeed, a certain disposition of rooms is habitually held as being 'typical' of the Roman house. As is now well understood, this layout is arranged around an axial line that runs from the main door to the street, through the *fauces*, the *impluviate atrium*, with its side rooms (*cubicula*) and *alae*, and the *tablinum*, to an ornamental garden or peristyle (Fig. 10.2). The idea that there is something 'standard' about the spatial layout of the Roman house has a long history in Western scholarship. It was one of the pre-eminent excavators of Pompeii, August Mau, who argued, at the turn of the century, that the distribution of the rooms in the excavated houses was 'characterised by a certain regularity' that made it possible to indicate their arrangement 'by reference to an ideal or normal plan' (1899, 341).

However, there is a difficulty with the concept that there was a standard Roman house and that becomes all too apparent if we examine a cross-section of houses in region VI of Pompeii (Fig. 10.3). Instead of a 'certain regularity' we find instead a complex interlocking mosaic of houses of different sizes and shapes. Indeed, the picture is so confusing it is difficult to recognise the boundaries of the individual properties at first sight. This would seem to challenge the idea that there was a typical Roman house design and not support it. Indeed,

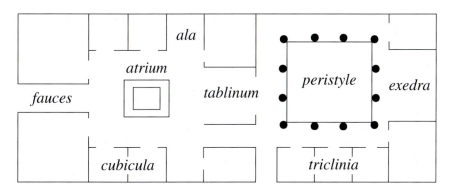

Figure 10.2 Idealised ground plan of a Roman house (Mau 1899, fig. 115)

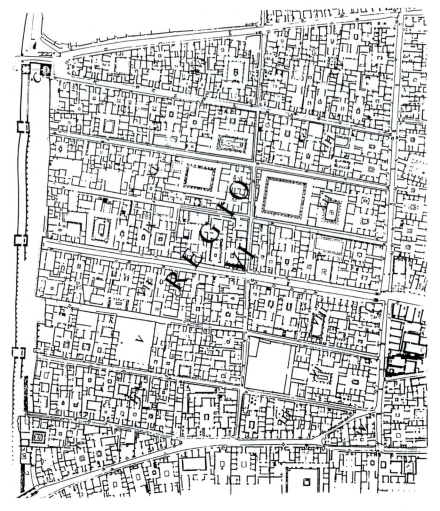

Figure 10.3 Ground plan of region VI of Pompeii (Van der Poel 1987)

Evans has noted that attempts to apply the concept of the traditional 'Roman house' has occasionally led to some bizarre interpretations. She illustrates the point with the example of two houses in region VIII, which at the time of the destruction of Pompeii by Vesuvius did not have side rooms leading off their *atria*, but it has been unwarrantedly assumed that they must have been built with them (1978, 175).

Packer's (1975) study of 'lower and middle class' houses has shown very clearly that many houses do not possess the standard layout in any way whatsoever, and that they are far from exceptional. Furthermore, many of these residences had fine decoration and furniture, suggesting that they were not hovels. This conclusion has been recently echoed by Wallace-Hadrill, who has shown that even relatively small abodes had their touches of luxury (1990, 192).

All this suggests that there was not a standard Roman house *in practice*, but nevertheless, none of this has dented the conception that there was at least a standard house plan *in theory*. We might ask: how it is possible to reconcile these apparently conflicting ideas?

Explanations have been offered for the variation between houses in terms of a model that conceptualises 'luxury' as 'trickling down' from the elite to those lower down the social hierarchy. Zanker (1979) has argued that the architectural features of the luxurious 'aristocratic' villa served as a model that was imitated by those of lower status, with the consequence that grand architectural features are found in miniature within the urban housing. Of course, the constraints of space make exact duplication impossible, so peristyles, ornamental gardens and *oeci* (reception rooms) have to be fitted in where they can. Occasionally this results in modifications of the standard design. For instance, in the House of Octavius Quartio (II. ii. 1–4) the view from the *fauces* ends not in a *tablinum* but in a three-sided portico surrounding a small garden.

Wallace-Hadrill (1990) has developed Zanker's model and argues that there was a spread of social luxury driven by a desire on the part of those of lower status, especially the socially disadvantaged freedman 'class', to emulate the elite in order to assert their acquisition of Roman citizenship, received on manumission. Naturally enough, they were not always able to afford to reproduce exactly, in terms of scale, proportions or quality of construction, the architectural features of elite residences. A further, and intriguing, suggestion by Wallace-Hadrill is that freedman may not have always understood how to use elite culture appropriately, with the consequence that they may have blunderingly parodied the cultural language of Roman luxury rather than communicating in it (1988, 48).

So the lack of standardisation in the house plans can be reconciled with the idea of a standard house design by arguing that the surviving houses were derived from a typical house, even if some were more typical than others. However, the considerable variation in house design is still problematic if we are to argue that the Pompeian house embodies and expresses a uniquely 'Roman' cultural identity. Identity is not an abstraction, it is part of the real life experience of the individuals who 'possess' it. If the house expresses and engenders a cultural identity, it follows that the actual layout experienced by individuals will have a profound effect on how they perceive themselves and their relations with others. Different spatial layouts suggest different ways of encountering others and different perceptions of self and relations to others. So, although the lack of a standard spatial layout amongst Pompeian houses may be explained away by positing that the standard was an ideal aimed for but rarely achieved, this does not allow us to reconcile differences in layout with the presence of a Roman cultural identity.

It was suggested above that house design and settlement layout (the two run into one another) can be used to express ethnic affiliations. Indeed, there is plenty of ethnographic evidence to suggest that house design and settlement layout are often emblemic of ethnic identity. The Bororo (Lévi-Strauss 1963) and Lele (Douglas 1972) villages have regular layouts, as do the ground plans of Betsileo (Kus and Raharijaona 1990), Thai (Tambiah 1969) and Swahili (Donley-Reid 1990) houses. Because Pompeian houses do not exhibit the same kind of regularity in their layout we may be tempted to argue that in contrast to Knights they do not embody and express a specially Roman cultural identity. However, this does not answer the question, what do these spatial layouts signify? We need to address this question, particularly as there is obviously *some* regularity in the spatial layout of *certain* houses.

Describing variation in spatial layouts

If we are to answer this question we clearly need a way of describing variation in spatial layouts, but before we can do this we need to study a particular case, as attempting to examine all the houses of Pompeii is obviously impractical. The case study selected here consists of 144 houses from region VI of Pompeii. The term 'house' as used here is not meant to convey any significance other than an 'architectural unit'. Consequently, buildings that are not usually considered to be 'residential' have been included in the sample. All the houses examined here have at least four interior spaces. The reason for this limit is that we are concerned with the patterning in spatial layout. If there are one, two or three interior spaces, there is only one basic pattern which they can take. However, once there are four interior spaces their arrangement can vary. Obviously enough, the more spaces there are the greater the number of possible arrangements. It follows that, if one particular arrangement is preferred, that fact will be significant.

If we are to describe spatial layouts, how are we to do it? The traditional layout of the Roman house has it centred on the *atrium* and peristyle. Although we draw a distinction between these spaces, from a purely *spatial* point of view they are actually similar. Both may be described as *courtyard spaces*. A 'courtyard' as defined here has several important properties that need to be specified. First, it has to be one of the largest spaces in the house. Second, it must be 'square' enough to permit circulation. Obviously enough, narrow passageways will more readily serve as conduits of movement than as loci for interaction. Finally, a courtyard space should provide and control access to a series of surrounding spaces. The courtyard is an important architectural feature because it provides a certain order to the arrangement of space and so we can consider it to be a basic 'building block' of spatial layouts.

Using the above criteria, we can identify the number of courtyards in each house and these are given in Table 10.1. The first observation that we can make is that there are a significant number of houses that do not have courtyards at all. Some 29.1 per cent of the sample are non-courtyard houses. Second,

Table 10.1 The number of courtyards in each house

Address	Spaces	Courtyards	Address	Spaces	Courtyards
VI i 18, 20	5	0	VI xv 2, 26	15	2
VI xvi 13	5	0	VI xv 23	15	1
VI iii 24	6	0	VI xv 7–8	15	2
VI xvi 18	6	0	VI xiv 39	15	1
VI vi 4–5	6	0	VI v 10	15	1
VI iii 14–15	6	0	VI v 14	15	1
VI xvi 12	6	0	VI ii 26	15	0
VI i 13, 22	6	0	VI vii 3	16	1
VI i 17	6	0	VI xv 13–15	16	1
VI i 1	7	0	VI x 3–4, 18	16	1
VI xv 21	7	0	VI v 5–6, 21	17	2
VI xiv 35–6	7	0	VI vii 8–11	17	1
VI iii 18–20	7	0	VI viii 8	17	0
VI xvi 20–4	7	0	VI v 4	17	1
VI xvi 11	7	0	VI v 16	17	1
VI xv 22	8	0	VI xvi 29–30	17	1
VI iii 12–13, 22	8	0	VI vii 16	17	1
VI i 14–16, 21	8	0	VI ii 28	18	1
VI ii 29	8	0	VI ii 15, 22	18	2
VI ii 13	8	1	VI xi 6, 15	18	2
VI xiv 8–9	8	0	VI xiv 21–2	18	2
VI ii 27	8	0	VI vii 4–6	19	1
VI xvi 1–2	8	0	VI xiii 13–14, 18	19	2
VI i 5	8	1	VI ii 18, 19	19	2
VI iv 1–2	8	0	VI v 8, 20	19	1
VI vi 9	8	1	VI iii 7, 25–6	19	2
VI xvi 39–40	9	0	VI xv 6	20	1
VI xvi 10	9	0	VI xiv 40	20	2
VI xv 9	9	1	VI i 2–4	20	1
VI vi 17–21	9	0	VI ii 16, 21	20	2
VI xi 8	9	1	VI x 6, 17	21	2
VI ii 9–10	9	1	VI xi 11–12	21	2
VI ii 11	10	1	VI xiii 6, 9	21	2
VI ii 7–8	10	0	VI vii 19	21	2
VI iii 10–11	10	0	VI xiv 38	21	2
VI xiv 37	10	1	VI viii 3–6	22	2
VI xv 11–12	10	1	VI xiii 16–17	22	2
VI iii 21	10	1	VI x 1–2, 19	22	2
VI iv 11–12	10	1	VI ix 5, 10–11	23	3
VI xvi 35	10	1	VI xiv 41–2	23	1
VI vi 10–10a	10	0	VI ix 3, 12	23	2
VI xi 14	11	0	VI ii 17, 20	24	2
VI v 15	11	0	VI viii 1, 22	24	2
VI xvi 32–3	11	1	VI vii 1–2, 18	25	3
VI xvi 28	11	1	VI x 7,16	26	3
VI vi 6–7	11	1	VI xiii 12, 19	26	1
VI xiii 10–11	12	1	VI i 9–10, 23	28	1
VI v 17–18	12	1	VI xiv 18–20	28	3

Table 10.1 continued

Address	Spaces	Courtyards	Address	Spaces	Courtyards
VI v 12–13	12	1	VI x 8–9, 11	28	2
VI v 7	12	1	VI xvi 7, 38	28	2
VI xiv 5	12	1	VI viii 23–4	29	3
VI xi 3	12	0	VI xiv 28, 30–2	29	0
VI iv 3–4	12	0	VI vii 23	29	3
VI xiv 25	12	0	VI v 9, 19	30	2
VI xiv 27	12	0	VI xiv 12, 16–17	30	2
VI ii 25	13	1	VI xvi 19, 26–7	31	2
VI vii 7	13	1	VI xiv 2, 43	31	3
VI xv 16–18	13	0	VI xv 1, 27	33	3
VI xv 20	13	1	VI xiii 1–4, 20–1	33	2
VI xvi 15–17	13	1	VI xv 4–5, 24	33	2
VI vii 25	13	1	VI vi 1, 8, 13, 22	35	2
VI xvi 36–7	14	1	VI ii 3–5, 30	37	3
VI viii 9–10, 12–13	14	0	VI ix 1, 14	39	4
VI xvi 31	14	0	VI ix 2, 13	39	2
VI vii 15	14	0	VI viii 2, 20–1	39	2
VI ii 23, 24	14	1	VI vii 20–2	43	4
VI xiv 33–4	14	1	VI xi 4–5, 15–17	44	0
VI ii 14	14	2	VI v 1–3, 22	48	2
VI x 14	14	1	VI i 6–8, 24–6	52	3
VI xi 18–20	14	1	VI xii 1–3, 5–8	52	4
VI ii 12	14	1	VI ix 6–9	60	4
VI iii 3, 27–8	15	2	VI xi 9–10	60	3

amongst the houses that do have courtyards there is variation in the number that each has. As we can see from the table, there are also variations in the number of spaces in each house, so it will be of some interest to understand how the number of courtyards varies with respect to the number of spaces.

To understand this a decision was taken to divide the houses into four groups according to the number of spaces in each. As we can see, in Fig. 10.4, the distribution of houses is skewed in the direction of those houses with fewer spaces, with the result that we cannot simply divide the distribution into four equal parts. Because of the skewed nature of the distribution the median serves as the most reliable measure of central tendency and this is calculated by ensuring that half the observations lie above and below it. Extending the principle we can construct four quartiles, which contain more or less an equal number of cases. These quartiles are five to ten, eleven to fifteen, sixteen to twenty-two and twenty-three to sixty spaces. Using pie charts (Fig. 10.5 A–D), we can see what proportion of the total number of houses within each quartile is made up of layouts with different numbers of courtyards.

If we examine these charts we can discern two significant trends. First, there is a shift from non-courtyard to courtyard houses as the layouts become larger. In the first quartile (Fig. 10.5 (A)) the non-courtyard houses are in the majority,

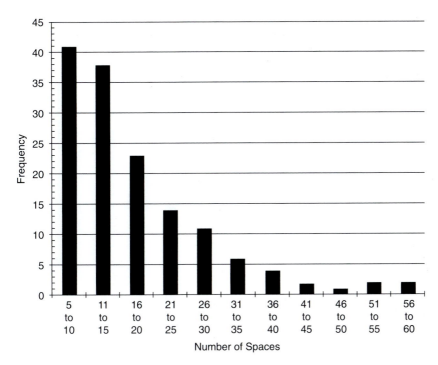

Figure 10.4 The frequency of occurrence of houses with different numbers of spaces

comprising just over 70 per cent of the forty-one houses in the group. This declines to 28.9 per cent in the second quartile (Fig. 10.5 (B)) and to just 3.2 per cent in the third (Fig. 10.5 (C)). Given that 29.9 per cent of all houses are of the non-courtyard type, the proportion of this total found in the first two quartiles is 27.8 per cent. Indeed, there are only three non-courtyard houses with more than fifteen spaces, allowing us to conclude that they have exceptional layouts.

The second trend is among the courtyard houses. As the layouts become larger, those with a single courtyard are displaced by those centred on two or more. Some 60.5 per cent of the layouts in the second quartile have one court-yard, with only 10.5 per cent of the houses having two (Fig. 10.5 (B)). This is reversed in the third quartile (Fig. 10.5 (C)), with 54.8 per cent of the houses being centred on two courtyards as opposed to only 41.9 per cent centred on one. The number of single-courtyard houses declines dramatically in the fourth quartile (Fig. 10.5 (D)) in that only 8.8 per cent of the thirty-four houses in this group have one courtyard. Two courtyards are still in the majority, in that they comprise 41.2 per cent of the group. However, there is an indication that if the houses were even larger they would also be displaced by houses organised around three or more courtyards. Some 32.4 per cent of the houses in the fourth

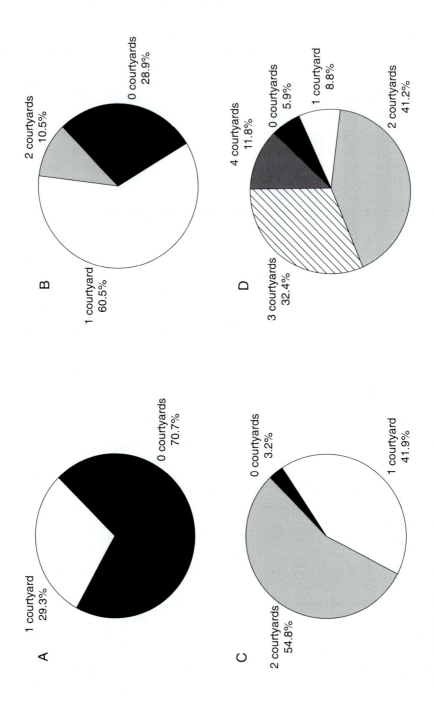

Figure 10.5 Pie charts showing the proportion of houses with different numbers of courtyard spaces for each quartile: (A) five to ten spaces, (B) eleven to fifteen spaces, (C) sixteen to twenty-two spaces, (D) twenty-three to sixty spaces

quartile are organised around three courtyards, while 11.8 per cent are centred on four.

Combining these trends, we can see that there is a strong positive correlation between the number of spaces in a layout and the number of courtyards. We can reasonably assume that houses with more spaces are indicative of wealth and status, since the construction, or modification, of a large layout requires more wealth and labour. The courtyard itself also 'consumes' a considerable amount of space and so cannot be fitted into very small house plots. This would explain why the courtyard occurs more frequently in houses that are physically larger, and so we can reasonably consider it to be symbolic of power and social status. It follows that the courtyard must have been an elite architectural form, with more courtyards expressing higher status.

The Pompeian house and cultural identity

What does this analysis show about the constitution of identity? Drawing on the examination of style earlier, I should like to begin by arguing that the non-courtyard houses demonstrate *isochrestic variation*. The surviving houses show little regularity in their layouts, suggesting that there was no 'standard' non-courtyard design. I would suggest that decisions about where to place architectural boundaries were based on a combination of the preoccupations of those responsible for organising the construction and alteration of these houses and the prevailing availability of space. The impression is that there was no overarching perception of how these houses should be laid out, with the result that their layouts seem to be almost random. Having only a few spaces, we might suspect that the non-courtyard houses belonged, or were at least inhabited by, those low down the social hierarchy. Most likely these individuals lacked the financial and political muscle to construct their houses as perhaps they would have wished. All this means that the non-courtyard houses have little or nothing to tell us about the presence of a cultural identity.

We move on to more fruitful ground when considering the courtyard houses. As was said earlier, courtyards provide a certain order to the spatial layout. The prevalence of courtyards would seem to indicate that they were a deliberate choice and so their presence may be interpreted as active style. This means that there was a conscious desire on the part of the those responsible for the construction or alteration of spatial layouts to incorporate this architectural feature. The question, of course, is whether we can consider this style to have been assertive or emblemic.

The answer to this question is not at all straightforward, since a case can be made for the courtyard houses as having been assertive *or* emblemic, depending upon whether we consider the spatial layout itself, or the presence or absence of certain room types. The variation in the number of courtyards and their arrangement with respect to one another indicates that ideas about how the house should be organised spatially were highly individualistic and this suggests assertive, rather than emblemic, style. If so, then we can conclude that layout was not supposed to signify anything, in contrast to the arguments put forward by Knights, outlined above; it simply asserted the personality of the householder.

However, if we bring back into consideration the traditional Latin nomenclature of the individual spaces, we know that most of the courtyards are *atrium* or peristyle spaces. Indeed, of the 101 courtyard houses 81.2 per cent have *atria* and, although only 39.6 per cent have peristyles, the peristyle is usually found in conjunction with an *atrium*, there being only two houses in region VI that have a peristyle but not an *atrium*. In houses with three or four courtyards the *atrium* is often duplicated with the addition of one or two peristyles.

The criterion used here for the identification of the '*atrium*' is the presence of the *impluvium*. The *impluvium* is a basin set in the floor for catching rainwater and so can be easily recognised from the ground plan. However, as Wallace-Hadrill has recently pointed out, there is also the *displuviate atrium*, which shed rainwater outwards instead of inwards and so does not have an *impluvium* (1990, 167). These are consequently not so easily located with any certainty and, for this reason, we should think of the number of *atria* identified here as being a *minimum*.

The peristyle is much more easily recognised by the presence of a colonnade. However, the 'classic' peristyle with its four-sided colonnade enclosing a garden is a rarity. Often there are so-called 'pseudo-peristyles' which have colonnades on only two or three sides. No discrimination has been made between peristyles on the basis of the number of colonnades, because they are all located in, and help define, a courtyard space.

The repeated use of the *atrium* and peristyle in courtyard houses with layouts of all sizes suggests that the spaces themselves were emblemic of social group membership rather than the layout of which they were a part. In other words, we can conclude that the *atrium* and peristyle had a specific referent beyond the assertion of personal identity.

The problem that now confronts us is: how can we reconcile both the assertive and the emblemic elements of house design? We can do so by understanding the social processes that resulted in the 'urban texture' that survives into the present. To uncover these processes I would like to draw on Wallace-Hadrill's (1990, 1994, 143–74) discussion of the social spread of luxury in Pompeii. Wallace-Hadrill argues that the *atrium* and peristyle had special significance in that they gave '*dignitas* to the home in a society in which so much turned on social standing' (ibid.). Because these architectural elements carried with them such symbolic overtones they may be understood as indicators of status and so were emulated by those lower down the social hierarchy who wished to wrap themselves in the prestige of the elite. Consequently, Wallace-Hadrill argues, such status indicators became commonplace, forcing the elite to 'innovate' in order to symbolise the difference between themselves and other groups in society.

These ideas accord well with those of Wiessner discussed earlier. Those in positions of power and status are likely to be emulated by those who see employing the cultural symbols of the elite as a way of developing a positive self-image. Emulation, after all, is a process of self-identification by comparison. The effect on the material symbols is interesting, because as they disseminate through the social hierarchy their meaning changes. In terms of style, they cease to be assertive and become emblemic of a more general cultural affinity and, indeed, this is the conclusion that Wallace-Hadrill reaches. As we saw above, one of the defining features of ethnicity is that it transcends class boundaries, and the distribution of *atria* and peristyles in Pompeian houses certainly suggests that these architectural features had become emblemic of a wider understanding of what it meant to be 'Roman'.

However, this does not explain the diversity of the spatial layouts of Pompeian houses. If we analyse various combinations of the traditional spaces in the courtyard houses (Table 10.2) we find that there is little in the way of a standard layout. The *fauces–atrium* combination occurs the most frequently, but, if we take into consideration the *tablinum*, fewer than half the courtyard houses have a *fauces–atrium–tablinum* arrangement and just under a quarter have a peristyle of some description added to the layout. The 'ideal' *atrium* house design of *fauces–atrium* with *alae–tablinum* is a rarity; in less then 20 per cent of the courtyard houses can this pattern be recognised. If we include those parts of the house often neglected because they are 'humble' or 'servile' then each layout emerges as unique.

Table 10.2 The frequency of occurrence of various combinations of the 'traditional' spaces found within the courtyard houses of region VI

Combination of spaces	Frequency	% of total
fauces–atrium	82	81.2
fauces–atrium–tablinum	48	47.5
fauces–atrium–tablinum–peristyle	25	24.8
fauces–atrium with alae–tablinum	19	18.8

How can we explain this lack of standardisation, despite the repetition of standard elements? First, we need to introduce the concept of knowledge into our discussion. If individuals are going to emulate others, they have to experience directly the object that serves to represent the attribute that they are trying to emulate. In the case of architecture it means that they would have to enter the space deployed as an indicator of status. It has long been recognised from the ancient literary sources that the receiving of visitors into the house played a central role in Roman social life (e.g. Wallace-Hadrill 1988). The morning reception by the *patronus*, seated in the *tablinum*, of his dependent clients, assembled in the *atrium*, is one of the most powerful and enduring images associated with the Roman house (e.g. Wallace-Hadrill 1989). We do not have to accept that this ritual occurred in every house with an *atrium* in exactly the way described in the sources, but, given the central location of the *atrium* in most houses, this would seem to give credence to the idea that the *atrium* was the main locus for the reception of visitors. It follows that it was therefore probably one of the most commonly experienced of all spaces in the house and as such it would have been the space most likely to be emulated, especially if Wallace-Hadrill is correct and the *atrium* endowed the house with dignity and social grace.

If the *atrium* was an elite form of architecture, its adoption by those of inferior social status may have caused alarm amongst the elite. According to the model presented by Wallace-Hadrill this should have forced the elite to innovate in order to maintain social distinctions. However, 'innovation' is socially very dangerous. There is always the possibility that the innovation will be rejected, bringing shame on to the innovator. The more 'original' the innovation, the more likely it is that it will be rejected, since the more unique it is the more difficult it will be to integrate it into existing social practices. A more reliable procedure is to modify an existing form. Such differences are small enough to make the modification acceptable, but large enough to indicate status differences.

In Pompeian houses the most reliable strategy would have been to reproduce existing architectural forms – two *atria* being better than one – and there are indeed some so-called double-*atrium* houses. However, an objection to this proposition may be that the *atrium* was not reproduced in most cases; rather, a peristyle was added. This architectural form was not an indigenous development, but was imported from the Greek east. However, a peristyle is just another form of courtyard and so is not as 'alien' as might first appear. We may, then, anticipate that this aided its adoption, since the 'logic' of the courtyard would already have been familiar to the Romans through the *atrium*. Furthermore, the peristyle appears not to have displaced the *atrium* but to have been added to it. This juxtaposition of 'old' and 'new' forms would have given a certain legitimacy to the new. Once *in situ* the peristyle would have become 'Romanised', losing its Hellenistic associations and obtaining a new, and local, set of cultural meanings. In effect, it became as 'Roman' as the *atrium*. The houses of the elite became composed of multiple *atria* and peristyles, enabling differences in social rank to be displayed to visitors, while at the same time deploying familiar symbols.

This, then, explains the differences in spatial layout amongst Pompeian houses and the fact the *fauces–atrium* combination is the most frequently occurring. Peristyles are even more elaborate and space-consuming than *atria* and so are harder to emulate. This is no doubt why the full classical peristyle is a rarity in Pompeian houses. Smaller houses do have peristyles, but often only two or three sides have columns. The peristyle had to be 'fitted in' in the best way possible and that meant modifying its form, but there is a limit to how much a peristyle can be manipulated and so we may assume that peristyles are indicative of higher social standing.

So, although the *atrium* and peristyle may be taken to be emblemic, they are more emblemic of 'status' than of 'etiquette', something confirmed by the fact that nearly 30 per cent of the houses analysed here do not have a courtyard space, let alone an *atrium* or peristyle. This means that it is unlikely that there was a strong and stable Roman ethnic identity, *in practice*. This distribution of emblemic features can be explained as arising from social competition and the desire of those of lower social status to emulate the elite. A cultural identity consequently emerges as a largely unintentional outcome of this process. In other words, there was not a conscious attempt to construct an ethnic identity, it was continuously being negotiated and renegotiated through practice. Although emergent, we may suspect that any sense of ethnic affinity was fairly weakly defined and that social status was a far more pressing day-to-day concern. If Wallace-Hadrill is correct about the process behind the social spread of status indicators, and the evidence from Roman houses does not contradict it, then we can assert with some confidence that the social processes that support ethnic identity formation were simply not present in Pompeii.

Romanisation and cultural identity

The central conclusion of this chapter is that a Roman cultural identity did not just 'exist', but rather was 'emergent'. This means that a cultural identity was not in any way 'fixed', but was being continually transformed over time. This conclusion has obvious implications for the process or processes of cultural diffusion usually referred to as 'Romanisation'. Although this is not the place for a radical deconstruction of the concept, the above conclusion does seriously throw into doubt whether 'Romanisation' is an analytically useful concept, particularly when thinking of cultural change in the provinces.

The term 'Romanisation' literally means 'to become Roman', whatever other connotations scholars have attempted to overlay on to it (e.g. Millett 1990). Consequently, we can hardly gauge the extent to which a conquered society 'became Roman' unless we already have an *a priori* understanding of what it meant to be 'Roman' in the first place. The degree of Romanisation is usually measured through the presence of material objects that are taken to be stylistically 'Roman' or largely influenced by Roman styles. The more frequently these 'Roman' or 'Romanised' objects occur the greater the degree of cultural influence. This, then, enables us to assess to what extent different parts of the Empire were, or were not, 'Romanised'. As a consequence, the literature on Romanisation has tended to concentrate on specifying the processes that resulted in the degree of observed Romanisation, with the result that the question of whether there ever was a Roman cultural identity has been neglected. Indeed, the perception seems to be that by the imperial period Italy was united, at peace and had become fully Romanised. The main phase of upheaval and change belonged instead to the Republic. This then indicates a stable Roman cultural identity against which the degree of Romanisation in the provinces may be measured. However, in contrast to this view, the evidence from Pompeii shows a vital and dynamic society right up to the time of the city's destruction in AD 79. More important, there is no indication that the processes of 'self-assimilation' and social competition discussed above were slowing – indeed, they may have even been intensifying. Consequently, the often implicitly held view that Italy under the Empire was somehow a static 'museum' of 'Romanness' must be dismissed.

Another difficulty with studies of Romanisation in the provinces is that scholars have tended to work with objectively defined units. As we saw, when discussing Bentley's work, analytical units cannot be based on the observer's criterion, but must be grounded on indigenous distinctions. Archaeologically, this means that identifying an assemblage of material is not sufficent in itself for the recognition of a cultural identity. Consequently, in Roman studies we must abandon objectivist models of cultural change such as 'acculturation' (e.g. van der Leeuw 1983) and world systems theory (e.g. Woolf 1990).

As a consequence of this we need to shift the level of analysis to the local, since we can no longer be sure that so-called 'Roman' or 'Romanised' material culture necessarily, and automatically, indicates a desire to adopt these styles because they were consciously perceived as being 'Roman'. Instead I would argue that the target population for stylistic referents was predominantly local. The reason why is clear if we ask how the individuals concerned gained knowledge of the appropriate symbols and how to use them. We can reasonably assume that all those individuals who lived out their lives in a way that *we* would recognise as Roman did not always go to Rome and experience Roman culture first-hand. Indeed, as Wiessner's research demonstrates, one individual might simply copy another because he or she appeared to be socially more successful. Because a Roman cultural identity is not automatically implied by the adoption of apparently Roman ways of doing, to speak of Romanisation is simply to assume what needs to be proved. Rather than demonstrating the presence of a Roman identity, 'Roman' and 'Romanised' styles of material may be asserting something else, and, given the conclusion of this chapter, it was probably social status.

Acknowledgements

I would like to thank the editors, Ray Laurence and Joanne Berry, for inviting me to contribute to this volume. I would also like to thank them for their helpful comments on a draft of this chapter. Needless to say, they are not responsible for any errors or omissions.

Bibliography

Bentley, G. C. (1987) 'Ethnicity and practice', *Comparative Studies in Society and History* 29: 24–55.

Childe, V. G. (1956) *Piecing Together the Past*. London: Routledge.

Conkey, M. W. and C. A. Hastorf (1990) 'Introduction' in M. W. Conkey and C. A. Hastorf (eds), *The Uses of Style in Archaeology*, 1–4. New Directions in Archaeology. Cambridge: Cambridge University Press.

Donley-Reid, L. W. (1990) 'A structuring structure: the Swahili house' in S. Kent (ed.) *Domestic Architecture and the Use of Space. An Interdisciplinary Cross-cultural Study*, 114–26. New Directions in Archaeology. Cambridge: Cambridge University Press.

Douglas, M. (1972) 'Symbolic orders in the use of domestic space' in P. J. Ucko, R. Tringham and G. W. Dimbleby (eds) *Man, Settlement and Urbanism*, 513–21. London: Duckworth.

Evans, E. (1978) 'A group of *atrium* houses without side rooms in Pompeii' in H. McK. Blake, T. W. Potter and D. B. Whitehouse (eds) *Papers in Italian Archaeology* I (i), BAR S41: 175–95.

Fried, M. H. (1967) *The Evolution of Political Society*. New York: Random House.

Knights, C. (1994) 'The spatiality of the Roman domestic setting: an interpretation of symbolic content' in M. Parker Pearson and C. Richards (eds), *Architecture and Order. Approaches to Social Space*, 113–46. London: Routledge.

Kus, S. and V. Raharijaona (1990) 'Domestic space and the tenacity of tradition among some Betsileo of Madagascar' in S. Kent (ed.) *Domestic Architecture and the Use of Space. An Interdisciplinary Cross-cultural Study*, 21–33. New Directions in Archaeology. Cambridge: Cambridge University Press.

Leach, E. (1954) *Political Systems of Highland Burma*. London: Bell.

Leeuw, S. E. van der (1983) 'Acculturation as information processing' in R. Brandt and J. Slofstra (eds), *Roman and Native in the Low Countries*, BAR S184: 11–41. Oxford.

Lévi-Strauss, C. (1963) *Structural Anthropology*. London: Allen Lane.

Macdonald, W. K. (1990) 'Investigating style: an exploratory analysis of some Plains burials' in M. W. Conkey and C. A. Hastorf (eds) *The Uses of Style in Archaeology*, 52–60. New Directions in Archaeology. Cambridge: Cambridge University Press.

Mau, A. (1899) *Pompeii. Its Life and Art*. Washington, DC.

Millett, M. (1990) *The Romanization of Britain. An Essay in Archaeological Interpretation*. Cambridge: Cambridge University Press.

Packer, J. E. (1975) 'Middle and lower class housing in Pompeii and Herculaneum: a preliminary survey' in B. Andreae and H. Kyrieleis (eds) *Neue Forschungen in Pompeji*, 133–42. Recklinghausen.

Parker Pearson, M. and C. Richards (1994) 'Ordering the world: perceptions of architecture, space and time' in M. Parker Pearson and C. Richards (eds) *Architecture and Order. Approaches to Social Space*, 1–37. London: Routledge.

Poel, H. B. van der (ed.) (1987) *Corpus Topographicum Pompeianum* IIIA. Austin: University of Texas Press.

Sackett, J. R. (1982) 'Approaches to style in lithic archaeology', *Journal of Anthropological Archaeology* 1: 59–112.

Sackett, J. R. (1985) 'Style and ethnicity in the Kalahari: a reply to Wiessner', *American Antiquity* 50: 151–9.

Sackett, J. R. (1990) 'Style and ethnicity in archaeology: the case for isochrestism' in M. W. Conkey and C. A. Hastorf (eds) *The Uses of Style in Archaeology*, 32–43. New Directions in Archaeology. Cambridge: Cambridge University Press.

Shennan, S. J. (1989) 'Introduction: archaeological approaches to cultural identity' in S. J. Shennan (ed.) *Archaeological Approaches to Cultural Identity*, 1–32, One World Archaeology 10. London: Unwin Hyman.

Tambiah, S. J. (1969) 'Animals are good to think and good to prohibit', *Ethnology* 8: 423–59.

Tylor, E. B. (1865) *Researches into the Early History of Mankind and the Development of Civilization*. London: Murray.

Wallace-Hadrill, A. (1988) 'The social structure of the Roman House', *Papers of the British School at Rome* 56: 43–97.

Wallace-Hadrill, A. (1989) 'Patronage in Roman society: from Republic to Empire' in A. Wallace-Hadrill (ed.) *Patronage in Ancient Society*. London: Routledge.

Wallace-Hadrill, A. (1990) 'The social spread of Roman luxury: sampling Pompeii and Herculaneum', *Papers of the British School at Rome* 58: 145–92.

Wallace-Hadrill, A. (1994) *Houses and Society in Pompeii and Herculaneum*. Princeton: Princeton University Press.

Wiessner, P. (1983) 'Style and social information in Kalahari San projectile points', *American Antiquity* 48: 253–76.

Wiessner, P. (1984) 'Reconsidering the behavioural basis for style', *Journal of Anthropological Archaeology* 3: 190–234.

Wiessner, P. (1985) 'Style or isochrestic variation? A reply to Sackett', *American Antiquity* 50: 221–4.

Wiessner, P. (1989) 'Style and changing relations between the individual and society' in I. Hodder (ed.) *The Meanings of Things. Material Culture and Symbolic Expression*. One World Archaeology 6: 56–63. London: HarperCollins.

Wiessner, P. (1990) 'Is there a unity to style?' in M. W. Conkey and C. A. Hastorf (eds) *The Uses of Style in Archaeology*. New Directions in Archaeology, 105–112. Cambridge: Cambridge University Press.

Woolf, G. (1990) 'World-systems analysis and the Roman Empire', *Journal of Roman Archaeology* 3: 44–58.

Zanker, P. (1979) 'Die Villa als Vorbild des späten pompejanischen Wohngeschmacks', *Jahrbuch des deutschen archäologischen Instituts* 94: 460–523.

NEGOTIATING IDENTITY AND STATUS

The gladiators of Roman Nîmes

Valerie M. Hope

Everyone who has done some great and memorable deed should, I think, not only be excused but even praised if he wishes to ensure the immortality he has earned, and by the very words of his epitaph seeks to perpetuate the undying glory of his name.

(Pliny to Cremutius Ruso, *Letters* 9. 19)

A funerary memorial is an aid to memory; it indicates where human remains are interred to prevent future interference and to ensure future respect. Simultaneously it may also memorialise chosen features of the identity of the deceased. If inscribed the memorial may preserve the name, gender, age or occupation of the dead individual. Sculpture may similarly capture facial features, while carved tools and equipment may indicate employment. The size, location and permanence of the memorial may also intimate relative wealth and social status. Thus the identity of the deceased has the potential to be remembered by the words and design of the funerary monument. This makes the hundreds of thousands of funerary memorials which survive from the Roman world a valuable source, as how individuals are presented in death should relate to their role and position in the living society. It has been noted, however, that the image created in death may not be a direct reflection of the reality of life (Hodder 1982, 146; Morris 1992, 21–4). The tombstone can be persuasive in the image it creates, and the identity of the deceased may be an idealised creation rather than a representation of reality.

Pliny speaks in praise of Verginius Rufus, who had composed his own epitaph and planned his own funerary memorial. Verginius Rufus' expectations were, however, frustrated, as nine years after his death his monument remained unfinished (Pliny, *Letters* 6. 10). It was not unusual in the Roman era for people to circumvent such difficulties by anticipating death itself and overseeing the inscribing of their own epitaph and the construction of their own tomb. Among

Pliny's generation the creation of large funerary edifices and the composing of flattering epitaphs may have been condemned by some members of the elite (Pliny, *Letters* 9. 19) but human remains had to be disposed of and in many cases the site of interment received some form of marker, however simple (Toynbee 1971, 101). It was not just the great and the glorious who aspired to be commemorated in a tangible form and thus remembered. Indeed, for the majority who had performed no famous deeds by which posterity would recall them, the funerary monument may have had a particular appeal.

The image fashioned by the tombstone could become an act of self-presentation. For those who created their own memorial before death this may have been particularly true. The monument represented how they wished to be remembered rather than how others might actually remember them. For memorials set up by the survivors of the deceased a similar principle could still apply; the representation of the deceased and the loved one could champion and recall elements thought insignificant by others or might reflect aspects of the identity of the commemorator rather than of the deceased.

The text, decor, scale and location of the Roman tombstone were manipulated to create a specific impression upon the viewer. An illustration of this is the use of the tombstone as a statement and symbol of integration. Roman society was complex and multi-layered and the funeral memorial was a method of expressing cultural and social alignment. In a recently conquered province of the Empire, for example, the inscribing of a Latin epitaph by a native inhabitant represented the adoption of Roman customs and the fusing of cultural forms. Furthermore for certain groups enduring persistent inconsistencies in their social or legal status, and thus occupying liminal positions, the Roman tombstone had a particular significance as a symbol of legitimisation. Freed slaves, for example, during the late Republic and early Empire used memorials decorated with funerary portraiture to lay claim to citizenship and as a symbol of their integration into society (Zanker 1975; Kleiner 1977, 1987). The message created and conveyed by the tombstone was not, however, a static one. As a medium of communication how and by whom the tombstone was exploited was constantly redefined (MacMullen 1982; Meyer 1990; von Hesberg 1992; Cannon 1989).

The intention of this chapter is to explore the presentation of the dead through a specific group of funerary memorials. The tombstones commemorating the gladiators of Roman Nîmes will be investigated to establish how this particular social group were presented in death and how the identity created related to the reality of their lives and the lives of those around them. The amphitheatre and the gladiator are identifiable symbols of Roman culture. Yet despite his cultural importance the social status of the gladiator was complex and ambiguous. How did the reaction of the community towards the gladiator and the response of the gladiator to his own position manifest themselves in the act of commemoration?

The memorials of Roman Nîmes

Nîmes came under Roman control in 120 BC and was probably established as a colony under Augustus (Rivet 1988, 162–3). The *colonia* Nemausus became a flourishing town and several notable landmarks survive, such as the Maison Carrée, the Tour Magne, the Porte d'Auguste and the amphitheatre (Rivet 1988, 163–7; Bromwich 1993, 93–108). The line of the town walls has been established and the sites of the cemeteries of Nîmes have been approximately located along the roads which radiated from the town (Rivet 1988, 16). Several hundred funerary memorials have been recovered but rarely were the monuments discovered still associated with the human remains they were intended to protect and commemorate. The majority of the stone monuments survive because of reuse, especially in the construction of the early Christian centres of the town. These funerary memorials mainly date to the first and second centuries AD and in terms of scale and decor are not particularly striking; there are, for example, no towering structures such as those surviving in Glanum (Rolland 1969). A few blocks exist which may have originated from large-scale monuments but this involves speculative reconstructions (Varène 1970).

The majority of the funerary monuments of Nîmes take the form of either *stelae* or small altars. The decorative range of these memorials is limited. A few are adorned with portrait busts, often arranged in rows with the names inscribed beneath (see, for example, Devijver 1989). The vast majority of the memorials are decorated with floral designs. On the *stelae* (Plate 11.1) these are very simple, often consisting of a single rosette in the gable, sometimes accompanied by palmette acroteria. On the altars (Plate 11.2) the floral designs could become extremely ornate, twisting their way around the inscription panel, forming a border incorporating flowers, vines, leaves and even small animals and birds (Sauron 1983).

A large number of Roman funerary monuments survive from Nîmes but we cannot assume that they provide us with a cross-section of the population of the town. It has been argued that inscribed tombstones were within the reach of people of modest incomes (Saller and Shaw 1984, 128). But even if this generous prediction is accepted we must acknowledge that not all burials would have been marked in this way. Markers made of more perishable materials such as wood and pottery have been identified as indicators at other Roman sites (Toynbee 1971, 101–3). In communal tombs individual graves and remains were frequently not indicated by a separate inscription or memorial (Eck 1987, 65–8) and the possible use of mass anonymous graves (*puticuli*) in large urban centres cannot be ignored (Hopkins 1983, 207–11; Bodel 1986 [1994], 38–54). In addition we know that inscribed tombstones were not constantly in production throughout the Roman period (MacMullen 1982). It is these variations in use and occurrence which make the exploration of the tombstone record potentially fruitful as we need to understand who was commemorated and how.

Plate 11.1 Tombstone with a triangular gable decorated with a single rosette. The epitaph commemorates a young woman (*CIL* XII. 3467)

A small group of tombstones found at Nîmes can be related to one of its famous Roman landmarks, the amphitheatre. There survive from Nîmes fourteen attested funerary monuments which recall gladiators. This is one of the largest collections of memorials set up to gladiators known from the Roman world and as such it provides an opportunity to assess how these tombstones functioned.

A cemetery of gladiators?

Observations can be made initially about the original location of these gladiatorial tombstones. Of the fourteen tombstones eight have attested find

Plate 11.2 Funerary altar with an ornate floral border encircling the inscription. The epitaph commemorates Gaius Aurelius Parthenius, an honorary decurion and *sevir augustalis* (*CIL* XII. 3203)

spots (Haon 1969, 88). Three of these (*CIL* XII. 3325, 3326; *ILGN* 435) are definitely associated with reuse and this also seems likely of a fourth (*ILGN* 433), the circumstance of the discovery of which is uncertain. The remaining four memorials (*CIL* XII. 3327, 3329, 3332; *ILGN* 436), however, were found, *in situ*, close together. They were discovered at the end of last century to the south of the amphitheatre at the crossroads of the rue de Saint-Gilles and the rue Charlemagne (Haon 1969, 90). Cinerary urns were also found in this area, with one accompanying the tombstone of the gladiator Lucius Pompeius (*CIL* XII. 3327). The discovery of these four associated tombstones suggests that the area may have been preferred for the burial of the gladiators of Nîmes (Haon 1969, 90–1).

Other examples survive from the Roman world which indicate similar group burial for gladiators. At Salona or Split in the former Yugoslavia, for example, a group of gladiatorial funerary urns was uncovered near the town's amphitheatre (Cambi 1987, 260). It is possible that the associated burial of gladiators was deliberately and freely chosen as an expression of group affiliation in death: the gladiators lived, fought and died together. The existence of a sense of community among gladiators is illustrated by attested gladiatorial *collegia* which may have had a funerary function (Wiedemann 1992, 117–18). A second possibility is that the site of gladiatorial burial may have been donated by the troop leader or a generous patron. Communal tombs erected by the organisers of gladiatorial shows for the burial of the dead combatants are known from Trieste (*CIL* V. 563;

EAOR II. 19) and Venusia (*CIL* IX. 465; *EAOR* III. 67). Such structures served to promote the name of the donor and to commemorate the splendour of his games as much as to recall the dead gladiators (Wiedemann 1992, 17).

An alternative explanation, although not mutually exclusive of the existence of a *collegium* and/or the benefactions of the wealthy, is that gladiators may have been buried communally more from coercion than from choice. It is probable that as victims of a violent death and as members of a stigmatised profession gladiators were excluded from normal burial areas and were segregated in death (Ville 1981, 340, 462–3; Hopkins 1983, 23; Wiedemann 1992, 30). The possibility that those stigmatised by profession and behaviour could be excluded is supported by a surviving inscription from Sarsina (*CIL* XI. 6528). Horatius Balbus, of Sarsina, donated some land for the burial of his fellow citizens but it was stated that burials of suicides and those living by immoral activities were not to be allowed. The gladiator was probably included among the excluded, as he suffered from the legal penalty of *infamia* and was socially stigmatised (Ville 1981, 339–45; Wiedemann 1992, 28–9; Gardner 1993, 135–40). The gladiator was of low status, he lived by killing and would himself be the victim of a violent end. The gladiator, like a prostitute, was viewed as selling and exploiting his body (Wiedemann 1992, 26); through performance and entertainment the gladiator was the common possession of the people (Funari 1993, 143). Thus the location of the gladiatorial tombstones at Nîmes supports the existence of the interment of gladiators within a separate cemetery or a segregated area of a cemetery. The location of this gladiatorial burial ground in proximity to the amphitheatre would have facilitated easy removal of the corpses of the dead gladiators from the city. Polluted by death, penalised by the law and stigmatised by society, the gladiator was contemptible and unworthy of contact in life, or burial in death, with decent and upright citizens.

The gladiatorial monuments

The tombstones of the gladiators are *stelae*; simple slabs of stone which would have protruded from the ground, indicating the place of interment (Plates 11.3–4). None of these *stelae* has any sculptural decoration; the stones are simply shaped with a rounded or semi-circular upper edge. These memorials, in terms of what was available in stone at Nîmes, must have been at the cheaper end of the scale. The simplicity of the execution is emphasised by the quality of the inscription. The characters of the text are of irregular size and the lines are frequently not horizontal (Plates 11.3–4). The memorials give the impression of having been produced hurriedly or created by people inexpert in the production of such items. Nevertheless the similarity in design and execution between the memorials of the gladiators creates a strong sense of group identity which would have been intensified had the memorials been placed together.

Similarities are also apparent in the content of the inscriptions. The epitaph composed to the gladiator Aptus (Plate 11.3) will serve as an illustration.

Plate 11.3 Tombstone of the 'Thracian' gladiator Aptus (*CIL* XII. 3329). Photograph courtesy of the Musée Archéologique, Nîmes

TR(ex)
APTVS NAT(ione) ALEXSAND
RINUS(annorum) XXXVII
OPTATA COIVX *sic*
DE SVO.

(*CIL* XII. 3329)

The epitaph indicates, by abbreviation, the type of gladiator commemorated; *thraex, myrmillo, retiarius.* Aptus was a 'Thracian' gladiator which entailed him fighting with a curved sword and a small shield. The age of the deceased is given in eight of the inscriptions. Aptus lived to the age of thirty-seven, outstripping his colleagues, who were killed at the ages of twenty (*ILGN* 434), twenty-one (*ILGN* 433), twenty-five (*CIL* XII. 3323, 3325, 3327, 3352) and thirty (*CIL* XII. 3331). The frequency of the occurrence of ages divisible by five suggests uncertainty as to the precise length of life of those involved (Duncan-Jones 1977, 1990). Eight of the epitaphs also give the number of appearances in the arena: these range from three (*CIL* XII 3332) to thirty-seven (*CIL* XII 3324); presumably the final combat resulted in death.

The names of the deceased, often single names such as Aptus, Calistus (*ILGN* 434) or Orpheus (*ILGN* 435), suggest that most of the gladiators were slaves. Some of these single names may also represent stage or nick names reflecting skills, nationality or qualities associated with heroes and precious items; the name Beryllus (*CIL* XII. 3327), for example, recalls a precious stone (Luca Gregori 1994, 55–6). A few of the gladiators were former slaves who had obtained their freedom – for example, Beryllus (*CIL* XII. 3323) was freed after twenty appearances in the arena, although only one (*CIL* XII. 3324) of the ex-slave gladiators has the *tria nomina* of a Roman citizen. Four others have the *tria nomina* (*CIL* XII. 3327, 3328, 3330, 3332) with no indication of former slavery or free birth; it is unlikely but not impossible that these were freeborn Roman citizens (Hopkins 1983, 23–4; Wiedemann 1992, 106–7; Gardner 1993, 40).

Several of the gladiators have their nationality stated; three were from Gaul (*CIL* XII. 3325, 3327; *ILGN* 436), but a Spaniard (*CIL* XII. 3332), a Greek (*CIL* XII. 3323) and an Arab (*CIL* XII. 3324) were also commemorated. Aptus was originally from Alexandria in Egypt. The inclusion of gladiators of foreign extraction in the combats at Nîmes may have added to the excitement of the arena but the mixed nationalities also reflect the potential geographical mobility of an individual gladiator and of gladiatorial troops (Wiedemann 1992, 114).

The commemorators, or those setting up the tombstones, are often identified as friends or the female partners of the gladiators. Aptus, for example, was commemorated by Optata, his *coniunx*. The sexual attraction of gladiators has often been expounded, with suggestions that they attracted female followers who were the ancient equivalent of 'pop groupies' (Ville 1981, 339–2; Hopkins 1983, 22–3; Wiedemann 1992, 20; Gardner 1993, 137–8). The women mentioned

Plate 11.4 Tombstone of the 'Thracian' gladiator Orpheus (*ILGN* 435). Photograph courtesy of the Musée Archéologique, Nîmes

in these epitaphs, however, cannot be labelled as such; they may not have been legally married but they could still be committed partners, even if the relationship was, by nature, of short duration (Wiedemann 1992, 115; Gardner 1993, 137). In general the transient, dangerous and unstable aspects of the gladiator's work must have severely limited opportunities for the development of family life and thus professional associations and activities may have provided a substitute (Joshel 1992, 92–122).

The content of the gladiatorial inscriptions is highly reminiscent of military epitaphs, which commonly state rank, age at death, years of service and place of origin, and were often set up by fellow soldiers or female partners with few references to familial relations (Keppie 1991, 81). The gladiators were soldiers of the arena and their identity is couched in military terminology. An additional shared characteristic of military epitaphs and those of the gladiators of Nîmes is the absence of ante-mortem commemorations, although this was commonplace in the town. Professions which involved frequent mobility and regular risk to life rendered anticipating death and preparing a tomb highly inappropriate. Instead this responsibility fell to the survivors of the gladiators – their womenfolk and friends, whose own lives probably revolved around the exploits of the arena.

The epitaphs with their standardised information unite the gladiators as a group, as does the location of burial and the memorial design. The most striking feature of these epitaphs is, however, not the content but the organisation and layout. The identification of the deceased as a gladiator repeatedly takes precedence over all other information. In eleven of the epitaphs the abbreviated occupation is placed first in the epitaph on a separate line. The epitaph of Aptus makes his occupation as a gladiator visually prominent on his memorial (Plate 11.3). Other attested professions generally do not imitate this ordering of information. Most Latin epitaphs place the name of the deceased first, followed by an indication of profession, if indeed the latter is included at all. Even soldiers, whose epitaphs in general bear many similarities to those of the gladiators, have their names placed first and their military career second. A brief survey suggests that this epigraphic format is characteristic of gladiators commemorated in Gallia Narbonensis and Spain; thus, for example, two memorials set up to gladiators in nearby Orange (*CIL* XII. 5836, 5837) have occupational title first, as do five examples erected to gladiators in the Spanish town of Cordoba (Garcia y Bellido 1960, 123–44). However, epitaphs set up to gladiators in Rome and Italy do not follow this pattern (*EAOR* I. 63–100, II. 40–54). This suggests that it was customary for the commemorators of the gladiators of Gaul and Spain to direct attention to the profession of the deceased.

A parallel case – the *Seviri Augustales*?

The ordering of information within the gladiatorial epitaphs is both unusual and visually striking. There is, however, another social group from Nîmes whose funerary inscriptions are similarly organised, namely the *seviri augustales*. It would seem that the gladiators had little in common with the *seviri augustales*, who were distinguished and wealthy office-holders, and that any specific similarities between their epitaphs was coincidental. But a closer examination of the *seviri augustales* of Nîmes and their funerary monuments suggests certain parallels with the gladiators and their tombstones.

Collegial associations of *augustales* arose under Augustus and were to be found across Italy and the western provinces, although the precise origin of the institution is uncertain (Ostrow 1990, 364–7). A *sevir augustalis* was a priest of the imperial cult but the position involved more than religious authority. The holders of the office were primarily recruited from the ranks of wealthy freed-men who were excluded on the basis of their birth from holding magisterial posts.[1] Thus the position allowed access to the symbols of power and authority normally denied to the majority of its members (D'Arms 1981, 127; Ostrow 1990).

At Nîmes *seviri augustales* are well represented in the funerary record, often commemorated by, or creating for themselves, funerary altars decorated with elaborate and complex floral borders (Plates 11.2, 11.5). In terms of quality and standard of execution these memorials are the antithesis of the shabby memorials received by the gladiators of Nîmes. The *seviri augustales*, however, do share in common with the gladiators the organisation of the associated epitaph. An indication of membership of the *augustales* is placed repeatedly before the name of the deceased; their office-holding takes precedence over all other information (Plate 11.5). A survey of epitaphs to other *seviri* in Gaul, and indeed through-out the Empire, indicates that this is a distinctive trait of the *seviri augustales* of Nîmes.[2]

The comparative grandeur of their memorials and the prominence given to their office created a special identity for the *seviri augustales* of Nîmes both as individuals and as members of a group. The burial of these successful members of the community was not controlled and monitored. There was no question of their being buried together by coercion, removed from other members of the community. It is possible, however, that the memorials of the *seviri augustales* were placed together. Demand for prime burial space, for example, near the town gates and walls may have led to the clustering of memorials associated with these wealthy and successful freedmen. Evidence from Pompeii indicates that elaborate memorials erected to *seviri augustales* occupied prominent positions, often fronting the roads, with some located near the town walls, erected in the *pomerium* as a gift of the town (Kockel 1983, 11–13). This is not to suggest that the *seviri augustales* created their own private cemetery, but the style and prominence of their memorials could come to dominate the existing cemetery areas.

The majority of the memorials associated with the *seviri augustales* of Nîmes are, unfortunately, of unknown provenance. For that reason the physical impact of these memorials on the surrounding environment remains uncertain. The organisation of the epitaph and the visual prominence given to title is, however,

Plate 11.5 Funerary altar decorated with a floral border. The epitaph commemorates Gaius Marcius Philologus, a *sevir augustalis* (*CIL* XII. 3251)

more than apparent. It is possible that at Nîmes this aspect of monument design was of fundamental importance, as there is limited evidence for large funerary structures and the use of funerary portraiture. The epitaph was a basic element which could be easily and subtly manipulated. Elsewhere in the Roman realm sculptured images were exploited to advertise status and success. In Rome and Italy successful freed slaves of the late Republic and early Empire were often depicted in portrait form on funerary memorials, representing, together with their relatives, an ideal citizen family (Zanker 1975; Kleiner 1977, 1987; Kockel 1993). The tombstones of Italian gladiators were often similarly adorned with portraits of fighting gladiators or depictions of gladiatorial equipment and weapons (*EAOR* I. 59, 83, 92, 97; II. 42, 44, 45, 47, 50; III. 69). In Nîmes the absence of a pictorial repertoire may have intensified the importance of the words of the epitaph and more specifically the organisation of the epitaph; prominent words replaced prominent pictures. The basic message conveyed by the tombstones remained the same but the details of the act of funerary commemoration were regionally defined.

The life of the gladiator and the life of the *sevir augustalis* must have varied greatly; they existed and functioned at opposite poles of society. These social differences were reinforced by the relative quality of the memorials erected to commemorate them. Nevertheless there were also similarities in the social position of gladiators and *seviri augustales*. Both could be viewed as successful but stigmatised. The gladiator was the champion of the ring, the hero of many, yet he was poor, often a non-citizen and a social outcast. The *sevir augustalis* was wealthy and successful but in origin a freed slave who was excluded from magisterial office. For both the gladiators and the *seviri augustales* of Nîmes, who shared in common their servile origins, occupation and office had a special significance: they became an emblem of success which, when given prominence, could eclipse social handicaps. The career in the arena or the role in the imperial cult was the key to identity and thus it received the greatest emphasis within the epitaph. For these groups the tombstone functioned as a symbol of success, but it also indicated their social isolation.

Conclusion

The amphitheatre was a symbol of Roman identity. Gladiatorial shows were an integral feature of Roman life which diffused across the Empire. It was necessary to the reputation of the emperor to attend such events in Rome and to appear to enjoy them; an essential aspect of being Roman was to take the games seriously. The gladiator embodied important Roman virtues: the ability to fight and die with honour (Barton 1993, 20, 32–6). The gladiator could become a popular hero, a conqueror, and many members of the upper classes and even emperors wished to fight as gladiators or to train among them (Wiedemann 1992, 109–11; Barton 1993, 25–31). Simultaneously the gladiator was often a slave or a criminal, with few rights or means; he was polluted by his association with death and was himself a victim of violence. The gladiator was stigmatised by *infamia*; like actors and prostitutes he suffered enforced legal disabilities even if he attained his freedom or was freeborn (Gardner 1993, 40). At Nîmes the method of burial and commemoration reflected the complex and ambiguous position that the gladiator occupied in life.

The Roman amphitheatre was often located on the margins of the town it was intended to serve (Wiedemann 1992, 46). The gladiator lived and worked on the periphery of society. In death his burial place was also marginalised; separated from other members of the community, the gladiator was isolated in death. The simple and crudely executed tombstones set up over the grave emphasised the poverty which confronted the daily life of the gladiator. A monument in stone, however, was expensive and not achieved by everyone (Duncan-Jones 1982, 79–80, 127–30). The remains of at least some gladiators must have fared better than the remains of many of the urban poor who had witnessed the arena combats. Indeed, despite the stigma of his profession the epitaph gloried in the gladiator's trade rather than ignoring it. The memorial captured this concept of triumph by emphasising victories and by placing the gladiator's profession first in the epitaph. The career in the arena may not have been freely chosen and it ultimately led to death yet it was the basis of the identity of such men (cf. Joshel 1992). For those commemorating the gladiators, perhaps themselves caught up in the glamour of the arena life style, the deceased was above all else defined by his few moments of fame. The gladiator was admired and despised; these conflicting aspects were captured in the poverty and isolation of his death, which was paradoxically accompanied by a sense of glory.

Legislation and social custom may have aimed to marginalise the gladiator, and lack of resources may have prevented flamboyant display, yet as a group the gladiators attained, nevertheless, prominence in death. The gladiators, being buried separately from others, and thus together as a professional group, created a striking impression within their own cemetery. Each memorial sought to differentiate the individual commemorated by stressing aspects such as method of fighting, age and nationality. Simultaneously the similarities between the memorials create a sense of community which emphasises the uncertain and transient elements of the gladiator's life and compensates for any absence of family. The individual memorials were simple but together they must have been impressive. Such gladiatorial cemeteries may have been visually reminiscent of military cemeteries located at civil settlements. At Rome the tombstones erected to members of the German bodyguard of the Julio-Claudian emperors conformed to a standard design and were not dissimilar to those of the gladiators of Nîmes (Keppie 1991, 86, plate 48). On the Via Tiburtina at Rome twenty tombstones commemorating members of the Praetorian Guard were found together, indicating a separate military burial area (Durry 1938, 60–3). A segregated cemetery could be associated with honour as well as disgrace.[3]

Tombstones construct identities. The identity represented is related to the reality of the life of the person commemorated, but it is often a limited view of reality. In the Roman town of Nîmes the funerary memorials of the gladiators and the *seviri augustales* captured a sense of glory and success which overshadowed the negative aspects of their life. A memorial is a limited form of communication and thus by nature it is selective in the image it portrays. This is not to deny that gladiators and *seviri augustales* were individually and collectively of high profile in the civic life of Roman towns. Indeed, it was their cultural importance which formed the basis of the claim to social status.

Prominence in death is not the sole preserve of the wealthy and the elite or the great and glorious (Cannon 1989, 437). The desire to perpetuate name and achievements in the Roman world, despite the expectations of the Younger Pliny, knew no such distinctions. The funerary record surviving from the first and second centuries AD of Nîmes does not present a mirror image of the social hierarchy; instead death can provide a medium for the compensation of the inequalities of life. The memorials present a view of the world through a rhetoric of language, images and places, but it is a view which may not conform to reality. The tombstones of the gladiators, in particular, exploited this rhetoric of symbols and funerary language as they borrowed from the code of military honour and social success. The gladiators were buried poorly and separately but by being aligned in death with soldiers and *seviri augustales* the stigma of their life became shrouded in the terminology of respectability. In the society of Roman Nîmes the gladiators occupied a marginal and ambiguous position; they existed on the edges of acceptance, and the memorials which commemorated them sought to redress the balance.

Acknowledgements

This chapter was originally presented at TRAC '95 and incorporates research from my Ph.D. thesis undertaken at the University of Reading. I would like to thank Joanne Berry, John Bodel, Michael Fulford, Ray Laurence, Andrew Wallace-Hadrill and Greg Woolf for commenting upon an earlier version of the chapter. Any errors, however, remain my own. I would also like to thank the curator (Dominique Darde) and staff of the Musée Archéologique of Nîmes for their assistance during my visits to the museum and for supplying Plates 11.3 and 11.4.

Abbreviations

CIL *Corpus Inscriptionum Latinarum.*

EAOR I P. Sabbatini Tumolesi, *Epigrafia anfiteatrale dell'Occidente Romano.* I *Roma.* Ricerche di Storia epigrafia e antichità. Vetera 3. Rome, 1988.

EAOR II G. L. Gregori, *Epigrafia anfiteatrale dell'Occidente Romano.* II *Regiones Italiae VI–XI.* Ricerche di Storia epigrafia e antichità. Vetera 4. Rome, 1989.

EAOR III M. Buonocare, *Epigrafia anfiteatrale dell'Occidente Romano.* III

VALERIE M. HOPE

Regiones Italiae II–V. Ricerche di Storia epigrafia e antichitá. Vetera 6. Rome, 1992.

ILGN E. Espérandieu, *Inscriptions Latines de Gaule Narbonnaise,* Paris, 1929.

Notes

1 Duthoy (1974) explores the status of *augustales* and concludes that the vast majority were freed slaves. At Nîmes some of the *seviri augustales* are explicitly identified as freed slaves, although the majority are not. The latter frequently have the *tria nomina* but it is never accompanied by an indication of free birth and many of the associated *cognomina* appear servile.
2 One exception is found nearby at Arles (*CIL* XII. 699).
3 There was no military garrison at Nîmes and few tombstones of military personnel, active or retired, are attested. Thus as the representatives of fighting skills the pseudo-military aspects of the gladiatorial tombstones and cemetery may have been particularly apparent.

Bibliography

Barton, C., 1993, *The Sorrows of the Ancient Romans. The Gladiator and the Monster,* Princeton.
Bodel, J., 1986 [1994], 'Graveyards and Groves: a Study of the Lex Lucerina', *American Journal of Ancient History* 11.
Bromwich, J., 1993, *The Roman Remains of Southern France,* London.
Cambi, N., 1987, 'Salona und seine Nekropolen' in H. von Hesberg and P. Zanker (eds) *Römische Gräberstrassen. Selbstdarstellung, Status, Standard,* Munich, 251–80.
Cannon, A., 1989, 'The historical dimension in mortuary expressions of status and sentiment', *Current Anthropology* 30, 437–57.
D'Arms, J., 1981, *Commerce and Social Standing in Ancient Rome,* London.
Devijer, H.,1989, 'Un des monuments Romains les plus connus de France', *Ancient Society* 20, 221–39.
Duncan-Jones, R., 1977, 'Age-rounding, illiteracy and social differentiation', *Chiron* 7, 333–53.
Duncan-Jones, R., 1982, *The Economy of the Roman Empire. Quantitative Studies,* Cambridge.
Durry, M., 1938, *Les Cohortes prétoriennes,* Paris.
Duthoy, R., 1974, 'La fonction sociale de l'Augustalité', *Epigraphica* 36, 134–54.
Eck, W., 1987, 'Römische Grabinschriften aussageabsicht und aussagefähigkeit im funerären kontext' in H. von Hesberg and P. Zanker (eds) *Römische Gräberstrassen. Selbstdarstellung, Status, Standard,* Munich, 61–83.
Funari, P. P. A., 1993, 'Graphic caricature and the ethos of ordinary people at Pompeii', *Journal of European Archaeology* 1. 2, 133–50.
Garcia y Bellido, A., 1960, 'Lapidas funerarias de gladiatores de Hispania', *Archivo Espanol de Arqueologia* 33, 1–14.
Gardner, J., 1993, *Being a Roman Citizen,* London.
Haon, A., 1969, 'Les gladiateurs à Nîmes', *Ecole Antique de Nîmes, Bulletin Annuel* 4, 83–99.

Hesberg, H. von, 1992, *Römische Grabbauten*, Darmstadt.

Hodder, I., 1982, *The Present Past. An Introduction to Anthropology for Archaeologists*, London.

Hopkins, K., 1983, *Death and Renewal. Sociological Studies in Roman History*, 2 Cambridge.

Joshel, S. R., 1992, *Work, Identity and Legal Status at Rome. A Study of the Occupational Inscriptions*, Oklahoma.

Keppie, L., 1991, *Understanding Roman Inscriptions*, London.

Kleiner, D. E. E., 1977, *Roman Group Portraiture. The Funerary Reliefs of the late Republic and early Empire*, New York.

Kleiner, D. E. E., 1987, *Roman Imperial Funerary Altars with Portraits*, Rome.

Kockel, V., 1983, *Die Grabbauten vor dem Herkulaner Tor in Pompeji*, Mainz.

Kockel, V., 1993, *Porträtreliefs Stadtrömischer Grabbauten*. Mainz.

Luca Gregori, G., 1994, 'Gladiatori e spettacoli anfiteatrali nell' epigrafia Cisalpina', *AAAd* 41, 53–67.

MacMullen, R., 1982, 'The epigraphic habit in the Roman Empire', *AJP* 103, 233–46.

Meyer, E., 1990, 'Explaining the epigraphic habit in the Roman Empire: the evidence of epitaphs', *JRS* 80, 74–96.

Morris, I., 1992, *Death-ritual and Social Structure in Classical Antiquity*, Cambridge.

Ostrow, S. E., 1990, 'The *Augustales* in the Augustan scheme' in K. A.Raaflaub and M. Toher (eds) *Between Republic and Empire. Interpretations of Augustus and his Principate*, Los Angeles, 364–79.

Parker-Pearson, M., 1982, 'Mortuary practices, society and ideology: an ethnoarchaeological study' in I. Hodder (ed.) *Symbolic and Structural Archaeology*, Cambridge, 99–113.

Rivet, A., 1988, *Gallia Narbonensis*, London.

Rolland, H., 1969, *Le Mausolée de Glanum (Saint-Remy-de-Provence)*, Paris.

Saller, R. and Shaw, B., 1984, 'Tombstones and Roman family relations in the Principate: civilians, soldiers and slaves', *JRS* 74, 124–56.

Sauron, G., 1983, 'Cippes funéraires à Rinceaux de Nîmes', *Gallia* 41, 62–110.

Toynbee, J. M. C., 1971, *Death and Burial in the Roman World*, London.

Varène, P., 1970, 'Blocs d'architecture découverts à Nîmes', *Gallia* 28, 91–115.

Ville, G., 1981, *La Gladiature en Occident des origines à la mort de Domitien*, Rome.

Wiedemann, T., 1992, *Emperors and Gladiators*, London.

Zanker, P., 1975, 'Grabreliefs römischer Freigelassener', *JDI* 90, 267–315.

INDEX